Guide to Backpacking
in the United States

Guide to

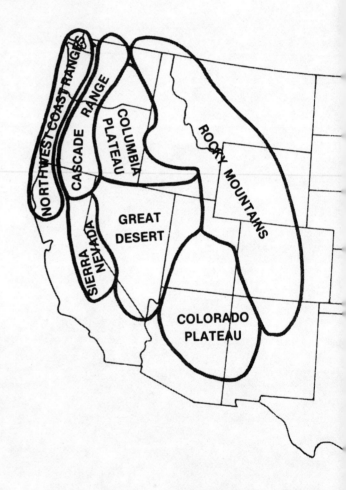

COLLIER BOOKS

A Division of Macmillan Publishing Co., Inc.

NEW YORK

Backpacking in the United States

by ERIC MEVES

UPDATED AND REVISED EDITION

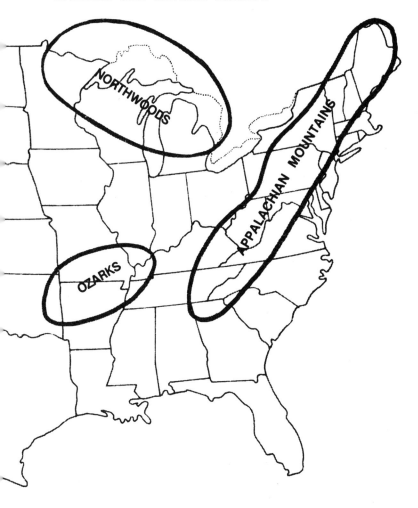

Macmillan Publishing Co., Inc.
866 Third Avenue, New York, N.Y. 10022
Collier Macmillan Canada, Ltd.

Library of Congress Cataloging in Publication Data

Meves, Eric.
    Guide to backpacking in the United States.

    Bibliography: p.
    Includes index.
    1. Backpacking—United States.   2. United
States—Description and travel—1960–   I. Title.
GV199.4.M48   796.5   76–44352
ISBN 0–02–584500–4
ISBN 0–02–029330–5

FIRST COLLIER BOOKS EDITION 1979
Printed in the United States of America

Contents

Guide to Backpacking
in the United States

The Backpacking Experience

Why does one forsake the ease and comforts of civilization to confront nature on its own terms? Why does one endure the discomforts and hardships often encountered on a backpacking trip and call it a vacation? And why do most people go back for more?

For sport, for love, and for the intense experience.

Backpacking is a test of the human body and spirit. It can be as easy or as rigorous as desired, but no backpacking trip is completed without a sincere sense of accomplishment. It is a deliberate, persevering effort extended over a period of days, a series of endurance tests, each followed by its own quiet triumphs. It is just as real and satisfying as those few minutes one shusses down a snow-covered slope or the moment one lands a prize trout. Best of all, it can be enjoyed by almost anyone.

On a deeper level, backpacking is love . . . love of nature. Backpacking strips away the façade of civilization we have placed between ourselves and nature. In a very short time and distance, the backpacker can put all the cares of civilization behind him and be left with nothing to interfere with his private communication with nature. For some, this love is expressed by a close study of nature, for others it means taking pictures, and for still others it means just being there to experience nature firsthand. The feeling exhilarates and, like all intense emotions, defies description. It is a nostalgic, comforting sensation, like returning home after a very long time.

But more than just sport or love, backpacking is a total, intense experience, something that civilized man has insulated himself from. Backpacking is an opportunity to use all one's senses again, to feel rain, wind, and sun, to hear the hush of the wind in the pines overhead, the roar of a waterfall, and uncivilized silence itself, to see mountain vistas and the micro-vistas of a patch of lichens, to smell damp woods and wildflowers, and to taste a smoky and sometimes burned dinner that seems better than a meal from a good restaurant.

During a day hike one spring, I became lost in the Gila Wilderness canyonlands of New Mexico. I was cold, wet, hungry, frightened, and exhausted. I nearly fell climbing out of a steep dead-end box canyon, only reaching safety by leaping to the top and clinging to a prickly pear cactus. Those spines are the only thing I don't remember of the entire traumatic experience. Everything else sticks in my memory as vividly as if it had happened yesterday. When I finally found my way back to camp after dark, and had time to collect myself, I realized that I had just experienced the most intense few hours of my life.

You don't have to be as careless as I was to experience such intense moments. Intense experience is what backpacking is all about. It's not equipment, it's not maps, it's not the natural environment. It's what all these things instill in you, the individual backpacker, as part of the backpacking experience.

Perhaps this is why backpacking has become so popular in our soft, insulated culture. Perhaps this is why we return time after time, even after cold nights spent in wet clothes, without dinner, after an exhausting day. The backpacking experience, at times elating and breath-taking, at other times miserable, is one you can take back with you to a comfortable home and a routine life to reflect upon when things seem just a bit too comfortable and routine.

The veteran backpacker is reading about something he already knows; the novice, about something he will soon discover. This book will introduce the novice to the backpacking experience, and it will introduce both the novice and the veteran to places in this country where the backpacking experience abounds.

2

Equipment and Techniques

Backpacking is an advanced form of hiking and camping. It is defined as hiking while carrying essential equipment and camping overnight on the trail. The growth in the ranks of backpackers is being matched by the "one-timers" who tried backpacking and, usually because their trip was ill-planned or ill-equipped, have sworn never to make that mistake again. This chapter is dedicated especially to the novice, the one-timer, and the potential one-timer in hopes of helping them over the rough spots. The experienced backpacker may wish to skip to the next chapter.

Planning a successful backpacking trip is a skill acquired through experience. The successful trip is a harmony among individuals, environments, and equipment, and the result of a well-thought-out choice of when and where to go, based on sufficient information. On his first trip the novice would do well to accompany an experienced backpacker. Your apprenticeship need not be long. One trip is usually sufficient, especially if complete with steep grades, rain, bears, and mosquitoes. In lieu of such experience, and as supplement to it, we offer the following discussion, and more importantly, the bibliography at the end of this book.

GETTING STARTED

The two basic considerations in backpacking are *planning* and *equipment*. This book concentrates on the planning aspects, although equipment considerations are also vital. The following paragraphs briefly summarize the backpacking equipment you will need. For more detailed information, refer to the books listed in the bibliography. Equipment for backpacking has become a science.

Boots

Good all-around boots start at about $30. Get a name brand built on American lasts. (A last is the form over which the boot is constructed.) European lasts are too narrow in the toe and too wide in the heel for many Americans. Look for one-piece construction, that is, no seams on the boot except at the heel. The heel piece should be offset toward the outside so the seams are not worn open where the two boots often knock together on the inside rear of the heel. Don't buy big, heavy boots suitable for climbing Mount Everest if you don't think you'll really need them that strong. Not only do they cost a mint, but an extra pound on your feet is like five on your back. Get the shoes one or two sizes larger in length than street-shoe size and about one size wider. Wear two pairs of socks, a pair of thick wool socks on the outside and a pair of thinner socks on the inside. These two pairs will slip against each other instead of your skin, helping to prevent blisters. Whether to waterproof boots is a matter of personal choice; but it's worth the bother. Waterproofing preparations are available where boots are sold. Finally, break in your boots *before* you use them on their first backpacking trip.

Pack

Expect to pay at least $25 (usually more) for a decent pack and frame. Conventional pack arrangements consist of a rectangular nylon pack with one or two large compartments and several smaller outside pockets, with a light tubular frame that holds the pack's shape and spreads the weight more evenly on the back. There are many styles to choose from. Some features to look for: The pack should be waterproof, not just water repellent, with covered zippers. The frame should have a full hip belt, not just a half belt. This allows the weight to be distributed between the shoulders and hips and makes for a more comfortable and stable load distribution. Buy the pack from a camping/backpacking store and be sure it fits. Packs come in different sizes, too, and getting the right size pack is just as important as getting the right size boot. The more you're willing to spend, the more frills you can get. One feature probably worth the money in terms of comfort is a pack frame with a yoke arrangement; ask to see it. A knowledgeable outfitter will know what you're talking about.

On or in your pack you should have the following:

Tent

Tents suitable for extensive backpacking use start at about $100. Of course, cheaper ones can be found (definitely cheaper), and some purists prefer to sleep under the stars with no tent at all. If you are all for stars, but don't think much of sleeping in the rain or in clouds of mosquitoes, you'll want to look for the following features in your tent: Weights are commonly in the 4-to-7-pound range for a two-person nylon tent. It should have a sewn-in floor of waterproof fabric and insect netting for the door and windows. The tent itself should not be waterproof, but should be equipped with a waterproof fly (a separate covering slung over the tent). This arrangement inhibits condensation and buildup of humidity inside the tent (a worse problem than it sounds). Also, the fewer stakes, the better. Some tents are freestanding, requiring few or no stakes. Better tents have floors that extend several inches up the walls to prevent puddling water from soaking through the lower wall and floor seams. Tents come in many styles, some interesting and unique. They are all designed for certain types of use. Take time to research before you buy. A tent will probably be your biggest single investment in backpacking equipment.

Sleeping Bag

A sleeping bag will probably be your second biggest investment, around $50 and up. Consider these factors when buying a sleeping bag: warmth, lightness, compactibility, and warmth when wet. Goosedown fill is the best on three out of the four; it's worthless when wet. Nevertheless, goosedown is the undisputed choice of most backpackers at present. As important as fill, though, is the construction. There should be no sewn-through seams, which make cold spots. Box and overlapping tube construction and variations on these styles avoid this problem.

Sleeping-Bag Pad

A sleeping-bag pad costs $5 to $10, less if you make it yourself. The most common type is a covered foam pad about 2 feet by 3 feet. Pads covered with waterproof fabric are easier to keep clean. The pad serves two purposes: In addition to providing cushioning, the foam insulates the sleeper underneath when the weight of the body compresses the sleeping bag fill (especially goosedown) and reduces its insulative efficiency. Air mattresses usually are heavier, don't insulate as well, and are inconvenient to inflate and deflate.

Cooking Equipment

You can choose from a variety of ready-assembled cook kits, or you can assemble your own. As the minimum, a cook kit should include one pot and lid and a cup and spoon for each member of your party. Many backpackers use the metal Sierra cup. To make meal preparation easier and your menu more varied, you may also want to add a coffeepot or tea kettle, a Teflon frying pan, a long-handled spoon, a nylon spatula, and an aluminum measuring cup. Although some backpackers prefer to eat from their cups, others carry a plastic bowl or a deep dish so that they can eat and drink at the same time. You may also want to include a pot gripper or lightweight pliers.

Food

Dehydrated foods are the backpacker's hallmark. Although special backpacking foods are more expensive than ordinary groceries, they are much cheaper than the restaurant foods that are normal vacation fare. The variety and quality of freeze-dried food become greater every year. The only way to discover personal preferences is through trial and error. Don't ignore common groceries that are dehydrated by their nature, such as rice, pastas, and other staples and convenience foods. They are less expensive than special backpacking foods and are just as good. Dry soy protein meat substitutes available in some grocery stores make excellent casseroles combined with rice or pasta. One-pot dishes are popular with backpackers because of ease of preparation and cleanup. (Imagine trying to prepare a five-course meal over one fire in the dark and eating it all before it gets cold or dumped.)

Backpack Stove

Most backpackers eventually break down and buy a backpack stove. They cost about $12 and up. The convenience of being able to prepare a quick meal or a cup of hot soup or a drink without the bother of a fire is well worth it. Many still build a fire for the evening meal for coziness, camp atmosphere, and psychological warmth. In areas where firewood is scarce and its use is ecologically unsound or banned, a backpack stove is a must.

Outerwear

Goosedown coats are lightweight, warm, and compactible, but if they get wet they are worthless. If you expect wet weather, wear woolen clothing. Because its fibers are hollow, wool is the only fabric that insulates while wet. Several layers of sweaters and heavy shirts are preferable because they can be put on or taken off in response to temperature changes, giving you a greater comfort range. For comfort, wear a layer of cotton next to your skin. You may also want to take a lightweight cotton shirt with long sleeves to wear in hot weather when you need protection from insects and too much sun.

Rainwear

In only a few places in the United States can you safely expect no rain. Always be prepared for rain if there is any chance of it. Nylon or thin plastic parkas are most common, but these channel the water down to the shins and thighs and allow the arms to get wet during camp activities. An outfit called a cagoule, a hooded, shin-length pullover rain coat, coupled with gaiters and waterproof boots, will keep you reasonably dry during extended wet periods. A rain suit will also keep the rain out, but it is more prone to interior condensation.

Checklist

A checklist of gear is as important to a successful backpacking trip as a comfortable pair of hiking boots. And just as your boots, with wear, adapt to the shape of your feet, so your checklist, with each trip, should become more adapted to your style of backpacking.

The checklist below is presented only as a general guideline to help you make your own. You certainly don't need to take every item on the list, and there may be items missing from the list that you couldn't imagine *not* taking.

More detailed discussions of equipment are found in some of the general backpacking books listed in the bibliography. You may also want to consult equipment catalogs.

You might expect that as a backpacker gains experience, he will acquire more equipment. The opposite is true. The experienced backpacker "goes light." It's the novice who falters along the trail under the weight of ice chests, camp stools, hurricane lanterns, and the like. One of the most common mistakes of beginners is to take more and heavier equipment than they need. This can be disastrous to the enjoyment and success of a backpacking trip, or very expensive—as the equipment is abandoned by the side of the trail. As a rule of thumb, a backpacker's load should equal no more than one-fourth of his or her body weight. The only exception to this is when the trip is exceptionally long, over seven days, for example, and food must be carried for the entire trip. In any case, a trip this length is not something the novice should attempt. The equipment list given here should be considered an upper limit. Depending on the trip, certain items will not be needed. In the Sierras in the summer, even a tent is often left at home.

Pack your pack. Weigh it. If it weighs more than one-fourth of your body weight, discard items. Do you really need the iron frying pan or the whole bottle of ketchup? The average backpacker on the average trip can be adequately equipped and provisioned with only 30 to 40 pounds.

TRIP PLANNING

Trip planning—where to go, when to go, how long to stay, how great a distance to hike, and what route to take—is a valuable skill every backpacker should develop. The general discussion that follows will introduce the beginner to this important part of every backpacking trip.

Where

The chapters that follow provide detailed information about where to go. Generally, in descending order of quality of the resource for backpacking, the opportunities are as follows: national forests (especially wilderness and primitive areas), national parks (backcountry), state forests, some state parks, and some county forests. A few wildlife refuges and some Bureau of Land Management areas are suitable for backpacking also. Chapter 4 discusses what these jurisdictions are. This country is fortunate to have such a wealth of natural backpacking areas. Although some

CHECKLIST

transportation

hiking boots
pack and frame

shelter

sleeping bag
stuff sack
foam pad
tent
ground cloth

small equipment

matches
fire starter (lighter fluid)
flashlight
extra batteries and bulb
pocket knife
nylon cord
water bottle
folding saw
map, compass
notebook
pen
lightweight pliers
small sewing kit

cooking gear

pot and lid
tea kettle or coffeepot
frying pan
long-handled spoon
spatula
measuring cup
collapsible water carrier
cup, bowl, and spoon for each
    person
fire grate
stove, fuel
food

clothes (including those worn)

nylon windbreaker
heavy wool shirt
wool sweater
long-sleeved cotton shirt
2 T-shirts
jeans
shorts
belt
2 briefs
2 pair cotton socks
2 pair wool socks
longjohns
sneakers or moccasins
swim suit
hat or cap
gloves
bandana
rainwear

for personal care and comfort

sunglasses
insect repellent
suntan cream
lip balm
first-aid kit
snake-bite kit
water-purification tablets
toilet paper
soap
small towel
comb
metal mirror
toothbrush
toothpaste

for entertainment

fishing gear
nature guides
paperback book
camera and film

regions have more and better opportunities, none are devoid of backpacking areas. The decision of where to go first depends on how far you wish to travel to get there. Then consult the following chapters for an area at about the distance that appeals to you. Of course, the farther you are willing to travel, the greater your selection.

When

Two environmental factors are involved in determining when it is best to backpack in a given area—weather and insects. A third factor, visitation levels, should also be considered if you are looking for solitude. Weather is an especially important consideration when traveling in the high country. The higher the elevation, the longer winter snow lingers on and the sooner it returns in the fall. Often, deep snow is encountered late into the summer. In these areas, backpackers who are not prepared for snow should limit themselves to summer visits. Insects, especially mosquitoes and black flies, usually are problems only at certain times of year and in certain environments. Unfortunately, these times and environments are also attractive to the backpacker. Late spring until mid-summer is the worst period, although insect populations vary from year to year depending on the weather. Both mosquitoes and black flies like it wet, and they are most frequently found in, although not limited to, wet woodlands. Mosquitoes breed in still water; black flies need fast-moving streams. People also seem to swarm in certain places at certain times of the year. They are most likely found in well-publicized areas near population centers between Memorial Day and Labor Day.

Length of Stay

It is often a mistake of the novice to plan too long an initial trip. Even many inveterate backpackers begin to miss civilization's conveniences—not to mention soft drinks and hamburgers—after about a week-long sojourn. For the beginner, it is especially important not to overdo. Individuals react to the wilderness dif-

San Juan Nat'l Forest Ⓞ

Weminuche Wilderness
Area

247-4874

Supervisor, San Juan Nat'l Forest
701 Camino Del Rio,
Durango Colorado, 81301

1 - 303 - 555 - 1212

ferently. The cultural shock of wilderness, or even just natural environments, on the uninitiated can be unpredictable. It is best to ease into backpacking slowly, with an initial trip of perhaps a few days. You can then lengthen your trips until you find a length that suits you best—long enough to become attuned to nature, but not so long as to lose your love for it. These lengths range from several days to several weeks and more for some. Of course, many trip lengths are determined by other commitments, such as jobs and school. One can justify traveling a longer distance to a backpacking area if the wilderness trip itself will be long. For the beginner, a weekend trip close to home would be good.

Length of Route

Route length rivals equipment weight as the most common pitfall for the beginner. The story is sometimes told about the three businessmen from the East who planned their first backpacking trip to include 50 miles along the Appalachian Trail over the weekend. After making arrangements to be picked up 50 miles down the trail on Sunday evening, they started out Saturday morning loaded down with their hurricane lanterns and iron frying pans, which were soon abandoned along with other equipment representing a considerable investment. They arrived at camp late Saturday night tired, blistered, and with only about a dozen miles behind them. Needless to say, a Sunday night arrival was unlikely.

Don't overdo. Ten miles a day may not sound like much sitting at home, but it's plenty if you want to enjoy yourself. Backpacking is not an endurance test, and there are many faster ways to travel. The most important consideration in planning trip length is terrain. Individuals in top condition can make about 2½ miles per hour on a good, level trail. In rugged, steep terrain, this can drop to less than 1 mile per hour—and this is for those in good shape. Here's a good rule of thumb for the beginner who is sitting down to plan a trip. When you think you've got a good length planned, cut it in half. That should be about right.

Route Selection

Route selection requires skill acquired through experience. The trip planner must obtain sufficient detailed information on an area and be clear as to what his personal preferences are. An experienced backpacker will sit down with a good map, usually a topographic map, and a general description of the area and plan a route that will provide him with just the variety of environments he desires. He may even be able to pick out the trailside camps he will want to make. For the novice, a few suggestions will be helpful. First, you may want to consider how to return to your starting point without backtracking. The obvious solution is to plan a circular route when possible. Second, you may wish to traverse a variety of environments. In hilly or mountainous terrain, trails often follow ridges and river bottoms. This is because ridges and river bottoms have fewest ups and downs and are easiest to travel. A model itinerary might consist of a circular route that leads out from the trailhead along a ridgetop or river bottom, then loops around, descends to a river bottom or climbs to a ridgetop, and returns the hiker to the trailhead. Which you take—river bottom or ridgetop—depends on the weather. If your trip begins with clear weather, start with the ridgetop. Otherwise, begin with the river bottom. The weather may clear up by the time you gain the ridgetop, providing beautiful vistas.

If solitude is part of the environment you prefer, stay away from those trails and areas that are most popular. Areas near population centers are often crowded. Even in heavily used areas, though, some trails are not used much. The ability to spot these on the maps is part of the skill of route planning. Of course the best way to get away from it all is to go cross-country, but this is not for the novice. More will be said about this in chapter 4.

Another important consideration is campsites. Good campsites generally have the following amenities: proximity to a water supply, good drainage in case it rains, good exposure to breezes if insects are a problem, and a few luxuries such as a good view, stumps, logs, or rocks to sit on, and firewood. Every so often one chances upon the perfect campsite. It might be located where a gurgling brook empties into a clear mountain lake. The lake is warm enough for swimming and the mouth of the brook provides good fishing. Mountains rise from the far side of the lake, and the sun will be setting over the lake through a draw in the mountains to the west. Shoreward breezes keep the insects in the forest behind the campsite, reserving the grassy shoreline for the camper. The forest provides convenient firewood as well as logs that serve as tables, chairs, and backrests. The forest even provides a fallen tree just the right height and texture to make an excellent latrine. These campsites are not found often, but just enough to keep the backpacker coming back.

ETHICS

To help ensure pleasant campsites for future campers, follow the often heard rule: take only photographs and leave only footprints. Here are some additional guidelines for the ethical camper.

In the past, campers were told to bury their garbage. Unfortunately, buried garbage sooner or later finds its way to the surface through animals or erosion. The new ethic is to pack out what you pack in. You can burn paper, but don't try to burn aluminum foil and other metals. They belong in the plastic garbage bag you should always carry with you. And if campers before you have left their garbage, carry it out too. It will give you a tremendous feeling .

If established campsites are available, use them. If you camp in an unestablished campsite, make sure it doesn't look like an established campsite when you leave. Scatter unused firewood in the woods and take apart your fire ring and place the rocks charred side down.

Use only deadfall for firewood. If there isn't enough deadfall for a campfire, don't make one. Never cut down living trees or branches.

A few frequently-used backcountry campsites have privies, but most don't. When you have to fend for yourself, which will be most of the time, follow the habits of the cat and bury all evidence that you were there. If you can't dig into the soil with your boot or a stick, cover the evidence with a small rock or dead bark. Stay away from watercourses, whether or not water is currently running, and don't spoil a potential campsite.

Never wash your dishes or yourself in a lake or stream. Use a cooking pot or a collapsible canvas basin for washing, and empty the soapy water into a rocky area without vegetation.

Don't contribute to noise pollution. If your campsite is within earshot of another campsite, try not to disturb the other campers. Make a special effort to control any barking dogs or squealing children you take along. Of course, no backpacker would even consider taking a transistor radio or a cassette tape recorder into the wilderness.

THE TYPICAL HIKING DAY

Everyone's hiking routine is unique. The following scenario will give you some idea of the wilderness backpacking experience.

The day begins as sunlight strikes the tent roof and you feel its radiant heat in your face. Now is the most difficult moment in the day—getting out of your warm sleeping bag to face the cold world. This morning it is below freezing, not unusual any time of the year in the mountains. If you are in an area with plentiful firewood, you might start a fire to break the morning chill, or if you are eager to begin the day's trek, you just pull out the camp stove to heat up water for breakfast. This morning, like most mornings, your meal is a bowl of instant oatmeal and a cup of instant hot chocolate.

It's now about an hour after sunrise. You don't know the precise time because you are intentionally keeping your watch in your pack. The sun and your biological clock are your only timepieces, and they tell you that it's time to break camp. The tent is taken down, sleeping bags are stuffed, and all other gear is repacked. You are ready to begin after a final look at the vista and the home that was yours for one night. You shoulder your pack and you're off.

Like many backpackers, you nibble your way down the trail,

keeping assorted candy, nuts, and raisins accessible. One of your favorite snacks is "gorp," a mixture of nuts, raisins, and other snacks. This snacking keeps your energy up and your mind off the more tiring parts of the trail. Your camera is also accessible. You are out to enjoy yourself, so no vista is passed without taking a shot or at least stopping to contemplate nature's beauty. Today's trek is 8 miles on gently rolling to moderate grades, and there's plenty of time for dawdling. You find yourself resting for about 10 to 15 minutes every hour.

After about 3 hours on the trail, it's lunchtime. You settle down in a sunny spot with good exposure to a steady breeze that helps keep away the few mosquitoes that have accompanied you on this trip. Lunch consists of instant soup and crackers with cheese from a squeeze tube. You heat up water for soup by placing your metal Sierra cup directly on the camp stove. Cleanup for this meal involves only a cup and a spoon. You have just a couple of miles still to go today, so it's time for a short nap and a little fishing or reading.

By early afternoon you're off again. After a short while on the trail, it begins to rain. Out with the rain gear. You're equipped for rain and it's no great inconvenience. You reach tonight's camp in the rain and decide to wait a bit before setting up camp in hopes that the rain will stop soon. You've reached camp early and there's plenty of daylight left.

You've chosen your camp on the basis of several criteria. You have chosen the eastern shore of a small lake where a stream flows into the lake. You enjoy the company of the stream's gurgling, and water and fishing are convenient. There is good exposure to the westerly breeze coming off the lake, which will keep the mosquitoes blown back in the woods behind you. There is a level spot for a tent, a large fallen log to sit on, and a large rock to serve as a table. This spot has been used before, but it is not overused. There is still plenty of wood around for a campfire, which, along with the sunset over the western shore of the lake, will make for a beautiful evening.

Now that the rain has stopped and the clouds are breaking up, it's time to make camp. First, you decide if you want to use the tent. If so, you choose the tent site on a level spot facing the lake between where the campfire will be and the woods behind you. Then you dig shallow contours, hip and shoulder holes, in the soil beneath the tent to conform to your body contours as you lie on your side. You've had much practice making these and so you do it quickly. (In the morning you will quickly fill them in again after you take down the tent.) The increase in comfort is well worth the inconvenience. You set up the tent and throw the un-rolled sleeping bags inside to give them a chance to fluff up.

Next, you gather the night's supply of firewood, using only dead-fall, of course, and build a fire. While the fire is burning down to a good cooking size, you get out tonight's dinner—a chicken-and-rice-casserole convenience dinner from the grocery store with freeze-dried pears from the camping store for dessert. You prepare orange drink to have with the meal, and take out tea bags for later on.

You cook the casserole on a lightweight grate over a slow fire in the one large pot you've brought. You roll a large log to a com-fortable distance from the fire. Using the log as a backrest, you sit on your sleeping pad placed on top of a ground cloth. Tired and relaxed, you sit back and enjoy your meal. Somehow, it always tastes better than if you ate it back in civilization.

With dinner finished, the pot and utensils are cleaned without dumping any refuse into the lake or stream. Tea bags and sugar are set aside for later. Before it gets dark, you hang all other food up in a tree out of the reach of bears and other wildlife. This is done by tossing a strong rope (nylon is best) over a high limb, tying one end to the food pack and the other to a stout stick for a better grip. The food is then hoisted up for the night (the farther out on a limb, the better).

There is still an hour or so of daylight. Time to do a little fishing or to contemplate the sunset. By dark, the campfire has been built up and you and your companion, if any, settle around it. The tea is steeping by the fire. Now is the best part of the day, and you can relax, converse, or just stare silently into the animate flames, think-ing of distant ancestors who were fascinated by other campfires.

Finally, it's time for bed. As you drift to sleep, you hope that the night won't be disturbed by visits from the larger forms of wildlife. Then your thoughts drift through the happenings of the day. How much fuller a day seems out here in the woods! Refreshingly tired, you sleep better than you have in a long time, and another backpacking day comes to an end.

3

Major Backpacking Environments in the United States

Many parts of the country are endowed with outstanding back-packing environments. These areas, because of their physiographic features, are the destination of most backpackers on moderate and long trips. It is helpful for the backpacker to be generally aware of these resources and their locations, and use this information as a starting point in trip planning.

For purposes of discussion, areas of the country have been classified into 11 physiographic zones. (See also the Physiographic Cross-Reference section, page 265.) Of course, these zones are not distinct but merge into one another. Descriptions of each of these areas give only a general idea of what natural and man-made elements these environments offer. More detailed discussions of the backpacking opportunities in each of these zones are given in later chapters.

ALASKA

This state is a zone in itself. For a discussion of its physiographic features, see chapter 5.

NORTHWEST COAST RANGES

Beginning in the extreme northwest corner of the United States, this area extends down along the coast into California. Although it is a mountainous zone, the tallest peaks are still less than

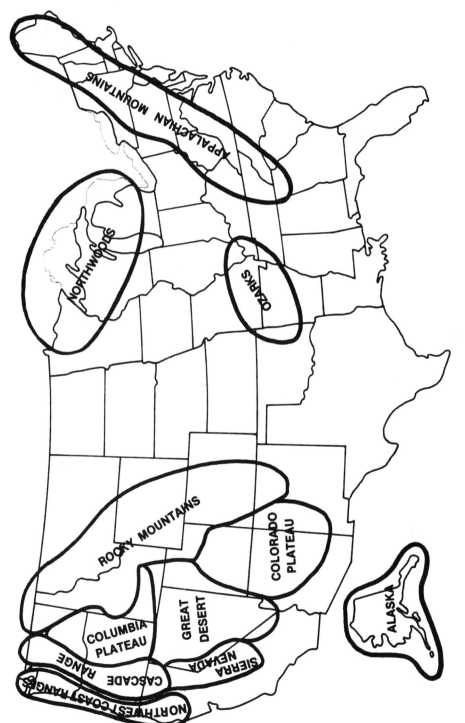

Major backpacking environments in the United States

8,000 feet, much lower than peaks in the Cascades and Sierra Nevada ranges found inland. It is not the physical terrain but the weather that distinguishes this area. Moderate temperatures, in all but the highest elevations, and abundant rainfall, up to an average of 200 inches a year in the north, combine to produce lush vegetation. Dense stands of immense cedars, hemlocks, firs, and spruces in the north and the world's largest trees, the redwoods, in the south, cloak the coast ranges. Beneath them flourish ferns, mosses, shrubs, wildflowers, and young trees, nourished by the thick, soft mat of decaying vegetation laid down over the ages.

On the higher peaks in the north, the plentiful snowfall has piled up to form some of the most impressive glaciers in the country. They have gouged and remodeled the mountains, sharpening the features that are smoothed out by the vegetation of the lower elevations. Another force constantly tearing away at the coast ranges is the Pacific Ocean, which forms the western boundary of this zone. This is an area of mostly rugged, picturesque coastline, with sand dunes, beaches, and cliffs.

For the backpacker, this zone is one of the finest. Trails in good condition are numerous, and most have moderate grades. The weather is kind, except in the highest elevations in the north where the thick blanket of winter snow lasts until mid-summer. Although rain is the rule rather than the exception, summer is the driest season in many parts of the range. As in any temperate, humid climate, be prepared for insects during summer. Use of trails is moderate, though there are many remote areas where you would have no difficulty avoiding other backpackers entirely to be alone with unspoiled wilderness.

The coast ranges are of particular appeal to those who are interested in botany. The climate nurtures a complex plant community, some members of which are very rare. The coast also supports sea mammals and birds, and the inland forests and streams are home for many other birds, mammals, and fish, including eagles, cougar, elk, mountain goat, and salmon. This zone is for those who are fond of searching among the rocks and cliffs of the Pacific shore amid the roar of the breakers, for those who would like to tread softly on a thickly carpeted trail of forest duff in a cathedral-quiet setting, and for those who like to careen down slopes of snow mass and glaciers.

CASCADE RANGE

Parallel and similar to the coast ranges, the Cascades have several notable differences. The peaks are much higher, with many over 10,000 feet, such as the tallest, Mount Rainier, at 14,408 feet. Volcanic activity has played an important part in creating this range and the tallest and most impressive peaks are volcanoes. These snow-covered symmetrical mountains tower all along the ridge of the Cascades, rising majestically from the surrounding plateaus and ridges.

The coast ranges intercept much of the moisture coming in from the ocean, and the precipitation in the Cascades is correspondingly lighter. It is still adequate to form many lakes, streams, and gorges, and to support dense stands of Douglas fir, lodgepole pine, and hemlock. Some areas, devoid of vegetation, are covered by recent (geologically speaking) lava flows. Likewise, lava flows have created many interesting caves, some of which are floored by ice the year round. Above the ground, crystalline-blue ice caves are found throughout the glaciated areas.

The Cascade Range is more popular among backpackers than the coast ranges. Perhaps this is because the area is larger, more remote, and with the taller peaks, the scenery is more awesome. Complementing the dense forest are beautiful alpine areas reminiscent of the Rocky Mountains and the Sierras. Many of the trails, though, are more rugged and steep than those of the coast ranges. Use is moderate, but there are many areas you can have alone to yourself. There is less rainfall here than in the coast ranges, but insects can still be a problem.

The Cascades, then, are generally a blend of dense northwest forest with its undulating verdant carpets and plunging gorges, and alpine areas with barren and snow-covered peaks jutting above them. The area has some of the finest wilderness remaining in the country and a good system of trails. One may even catch sight of a rare grizzly or timber wolf in the northern reaches of the range.

SIERRA NEVADA

Most West Coast residents will tell you that the Sierras are the best backpacking mountains in the country, in addition to being the most beautiful. They are well known as good hiking mountains, made famous by John Muir and the Sierra Club, which he founded.

The Sierras extend southward from the Cascades through California. The barren, glaciated peaks of granite that typify the Sierras are being thrust up by geologic forces. In many areas they rise to over 14,000 feet. These forces are still felt today, as in the recent past, as earthquakes. Unlike the coastal ranges and the Cascades, the Sierras receive little rain in the summer. This drier climate supports a different community of plants. As you move up from the lower elevations, you encounter ponderosa pine, white fir, and yellow pine. Farther up, red fir and lodgepole pine become dominant, finally dissolving at timberline into the austere landscape of alpine lakes and lichen-covered granite. Some of the notable inhabitants of the mountains are trout, coyote, bighorn sheep, and the rare cougar.

Trails are plentiful and well maintained, though some have difficult grades. The area is well known and popular, making it one of the most heavily used backpacking areas in the country. That should not discourage the visitor, only make him more resolved to plan his itinerary to take him into the more remote and lesser used areas. Because of the warm, dry summers, many do not take tents into the mountains during this season. Still, in alpine areas mosquitoes can be pesty.

These mountains have a mystique all their own. Perhaps it is the clean, stark granite monoliths that can be viewed through the clear air over such great distances, or the sight of Half Dome at sunset over Yosemite Valley, reputedly the most beautiful valley in the world. Whatever it is, every backpacker should experience the Sierras at least once.

COLUMBIA PLATEAU

This is a little known backpacking area, nestled between the Cascades and the Rocky Mountains, covering parts of Washington, Oregon, and Idaho. Threading through and defining this zone is the Snake River, confined generally by semiarid hills and canyons as it carves into the volcanic rock of the Plateau. In south-central Idaho, recent volcanic activity has left a moonscape of cinder cone and craters, only sparsely covered by the hardiest grasses and shrubs. Where the Snake forms the Oregon-Idaho border, it becomes a raging torrent within the Hell's and Snake river canyons. Northeastern Oregon is in the highlands of the Plateau, with the alpine areas of the Blue and Wallowa mountains, and the ponderosa pine parklands and meadows of the lower mountains to the southwest. This zone is the home of some of the largest populations of cougar in the country. Eagles and hawks can be seen soaring through the river valley, and salmon and huge sturgeon fight the currents of the Snake.

Except for parts of the several national forests in this zone, it is a little known and little used backpacking area. Float trips down the Snake are popular, but few venture from its shores. Roaming through the trackless dry lowlands and canyons is not recommended for the novice, but the experienced backpacker will find it an exciting challenge. The aridity of much of the Plateau keeps the bothersome insect population down, but at the same time the summer heat and dryness pose their own special problems. In addition, the razor-sharp lava beds can make short work of unsuitable footwear. With careful preparation, though, the backpacker can experience lonely, spectacular country that few ever visit.

GREAT DESERT

What seems an unlikely place for backpacking is the most wild and least used of any zone. For that reason alone, it should appeal to many. This is a largely misunderstood environment, in reality a far cry from hot, monotonous sand, the image held by many of those unfamiliar with this environment.

The Great Desert extends from southeastern Oregon, through and including all of Nevada, and onward into southern California and southern Arizona. Few areas in the zone are flat. Instead, the desert is cut by numerous mountain ranges of forest, scrub, or sculptured rock. Geographers have divided this zone into three types of desert: the Great Basin, mostly in Nevada; the Mohave in southern California; and the Sonoran of southern Arizona. The Great Basin is a land of sagebrush, with a few cottonwoods and willows along the streambeds. The ever present mountains drain enough moisture out of the passing winds to support piñon pine and juniper. The Mohave to the south is distinguished by the weird Joshua tree with its wildly flung limbs. This desert is the location of Death Valley, which is not as dead as you might think—over 600 species of plants have been identified here. Finally, there is the Sonoran Desert, the cactus land most people think of when they think desert. The saguaro cactus typifies this desert, though many species of plants and animals inhabit it.

Throughout the Great Desert, wildlife persists. Wild horse and burro, antelope, coyote, a variety of reptiles, birds, insects, and rodents all make their home here. It is an interesting area, but like the endemic animals and plants, the backpacker must adapt to the desert conditions. Except in national forests and other developed areas, there are few designated backpacking trails. Nevertheless, this environment can be enjoyed if you are prepared. Winter and early spring are especially good seasons. Of course, any extreme environment has its inherent dangers. This is not an area for novices or the unprepared. But for those who are willing to take the time to plan wisely, this zone affords an excellent, though somewhat different, wilderness experience.

COLORADO PLATEAU

As a land of fantastically shaped buttes, mesas, and canyons, including the Grand Canyon, this zone offers the backpacker the most bizarre landscape in the country. It includes western Colorado, eastern Utah, and northern Arizona and New Mexico, an area owing its unique appearance to the Colorado River. Back in its geologic past, layer upon layer of sediments were laid and compacted into sedimentary rock. Slowly, this zone was uplifted, but just as fast as the land would rise, the powerful, silt-laden Colorado, conspiring with the other elements, would grind it down. The river maintained about the same elevation above sea level, cutting through the rising land around it to do so. The bare land, unprotected by vegetative cover, fell easy prey to erosion. Varying rock hardness and colors caused them to be carved into the myriad of shapes and hues that embellish the landscape today.

The eroded plateau is generally arid and hot in the summer. Just as temperatures fall as elevation increases, they rise as elevation decreases, often making the canyon bottoms blisteringly hot. The environment of the interior of the plateau is similar to that of the Great Desert region, with many of the same plants and animals. Ringing the plateau, though, are the cooler mountain ranges—oases of piñon pine, juniper, and cottonwood, with aspen and spruce nearer the summits. In and around these mountains live cougar, elk, antelope, black bear, and a variety of smaller animals.

For the backpacker, this zone provides a great variety of environments, from desert to alpine. The many national forests, parks, and monuments provide excellent trail-hiking opportunities, while additional public land in the eroded lower elevations provides abundant room to roam and a year-round season. The cross-country traveler should be cautious: this topography can become a maze for the unwary traveler. In the heat and dryness of summer, being lost for even a short period can be serious. This type of confrontation with nature is unnecessary in this often eerie and thoroughly enchanting land.

ROCKY MOUNTAINS

By virtue of this zone's sheer size, it offers tremendous backpacking opportunities. The mountains begin in Canada, extend through Montana, Idaho, Wyoming, Utah, Colorado, and into

New Mexico, making a vast chain of wildernesses along the back-bone of the continent. The mountains are well watered, with jagged, barren summits, glaciers on the northern peaks, alpine lakes and meadows, rushing icy streams, forested slopes of conifers and deciduous trees. The most striking difference between these mountains and their closest rival, the Sierras, is the amount of precipitation they receive. Unlike the Sierras, the Rockies receive abundant precipitation the year round, including sometimes severe summer thunderstorms. Wildlife is also abundant here. The lakes and streams provide excellent trout fishing, and some of the largest herds of elk, bighorn sheep, and mountain goat, as well as black and grizzly bear, cougar, fur-bearers, and a variety of birds are found here.

More than 40 national parks, forests, and monuments make this a backpacking paradise with thousands of miles of good trails and many wilderness and primitive areas. Opportunities for cross-country travel are equally good. Many of the trails are steep and rugged, making a hike torturous for those not up to it. In addition, mosquitoes in the spring and first half of summer, even in the alpine areas, can be a problem. The season is as short as a couple of months in the high north country because of snow in the high mountain passes. Use is moderate.

This is the favorite area of many backpackers. The experience of camping above the timberline in an alpine meadow on a glacial lake at the foot of a stark, rugged peak is hard to surpass. The mountain wildflowers are beautiful, and the snow-capped peaks and rocky ridges seem to tumble away in all directions. Nature seems so alive here when it sends its violent thunderstorms up the mountain valleys, and then sets the sun glinting off the necklace of alpine ponds strung down along the mountainside.

OZARKS

This obscure zone includes the Ozark Plateau of southern Mis-souri and northern Arkansas as well as the Ouachita Mountains of west-central Arkansas (though, technically, these are not part of the Ozarks). This uplifted zone has been eroded in much the same way as the Colorado Plateau—as the sedimentary plains of sand-stone and limestone slowly rose, they were worn down by erosion at about the same rate. For this reason, the mountain tops here are all about the same height, with most less than 2,500 feet. But unlike the Colorado Plateau, abundant precipitation supports dense vegetation that shields the earth's surface from the worst of the watery onslaught, and the features are softer and more rounded, making it an area of low mountains and shallow valleys cloaked in forests of hardwoods. Also, as a result of the easily dissolved limestone substratum, many caverns, caves, and under-ground rivers honeycomb the landscape.

The Ozarks are a meeting ground for many of the northern and southern species of plants and animals. More than 3,500 species of plants, 160 species of fish, and hundreds of species of birds are found in this area. Most of the larger mammals have been hunted off, but deer and black bear are regaining their numbers. Interest-ingly, some of the warmer south-facing rocky slopes support pseudo-desert environments, complete with cacti and scorpions.

Of all the major backpacking areas, though, this is the poorest. There is an unfortunate dearth of good trails, and the area is fairly well settled with many roads. Some good trips can be had here, especially if you choose to travel cross-country into some of the many pockets of wilderness. It is a popular hunting, fishing, and river-floating area, but its backpacking use is light. A nice feature of the area is its long, 8-month season, although the summers may be uncomfortably warm with abundant insects.

NORTHWOODS

While most of the Northwoods are found in Canada, extensive Northwoods environments exist in northern Minnesota, Wisconsin, and Michigan. Unlike the other backpacking areas in the country, the Northwoods are relatively flat. The last major geological event to have an effect on them was the latest period of glaciation. The last of the glaciers melted away only about 6,000 years ago, leav-ing behind the Great Lakes and a scoured landscape, soon re-claimed by the forest.

The Northwoods of today are mostly flat to rolling forests of mixed conifers and deciduous trees, punctuated by abundant lakes, bogs, and streams, supplied by plentiful year-round precipitation. The zone is noted for its good fishing for muskelunge, northern pike, and walleye, and the forests are inhabited by moose, deer, black bear, lynx, bobcat, fur-bearers, and an occasional wolf. Birds are numerous here along the Mississippi Flyway. Perhaps the Northwoods' best-known residents, though, are the mosquitoes and black flies, which can be intolerable in some areas in late spring and early summer.

This is a zone of fair to good backpacking opportunities, with a few outstanding areas such as Isle Royale and Superior National Forest. The somewhat limited number of trails are mostly well maintained with easy grades, but are moderately to heavily used. Cross-country travel is possible in many areas, although dense undergrowth and bogs can sometimes make the going rough. This is a good area for snowshoe backpacking if you are so inclined and if you plan your itinerary to steer clear of the snowmobilers. The area is most attractive to Midwesterners, of course, because of its proximity. They are drawn to the quiet lakes and deep forests to hike, surrounded by the deep green of summer or the blazing colors of autumn and to camp beside a tranquil lake, the quiet of dusk broken only by the lonely cry of a loon or the rare howl of a distant timber wolf.

APPALACHIAN MOUNTAINS

This extensive zone includes most of the country's eastern backpacking opportunities, extending from Maine to Georgia. It is defined by the ancient Appalachian Mountains, which, unlike the younger Rockies and Sierras, have been eroded down to lower, more rounded peaks. From New York State north, the glaciers have scraped away the topsoil and the higher peaks are barren with the mountain slopes pocketed by lakes gouged out by the glaciers. South of New York, where the glaciers never reached, the mountains have retained their mantle of topsoil, which supports luxuriant vegetation. Here, there are fewer lakes but the mountains are well drained by extensive streams and rivers.

The northern half of this zone is similar to the Northwoods environment, except that it is mountainous with some peaks over 6,000 feet. This may not seem high compared to the Western mountain systems, but the impact of these mountains is impressive with many soaring 4,000 feet above the surrounding landscape. The most ancient exposed rock on earth, the Canadian Shield, thrusts through the surface in many places here. In the southern portion of the zone, the natural environment reaches its greatest glory in the Smoky Mountains, where the moderate climate and abundant rainfall support a diverse ecology of Northern and Southern species of plants and animals.

Backpacking in this zone is good to excellent. The famous Appalachian Trail traverses this zone and the trails are usually good, but sometimes steep. The season in the southern reaches of the zone is year-round. Unfortunately, the only part of the zone that is at all remote and lightly used is in Maine. You might expect company in most of the other areas. This zone's greatest asset, though, like the Northwoods, is its accessibility to major population centers. While not as spectacular as some of the scenery out West, the zone provides wilderness and natural-area experiences for millions of people within a day's drive. With its late fall and early spring, the southern portion also provides a haven for the backpacker not content to put away the pack in September and take it out in June.

4

Some Things You Should Know

This country is blessed with an abundance of well-managed backpacking regions, ranging from natural areas virtually in the backyards of big cities to remote wilderness areas out West. Only a few well-publicized areas, though, receive the bulk of backpacking use. This is unfortunate for the backpackers who use these areas, and for the areas themselves. Overuse is becoming a serious problem.

When using this guide, keep an eye out for those areas that seem a little less popular than others. Comments on visitation are often provided. The Great Smoky Mountains National Park, for example, is the most heavily visited national park in the country, but backcountry use is only moderate. This is not unusual in the national parks. Some lesser-known trails in the Smokies are virtually unused, while the segment of the Appalachian Trail within the park is one of the most heavily used trails anywhere. Skill for predicting visitation on the basis of available information is a combination of experience and a little common sense.

About one-third of this country is in federal ownership. Federally administered backpacking areas of significance are under several jurisdictions. These include the national parks, seashores and lakeshores, monuments, and recreation areas, usually administered by the National Park Service, U.S. Department of the Interior; the national forests, administered by the Forest Service, U.S. Department of Agriculture; general public lands, administered by the Bureau of Land Management, U.S. Department of the Interior; and wildlife refuges, administered by the Fish and Wildlife Service, U.S. Department of the Interior. There are also a few other areas of less significance administered by the federal government.

National parks (including the national seashores and the like) were established by Congress exclusively to preserve outstanding recreational, scenic, inspirational, geological, and historical values for the public to enjoy. Although national parks usually are heavily visited, most visitors do not leave the roadside, and the excellent trail systems in the backcountry receive much less use than one would expect. National monuments were established for the same purpose as national parks, but these are less developed for backpacking use, often requiring the backpacker to travel cross-country. The national recreation areas supposedly have outstanding recreational attributes of national significance, and many do offer excellent backpacking opportunities. Together, the national parks, monuments, and recreation areas provide some of the most interesting backpacking opportunities in the country. Generally, no motorized vehicles are permitted on backcountry trails and no hunting is allowed. Topographic maps are usually sold at the parks.

The Forest Service manages 155 national forests and 19 national grasslands, comprising 187 million acres in 41 states and Puerto Rico. These are managed on the basis of multiple use of resources —water, timber, forage, wildlife, minerals, outdoor recreation, and environmental quality. By virtue of their sheer size, they offer the most for the backpacker, and they contain more than 100,000 miles of trails. Recreation, natural environment, and wildlife habitat are important management functions in most forests. Forest boundaries define the area that is planned to come into complete public ownership someday. Out West, many forests are near this goal and there are few private in-holdings. In the East, though, some areas are so chopped up that they can barely be called national forests. These in-holdings are often owned by timber companies that don't mind backpackers on their land. Otherwise, the backpacker has to be careful of trespassing on the private in-holdings.

Specially designated areas in the national forests are of particular interest to the backpacker. These are the wilderness and primitive areas, which, more than anywhere else, represent this country as it once was. The federal government defines them as places "where the earth and its community of life are untrammeled by man . . . retaining its primeval character and influence, without permanent improvements or human habitation . . . generally appearing to have been affected primarily by the forces of nature, with the imprint of man's work substantially unnoticeable. . . ."

Sound like what you're looking for? They probably are. The two characteristics that make these areas good for backpacking are also responsible for sparing them from civilization. One is that these areas are unsuitable for intensive use such as cities or farms. This is good for the backpacker, because the attributes that make land bad for development, such as rugged terrain and extremes of climate, often make it especially attractive for backpacking. The second is that these areas are far from large populations. Although inconvenient for the backpacker because it means he will usually have to travel farthest for the best wilderness, this is a small price to pay for solitude.

Here's the terminology the federal government uses: a wilderness area is anything over 100,000 acres, a wild area is between 5,000 and 100,000 acres, and a primitive area is an area being studied for designation as a wild or wilderness area. Wild and wilderness areas are usually lumped together and referred to broadly as wilderness areas or just wildernesses. All totaled, these areas comprise about 14.6 million acres, or about 8 percent of the entire national forest system. A little livestock grazing and prospecting is allowed, but closely controlled. There is no development beyond trails and a few very primitive campsites.

Another federal agency, the Bureau of Land Management, manages all those lands no one else wants, 460 million acres. Generally these are the arid regions of the West and Southwest. While these are not the most popular areas, some do offer significant backpacking opportunities. The Bureau of Land Management also has designated a few primitive areas that are distinct from the primitive areas described above.

The Fish and Wildlife Service administers the wildlife refuges throughout the country. The chief purpose of these areas is to provide wildlife habitat. While it is not the prime goal of the Fish and Wildlife Service, some areas do provide recreation opportunities, including backpacking. The Fish and Wildlife Service allows this type of use when it is not in conflict with the objectives of wildlife management.

In any of the federally managed areas, as well as some state and locally administered areas, there may be restrictions on the use of fire and on dogs, and there may be registration requirements. Most areas require fire permits for backcountry travel. This simply involves granting permission to build fires. It gives the official an opportunity to caution the backpacker on the dangers of careless use of fire, and, if the fire danger is too great, to prohibit its use. There is no cost for fire permits.

Many areas do not permit dogs in the backcountry. There are good reasons for this, including the harassment of wildlife by dogs and vice versa. Check before taking your dog along.

There is usually no fee for registering before you enter the backcountry. Registration is for your protection so the officials will know where to look if you don't return on time. Also, in heavily used areas, registration is used to control overuse of certain areas. Sometimes you may not be permitted to go where you wanted simply because there are too many people there already. Most backpackers, once they know that, would rather choose a less crowded area anyway.

In addition to federal areas, some states have state and local forests and parks that provide significant backpacking opportunities. Generally, federal areas are better for backpacking. The policies covering these areas vary with the state, but many are open to backpackers.

Another resource is the private trail. Perhaps because of limited public land ownership, long-distance trails developed and maintained by private groups proliferate in the East, the Appalachian Trail being the most famous. Thousands of miles of such trails presently exist and more are being developed. Unfortunately, large portions of these trails are better suited to casual hiking than to backpacking. Often, the trails traverse the rather civilized environments of cities and farmlands, and trailside camping may not be provided for nor permitted. These long-distance trails all cross a substantial amount of private land and prohibitions against camping are common. In planning trips along these trails, a good rule of thumb to follow is that trail segments largely on public land are the best sections for backpacking. Furthermore, long-distance trails that are mostly on public land are generally superior overall. While there is a romantic lure to take a long trip of several hundred or thousand miles along these trails, few actually do and settle instead for hiking some of the better sections. If there are two cars in your party and no opportunity for a loop trip, you can spot one at the end point of your itinerary to avoid having to backtrack.

Insects should be considered when planning any trip. The most bothersome insects are mosquitoes and black flies. Black flies are forest-loving gnats with an often painless bite that swells and itches for many days. They need fast-running water to breed and are found mostly in the Northwoods. Everyone knows what a mosquito is. They need still water to breed and seem to be found just about everywhere there is water. Perhaps more than any other natural cause, these two insects are responsible for ruining backpacking trips. Other insects that can be a problem in some areas of the country are ticks, chiggers, no-see-ums, deerflies, and horseflies. The peak insect season is usually early summer. It's a good idea to inquire about insects before visiting an area.

Some backpackers abstain from their favorite pastime during late spring and early summer, or visit arid areas where insects are not a problem. Late summer and fall are a particularly attractive time for backpacking in many areas simply because insects as well as overuse are less of a problem then. If you intend to visit an area during bug season, prepare yourself. Not only can swarming, stinging insects ruin the trip, they may also turn you off to backpacking completely. Take long-sleeved shirts, long pants, and plenty of insect repellent if there is any chance of an insect problem.

During the beginning of deer season in mid-fall, armies of hunters in the more populous states transform normally serene forests into dangerous battlegrounds. Individual hunters are not the problem; it's only when too many crowd into too few acres that people begin to die. Few backpackers brave areas where hunting is permitted during this time, and for good reason. However, national parks are always closed to hunting and provide a refuge for backpackers as well as for wildlife.

Grizzly bears have their own hunting season—for humans. For more about the dangers of grizzlies, see the discussion on Montana, page 158.

A few words about traveling cross-country. Cross-country travel means leaving designated trails and letting only your maps and compass be your guide. Many experts advise against it for the novice, and well they should. However, cross-country travel is the only way to really get away from the crowds and experience true wilderness where your footsteps might be the first. A cross-country trip requires more detailed, careful planning than a conventional one, but it need not be significantly more dangerous Two things are of paramount importance for a cross-country trip: having good detailed maps (the topographic maps described below), and informing a responsible official or friend of your itinerary. If you have the first, you shouldn't need the second unless you have an accident (which isn't as common as might be expected). Should you get lost or run into trouble and not return on the specified date, a search party can be arranged. If nobody knows you went in, nobody will know you didn't come out.

Of course, traveling alone cross-country is more risky than traveling with companions, but solo cross-country travel is probably less dangerous than mountain climbing and driving race cars, and it may even be less hazardous than riding in a car to the trailhead.

Standard U.S. Geological Survey maps are indispensable to the cross-country backpacker, and they can be helpful, and fun, even for those who stick to the beaten path. These topographical maps or "topos" show the shape and elevation of the terrain and delineate a wide range of natural and man-made features in detail. They are not difficult to learn to use. Unfortunately, not all areas of the country are covered by topos.

Indexes to topographic maps for each of the 50 states, American Samoa, Guam, Puerto Rico, and the U.S. Virgin Islands and an information booklet on topographical maps and symbols are available free on request from USGS distribution offices: 1200 S. Eads St., Arlington, Virginia 22202; Federal Center, Denver, Colorado 80225; and 310 Fairbanks Ave., Fairbanks, Alaska 99701; and the National Cartographic Information Center (507), U.S. Geological Survey National Center, Reston, Virginia 22092.

For purposes of this guide, the country is divided into 6 geographic regions:

The Northwest, including Alaska, Idaho, Oregon, and Washington.

The West and Southwest, including Arizona, California, Hawaii, Nevada, New Mexico, and Utah.

The Midcontinent, including Colorado, Kansas, Montana, Nebraska, North Dakota, South Dakota, and Wyoming.

The Midwest, including Illinois, Indiana, Iowa, Michigan, Minnesota, Missouri, Ohio, and Wisconsin.

The South, including Alabama, Arkansas, Florida, Georgia, Kentucky, Louisiana, Mississippi, North Carolina, Oklahoma, South Carolina, Tennessee, Texas, Virginia, and West Virginia.

The Northeast, including Connecticut, Delaware, Maine, Maryland, Massachusetts, New Hampshire, New Jersey, New York, Pennsylvania, Rhode Island, and Vermont.

Backpacking areas in each state are discussed, usually beginning with federally administered areas, then state, and finally locally administered areas. For each individual state this is generally descending order on the basis of backpacking quality. For some states with many backpacking opportunities, areas are grouped geographically. Discussion of each area includes indication of its size, location, natural characteristics, potential for backpacking, and other pertinent information, followed by references for more detailed information. The description of each area is just an introduction. Top-quality detailed information is available for most areas from the administering agency. After you identify areas that interest you, write for maps and information to the addresses given throughout this book. Such information will contribute to the success of your trip and will provide many enjoyable winter evenings planning next summer's trips.

The following federal agencies, as discussed previously, administer the most extensive system of wild and natural areas in the country. General information is available from them as listed below. More detailed information can be obtained from specific sources listed in the regional guides. Although many of these publications carry a nominal charge when obtained from the Superintendent of Documents, they are frequently distributed by the land managing agencies for free.

U.S. Forest Service, U.S. Department of Agriculture

"Backpacking in the National Forests" (PA-585, 25¢), "National Forest Vacations" (FS-50, 55¢), and "Search for Solitude" (PA-942, 65¢) are available from the Superintendent of Documents, Washington, D.C., 20402. "National Forest Wilderness and Primitive Areas" and "Field Offices of the Forest Service" are available free from the Forest Service, U.S. Department of Agriculture, Washington, D.C. 20250.

National Park Service, U.S. Department of the Interior

"Back-Country Travel in the National Park System" (65¢) and "Winter Activities in the National Park System" (35¢) are available from the Superintendent of Documents, Washington, D.C. 20402.

Bureau of Land Management, U.S. Department of the Interior

"Room to Roam," "List of Primitive Areas," and "State Offices Mailing Addresses" are available free from the Office of Information, Bureau of Land Management, Interior Building, Washington, D.C. 20240.

Fish and Wildlife Service, U.S. Department of the Interior

"List of National Wildlife Refuges Permitting Camping" is available free from the Assistant Director—Public Affairs, Fish and Wildlife Service, Interior Building, Washington, D.C. 20240.

5

The Northwest: Alaska, Idaho, Oregon, and Washington

Each state in this region has outstanding backpacking opport
nities. Alaska is a wilderness region where the rugged topograph
and rigorous climate have preserved it in a natural state an
blessed it with more wilderness than in all the other states com
bined. Unfortunately, it is inaccessible to most backpackers
Idaho is another rugged land where much of the state is excellent
for backpacking. Low population densities in and around the
state contribute to the untrammeled character of its many backpacking areas. Oregon and Washington have magnificent mountain ranges, temperate rain forests, wild Pacific coastlines, and
sparsely settled inland areas to attract the backpacker.

ALASKA

This state is in a class by itself with wilderness the rule. The
state consists of a series of mountain ranges and valleys, generally
running east-west. These, along with the oceans on three sides,
influence the weather, which in turn determines the varied environments of the peninsula. The southern mountains include the
coast ranges in the panhandle with elevations to about 18,000
feet, the Alaskan Range in southern Alaska with 20,320-foot
Mount McKinley, and the Aleutian Range with elevations mostly

[41

under 6,000 feet. This southern portion of the state is wet, temperate, and heavily forested, the result of the warming influence of the Japan Current.

North of the Alaskan Range, the climate becomes drier and much colder. This interior land of low hills and ridges often endures winter cold of $-50°$ F or less, and receives less than 20 inches of precipitation. The landscape is sparsely forested, with extensive tundra.

The Brooks Range in the northern third of the state defines the northern boundary of the Alaskan interior. On the North Slope, the area between the Brooks Range and the Arctic Ocean, the temperature warms up a bit, again because of the warm Japan Current, but the area is technically a desert with less than 5 inches of precipitation a year. The North Slope is marshy nevertheless because the permafrost permits none of this moisture to percolate into the ground, creating a tundra environment where large trees cannot survive and all vegetation hugs the ground for protection against the dry, cold wind.

While Alaska has more acres of national forest than any other state, the wilderness is so pristine that there are few developments even for the backpacker. Anyone who is fortunate enough to make it to Alaska must be completely self-sufficient, because there are few conveniences to greet you there. It is not an area for novices, and experienced backpackers should be prepared to include cross-country travel plans in their itinerary. Even travel to and from the backpacking areas is often difficult and expensive. Roads are nonexistent in most of the state, so travel is mostly by air. The best time to visit Alaska is in June before the mosquitoes get bad and when daylight exists for almost 24 hours. Average summer temperatures range in the mid-50s. Black bear, brown bear, and moose can be dangerous. Here is a passage from a brochure describing a trail in Chugach National Forest: "This is brown bear country. Hikers should make noise and carry a 30.06 or larger rifle."

General tourism information is available from the State Travel Division, Department of Economic Development, Pouch E, Juneau, Alaska 99801.

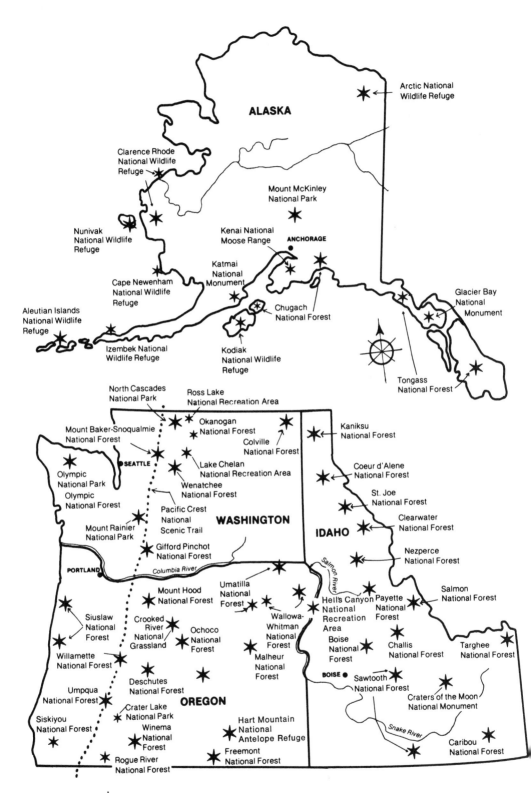

ALASKA

Arctic National Wildlife Refuge

Clarence Rhode National Wildlife Refuge

Mount McKinley National Park

Nunivak National Wildlife Refuge

Kenai National Moose Range

ANCHORAGE

Katmai National Monument

Cape Newenham National Wildlife Refuge

Chugach National Forest

Glacier Bay National Monument

Aleutian Islands National Wildlife Refuge

Izembek National Wildlife Refuge

Kodiak National Wildlife Refuge

Tongass National Forest

North Cascades National Park

Ross Lake National Recreation Area

Mount Baker-Snoqualmie National Forest

Okanogan National Forest

Colville National Forest

Kaniksu National Forest

Olympic National Park

Olympic National Forest

SEATTLE

Lake Chelan National Recreation Area

Wenatchee National Forest

Coeur d'Alene National Forest

St. Joe National Forest

Pacific Crest National Scenic Trail

WASHINGTON

Clearwater National Forest

Mount Rainier National Park

IDAHO

Gifford Pinchot National Forest

PORTLAND

Columbia River

Nezperce National Forest

Mount Hood National Forest

Umatilla National Forest

Salmon River

Hell's Canyon National Recreation Area

Payette National Forest

Salmon National Forest

Siuslaw National Forest

Crooked River National Grassland

Ochoco National Forest

Wallowa-Whitman National Forest

Boise National Forest

Challis National Forest

Targhee National Forest

Willamette National Forest

Malheur National Forest

BOISE

Sawtooth National Forest

Umpqua National Forest

Deschutes National Forest

OREGON

Craters of the Moon National Monument

Crater Lake National Park

Siskiyou National Forest

Winema National Forest

Hart Mountain National Antelope Refuge

Snake River

Caribou National Forest

Rogue River National Forest

Freemont National Forest

★ Relatively large-acreage area
✳ Comparatively small-acreage area

Mount McKinley National Park

The 1,939,000-acre park is located between Anchorage and Fairbanks, surrounding North America's tallest peak, Mount McKinley, at 20,320 feet. The park is a wilderness of alpine tundra, spruce forests, lakes, streams, and glacier-topped mountains. Wildlife is abundant and includes caribou, moose, Dall sheep, black and grizzly bear, wolf, wolverine, lynx, river otter and other fur-bearers, grouse, ptarmigan, and whistling swan.

For all its great size, the park has only 10 miles of hiking trails because it is well-suited for travel without them. Cross-country travel is unrestricted except for the required backcountry use permit. The season is from about June 1 to September 15. Access is by an all-weather road, by train, or by airplane.

For information and a map of the park, contact the Superintendent, Mount McKinley National Park, P.O. Box 9, McKinley Park, Alaska 99755.

Glacier Bay National Monument

With 2,804,000 acres, this is the largest unit in the national park system. Located just west of Juneau, the monument is an interface of land, ice, and water where huge blocks of ice sheer from glaciers and plunge into the sea, filling it with icebergs. Peaks rising to 15,300 feet are covered with dense coniferous forests below the timberline, home for brown bear, the largest land carnivore, and black bear, lynx, wolf, coyote, wolverine, mountain goat, deer, mink, and marten. The shoreline is also inhabited by seals, whales, porpoises, and a variety of shore birds. Fishing, both fresh- and saltwater, is good.

There are only 12 miles of trails in the monument, so the backpacker should plan to travel cross-country. There is no access by land; it is reachable by airplane and boat only. Obviously, solitude and wilderness are easy to come by here.

For information, contact the Superintendent, Glacier Bay National Monument, Gustavus, Alaska 99826.

Katmai National Monument

A close second in size to Glacier Bay, this 2,792,000-acre monument spans the base of the Alaska Peninsula southwest of Anchorage. It is a volcanic region that includes the Valley of Ten Thousand Smokes, the scene of a violent eruption in 1912. The monument is a mosaic of tundra, grassland, and forests, with many large lakes and streams. Wildlife includes brown bear, wolf, lynx, moose, wolverine, sea and river otters, northern sea lion, beaver, and many birds. Fishing is excellent.

There are no trails in the monument, so it is an area for experienced cross-country travelers only. Access is by airplane and boat only.

For information, contact the Superintendent, Katmai National Monument, P.O. Box 7, King Salmon, Alaska 99613.

Chugach National Forest

This 4,723,000-acre forest, the second largest in the national forest system, is located on the southern coast of the state near Anchorage. It is a land of islands, bays, inland lakes, rivers, glaciers, and mountains. Most of the area is tundra above Alaska's low timberline, with forested areas limited to the coast and valleys. Wildlife is abundant and includes moose, Dall sheep, brown and black bear, mountain goat, elk, wolf, lynx, a variety of birds, shellfish, and fish. Salmon fishing is especially good.

Because of the presence of 100 miles or so of trails and backcountry cabins, this is an excellent area for backpacking. There are good maps and detailed literature available on these trails, and access is by auto, boat, or airplane from Anchorage. Backcountry cabins must be reserved and a fee is charged for their use. Cross-country travel is possible on the extensive alpine tundra.

Information and a map of the forest is available from the Supervisor, Chugach National Forest, 121 East Fireweed Lane, Suite 205, Anchorage, Alaska 99503.

Tongass National Forest

By far the largest forest in the national forest system, Tongass National Forest contains 16,001,000 acres. It takes up most of the southeastern panhandle of the state, and is bordered on the north by Glacier Bay National Monument. It is similar to the Chugach, but is more heavily timbered, mostly with spruce and hemlock. Fjords lace the entire forest beneath towering mountains, and the famous Menderhall Glacier is found here. The warm Japan Current has a moderating effect on the climate and produces heavy rainfall. Deer, moose, wolf, coyote, wolverine, black and brown bear, eagle and other birds, and a variety of fish including 50-pound king salmon, are abundant.

Like in Chugach, there are backcountry cabins, some of them accessible by trail. These must be reserved and a fee is charged for their use. Trails are not abundant considering the forest's size, and cross-country travel is difficult in the dense forest and not recommended.

For information and maps of the forest, contact the supervisors: in the Chatham Area: P.O. Box 1980, Sitka, Alaska 99835; in the Ketchikan Area: P.O. Box 2278, Ketchikan, Alaska 99901; and in the Stikine Area: P.O. Box 309, Petersburg, Alaska 99833.

Alaska's National Wildlife Refuges

Most of the Alaskan refuges are remote, without facilities, and have few or no trails. However, all can provide rewards to the well-equipped backpacker, experienced in wilderness camping and willing to pay the price. For example, access to the Cape Newenham Wildlife Refuge is by float-equipped bush plane only and costs about $400 round trip from Bethel. Nunivak Wildlife Refuge is a real bargain via a scheduled mail flight serving the island's community of Mekoryuk—only $75! Travel in Alaska is not cheap.

For general information on the state's wildlife refuges, contact the Supervisor, Alaskan Wildlife Refuges, Fish and Wildlife Service, P.O. Box 280, Anchorage, Alaska 99501. Detailed information on refuges offering the best backpacking opportunities may be obtained from the addresses below.

ALEUTIAN ISLANDS NATIONAL WILDLIFE REFUGE

This is the third largest in the national system at 2,720,000 acres. It extends over 1,000 linear miles along the Aleutian Islands chain, encompassing 200 of them. A major sea otter habitat, it also supports sea birds, brown bear, caribou, and other flora and fauna of the Alaskan Peninsula. Access is by commercial airlines.

For information, contact the Refuge Manager, Aleutian Islands National Wildlife Refuge, Cold Bay, Alaska 99571.

ARCTIC NATIONAL WILDLIFE REFUGE

The largest in the national system at 8,900,000 acres, this refuge encompasses the northeast corner of the state. It is an undisturbed arctic environment and one of the most magnificent wilderness areas in North America. Polar bear as well as other large mammals, fur-bearers, and upland birds are present. Access is by private or charter plane only.

For information, contact the Supervisor, Alaskan Wildlife Refuges, P.O. Box 280, Anchorage, Alaska 99501.

CAPE NEWENHAM NATIONAL WILDLIFE REFUGE

Located on the southwestern coast, it includes 265,000 acres, terminating at the steep-cliffed Cape Newenham. This refuge is possibly the largest nesting colony in North America. There are also grizzly bears, but the most common mammals are hair seals, sea lions, and walrus. Hiking conditions are good on the mostly barren mountainous rock. Access is by chartered float plane.

For information, contact the Refuge Manager, Cape Newenham National Wildlife Refuge, P.O. Box 346, Bethel, Alaska 99559.

CLARENCE RHODE NATIONAL WILDLIFE REFUGE

The second largest refuge in the national system at 2,817,000 acres, this refuge is an area of low-lying tundra on the coast north of Cape Newenham. It is an extensive migratory bird nesting area accessible by charter plane. This is a wet area that is difficult to hike on, and would make a better combination hike-boat trip.

For information, contact the Refuge Manager, Clarence Rhode National Wildlife Refuge, P.O. Box 346, Bethel, Alaska 99559.

IZEMBEK NATIONAL WILDLIFE REFUGE

This refuge consists of 415,000 acres on the tip of the Alaskan Peninsula. It is a scenic combination of both upland tundra and lowland tidal lagoons and bays. Wildlife includes waterfowl, brown bear, and caribou. Access is by commercial airlines.

For information, contact the Refuge Manager, Izembek National Wildlife Refuge, Cold Bay, Alaska 99571.

KENAI NATIONAL MOOSE RANGE

This 1,730,000-acre area occupies the western slopes of the Kenai Mountains and the glaciated lowlands bordering the Cook Inlet southwest of Anchorage. In addition to moose, the upland is habitat for Dall sheep, mountain goat, brown and black bear, and fur-bearers. The lake-dotted lowland is excellent trout habitat and nesting grounds for the rare trumpeter swan. This is the most accessible (by land from Anchorage) and most developed (campgrounds, picnic sites, hiking trails, and canoe trails) of the state's refuges. Consequently, it is also the most heavily used, but by no standards but Alaska's own.

For information, contact the Refuge Manager, Kenai National Moose Range, P.O. Box 500, Kenai, Alaska 99611.

KODIAK NATIONAL WILDLIFE REFUGE

This 1,815,000-acre area encompasses the rugged, mountainous southwestern two-thirds of Kodiak Island off the southern coast of the state. The refuge is the home of the famous Kodiak brown bear, and extensive streams provide habitat for abundant salmon. Access is by commercial airlines or boat. Guide service, available in and around the island, is required for nonresidents. Needless to say, this can be expensive.

For information, contact the Refuge Manager, Kodiak National Wildlife Refuge, P.O. Box 825, Kodiak, Alaska 99615.

NUNIVAK NATIONAL WILDLIFE REFUGE

This refuge is a 1,109,000-acre, tundra-covered volcanic island off the southwest coast of the state. It is the home of the only musk-ox herd in the United States and is also shared by a large reindeer herd. Access is easy by regular air transportation, and the village of Mekoryuk provides guides if desired. The south side of the island is very scenic where musk-ox and traditional Eskimo fishing camps may be seen.

For information, contact the Refuge Manager, Nunivak National Wildlife Refuge, P.O. Box 346, Bethel, Alaska 99559.

Other Public Lands

There are over 1,000,000 acres of state parks (Chugach near Anchorage, Kachemak Bay on the south coast, and Denali near Mount McKinley) and much more public land that is wilderness or virtually so. This is all typical Alaskan environment—tundra, mountains, glaciers, lakes, streams, and abundant wildlife—and Chugach is the only state park with significant developments. Backpacking is mostly cross-country for the experienced only. An exception to this is the 80-mile White Mountains Trail, interior Alaska's first. Its access points are Mile 42 Steese Highway and Mile 25 Elliot Highway. This trail passes through all types of Alaskan terrain—bogs, alpine meadows, and mountain ridges. A variety of the state's wildlife, large and small, is represented along the trail and there is good grayling fishing.

For information on state land, contact the State of Alaska Department of Natural Resources, 323 East Fourth Avenue, Anchorage, Alaska 99501. For information on the White Mountains Trail and other federal land, contact the Bureau of Land Management, 555 Cordova Street, Anchorage, Alaska 99501.

IDAHO

Except for the Snake River Plain in the southern portion of the state, this state is almost entirely hills and mountains. This, combined with its low population density and distance from large population centers, makes Idaho an excellent state for backpackers. With plentiful public land, much of it is in a natural or wilderness state. It has the most acres of designated wilderness and primitive areas of all the states—the largest and most primitive protected wildland in the continental United States, the Idaho Primitive Area, and several other firstclass backpacking areas are found here. The season in the highlands is short, generally the summer months. Most backpacking opportunities are in the 12 national forests in the state, total acreage of which is second only to California. They are described below, beginning in the north. The Kaniksu, Coeur d'Alene, and St. Joe National forests are collectively referred to as the Idaho Panhandle National Forests, but each maintains its own identity.

General tourism information is available from the State Department of Commerce and Development, State Capitol, Boise, Idaho 83707.

Kaniksu National Forest

The 1,622,000 acres of this forest include most of the northern tip of the state north of Sandpoint and extend into Montana and Washington. Although elevations do not exceed 7,000 feet, the backcountry is very rugged. Several large lakes border the forest and lake and stream fishing is good. Wildlife includes black bear, door, a few grizzlies and cougar, bobcat, and no doubt occasional wolves wandering down from Canada.

The Cabinet Mountains Wilderness Area is partly in this forest, described under the Kootenai National Forest in Montana. There are hundreds of miles of additional trails in the forest proper, and due to the remoteness of this forest, they are very little used. The Selkirk Crest in the northern portion of the forest is particularly wild and has few timber company intrusions; there are over 100 square miles of roadless area here.

For information and maps of the forest, contact the Supervisor's office, U.S.D.A. Forest Service, P.O. Box 310, Coeur d'Alene, Idaho 83814.

Coeur d'Alene National Forest

Just south of the Kaniksu National Forest and east of the city of Coeur d'Alene lies this forest of 725,000 acres, extending partly into Montana. It is an area of low, timbered mountains that are home principally for elk and deer. The forest is neither particularly noteworthy nor wild as there is considerable mining and logging, but the Bitterroot Range on the east bordering the Kaniksu in Montana is fairly remote with elevations in the 5,000-foot range. There are few trails in the forest and wilderness lovers may want to pass up this forest in favor of those wilder areas to the south.

For information and a map of the forest, contact the Supervisor's office, same address as above.

St. Joe National Forest

Continuing south down the state is this 865,000-acre forest near St. Maries. Virgin stands of white pine grace the mountain sides, target for many of the large timber operations in the forest, as are the spruce, fir, cedar, and hemlock which are all clearcut. Elk, deer, black bear, and mountain goat may be spotted and the fishing is good in the streams. The forest is generally not very good for backpacking. Two areas are exceptions. The most remote and rugged area is the Bitterroot Range of the Idaho-Montana divide, which offers good hiking possibilities and the least possibility of getting in the way of someone's bulldozer. The Mallard-Larkins Pioneer Area is a 31,000-acre nonmotorized area, also good for backpacking. This subalpine area has a concentration of trout-filled lakes and rugged mountains.

For information and a map of the forest, contact the Supervisor's office, same address as above.

Clearwater National Forest

Lying just south of the St. Joe, the 1,823,000 acres of this forest of pine, fir, hemlock, spruce, and cedar is east and north of Orofino. It includes 3,000 miles of streams and 116 lakes, many of which offer good trout and salmon fishing. There are deep canyons and peaks to 8,800 feet. Elk, deer, and black bear frequent the large stands of white pine. A variety of other wildlife abounds, including a few elusive mountain goat and moose.

About two-thirds of the forest is roadless and undeveloped, and there are many miles of trails all over the forest. Two areas of particular interest to backpackers are the Selway-Bitterroot Wilderness described under the Nezperce National Forest and the Mallard-Larkins Pioneer Area mentioned above in the St. Joe National Forest description. The many miles of trails, lakes, large trees, and magnificent scenery all over the forest make for excellent backpacking. Naturally, in the roaded areas you are more likely to encounter motorized vehicles or logging activity.

For information and a map of the forest, contact the Supervisor, Clearwater National Forest, Orofino, Idaho 83544.

Nezperce National Forest

This 2,198,000-acre forest borders the Clearwater on the south just east of Grangeville, and with 2,700 miles of trails, it is one of the best backpacking forests in the state. The area has many mountain lakes and many hundreds of miles of streams. The range in elevation is from about 1,000 feet to 10,000 feet, providing a variety of environments, from warm, sometimes dusty lowland meadows, through cooler, forested mountainsides up to timberline. This variety of environments supports a variety of wildlife, including elk, deer, black bear, bighorn, cougar, mountain goat, smaller mammals, and about 200 species of birds. Since 1,500 miles of roads penetrate much of this forest, three roadless areas are of particular interest to the backpacker. See also Hell's Canyon National Recreation Area in Oregon, below.

Encompassing 1,240,000 acres, the Selway-Bitterroot Wilderness Area is the largest classified wilderness in the lower 48 states. It extends into four national forests in two states. Elevations range from 1,600 feet to about 10,000 feet, covered with wildflower meadows, forests of spruce, fir, pine, and cedar, and some very rugged terrain. Past wildfires have kept the forests young; few old patriarchs can be found except for the huge old cedars in the river valleys, where many of the trails are found. Trails are plentiful, but often traverse difficult terrain. An especially remote and wild area is along the Bitterroot Range on the east side of the wilderness. Many trails along this range receive very light use. Cross-country travel is also possible.

The Salmon River Breaks Primitive Area includes 217,000 acres and is an extension of and is physically similar to the large Idaho Primitive Area described under the Payette National Forest below. It lies on the north side of the Salmon River, "the river of no return," extending for 40 miles along riverbreaks, forests, and mountains. It is well serviced by trails, but otherwise is extremely rugged and remote. Bighorn sheep may be spotted on the mountains in the higher elevations.

The third area, the Gospel Hump Wilderness Area, contains 206,000 acres of scenic high country between Buffalo Hump and the Gospel Mountain, extending south to the Salmon River. There are only a few trails in this newly designated wilderness.

For information and maps of the forest, wilderness, and primitive area, contact the Supervisor, Nezperce National Forest, 319 East Main, Grangeville, Idaho 83530.

Payette National Forest

This forest is probably the most remote and wild of any in the continental United States. Its 2,313,885 acres are located in central Idaho, divided into two units bordering the Nezperce on the south. About half is timber-covered, with hundreds of miles of trails throughout. Although most of this forest is excellent for backpacking, the Idaho Primitive Area provides the best wilderness backpacking opportunities. Also see Hell's Canyon National Recreation Area in Oregon, below.

If you're going to Idaho looking for wilderness, the Idaho Primitive Area is the place. The huge 1,225,000-acre area is the wildest of all those designated areas in the continental United States. It is a rugged land of lakes, rivers, streams, peaks, canyons, forests, and parklands, stretching as far as the eye can see, with elevations from 3,000 feet to 10,000 feet. Deer, elk, moose, bighorn sheep, mountain goat, black bear, cougar, lynx, bobcat, fox, and other small mammals, as well as many birds, and good trout fishing are found here. The more than 2,000 miles of trails have good campsites and light use. Fire danger is high in the summer. This area also has the distinction of being the home of the last of the mountain men, Sylvan Hart, who deserted civilization in the 1930s to live a self-sufficient spartan life as a recluse-hunter-farmer, and succeeded. Backpackers often cross his hand-made suspension bridge to drop in and chat.

For information and maps of the forest and primitive area, contact the Supervisor, Payette National Forest, McCall, Idaho 83638.

Salmon National Forest

Bordering the Payette on the east and including part of the Idaho Primitive Area is this 1,768,000-acre forest of mostly high country between 6,000-foot and 10,000-foot elevation with spectacular scenery of jutting granite peaks, forests, and parklands. Wildlife is similar to that of the Idaho Primitive Area, with the addition of antelope in the lower areas. Most backpackers will want to visit the Idaho Primitive Area in this forest, but there are over 1,200 miles of trails throughout several units of the forest, and most of them are little used, so solitude is easy to find. The backpacker who is a bit unsure of himself in the primitive area may wish to try some of these other excellent and somewhat less remote trails. Access to this forest is generally good.

For information and a map, contact the Supervisor, Salmon National Forest, P.O. Box 729, Salmon, Idaho 83467.

Challis National Forest

While this 2,448,000-acre forest just south of the Salmon National Forest has no designated wilderness or primitive areas
exclusively within its boundaries, it is by no means nondescript.
The tallest peak in the state, Mount Borah at 12,655 feet, is within
its boundary as well as some of the largest herds of game animals,
including antelope. The terrain is often severe, glacier-carved
mountain peaks, interspersed with forest, parkland, meadows, and
over 900 miles of rivers and streams. Trails are plentiful, but
some are quite difficult to traverse. Three excellent areas for backpacking are the Idaho Primitive Area, which extends into this
forest and is discussed under the Payette National Forest, above;
the Sawtooth Primitive Area, discussed with Boise National
Forest, below; and the White Cloud Peaks in the Sawtooth National Recreation Area.

Although not designated as a primitive or wilderness area
because of its present and past mining activity, the 157,000-acre
White Cloud Peaks area is worthy of such designation as far as
the backpacker is concerned. It is an area of peaks in the 10 to
12,000-foot range, studded with lakes and laced with cascading
streams. Trails serve many of the lakes and follow streams. No
roads penetrate the Peaks area, and there are restrictions on
motorized use.

For information and maps of the forest and recreation area,
contact the Supervisor, Challis National Forest, Forest Service
Building, Challis, Idaho 83226.

Boise National Forest

This large, 2,639,000-acre forest, bordering the Challis National
Forest on the north and just east of the city of Boise, is a combination of mountains, canyons, forests, parklands, meadows, barren
peaks, and stands of virgin ponderosa pine. Black bear, elk, and
deer are present, though not in the numbers common for Idaho's
forests. Lake and stream fishing for trout is good. The forest is not
as remote as many in the state and is penetrated by many roads.

This, combined with the proximity of Boise, makes use in the more accessible areas relatively heavy. However, the backpacker can find refuge in the Idaho Primitive Area, discussed above under the Payette National Forest, which extends into this forest, or may choose the excellent Sawtooth Wilderness in the Sawtooth National Recreation Area.

The Sawtooth Wilderness is 216,000 acres of jagged, "sawtooth" mountains, gorges, timbered slopes, streams, waterfalls, meadows, and over 200 alpine lakes hidden among the high peaks which soar to over 10,000 feet. Trout are found in the lakes, and mountain goat, deer, elk, black bear, and smaller animals and birds abound. Access is good and 300 miles of trails connect many of the interior lakes. The trailless areas around many of the high lake basins also provide excellent cross-country travel opportunities. The lightest use of the area during the regular season is between June 1 and July 15, and during September.

For information and maps of the forest and wilderness, contact the Supervisor, Boise National Forest, 1075 Park Boulevard, Boise, Idaho 83706.

Sawtooth National Forest

Nestled between the Boise National Forest on the west and the Challis National Forest on the northeast are the 1,804,000 acres of this national forest. Several other small units of the forest are located on the south-central border of the state and extend into Utah. The large northern unit contains the Sawtooth Mountains and part of the Sawtooth Wilderness described under the Boise National Forest above. The scenic, jagged peaks form a spectacular backdrop to the fir, spruce, and pine forests that cloak their higher slopes. The forest is famous for the Sun Valley four-season recreation area, but most of the forest is wild and rugged enough to deter most of the "tourist" use. Wildlife includes deer, elk, mountain goat, bighorn sheep, antelope, cougar, bobcat, fox, and other fur-bearers. Trout and salmon are found in the rivers and lakes. The units to the south are more arid, with fantastically carved natural rock sculptures, but are less suitable for backpacking because of their smaller size, greater accessibility to the population, and poorer trail system.

The best area in the forest for backpacking is the Idaho Primitive Area, as already mentioned, and the Boulder Mountains in the Sawtooth National Recreation Area. The Boulder Mountains are masses of sheer, rocky ledges and spires climbing to almost 12,000 feet. This is a very rugged, wild area with few trails and very light use. Although there are few alpine lakes, streams are plentiful in this land of awesome and sometimes stark landscape.

For information and a map of the forest, contact the Supervisors, Northern and Minidoka Divisions, Sawtooth National Forest, 1525 Addison Avenue, Twin Falls, Idaho 83301.

Targhee National Forest

This 1,854,000-acre forest spreads along the northeast corner of the state into Wyoming, west of Yellowstone and the Grand Tetons national parks which it borders. The forest generally follows the timbered and alpine crests of several mountain ranges, including the Teton Range, and follows the continental divide along the Centennial Mountains on the Idaho-Montana boundary. Deer, black bear, elk, and a few grizzlies and bighorns are the larger mammals present, with moose most abundant in the Teton Range. Water is not abundant, in the Northern Plateaus, but streams and few lakes containing trout, salmon, and whitefish elsewhere in the forest provide excellent fishing. The lower reaches of the forest are well laced with roads, and only a few trails penetrate the alpine areas, which are quite wild. One of the best areas for backpacking is just west of Grand Teton National Park, where good but steep trails lead into the park, and in a large, virtually roadless area just south and west of the park. The trails are not always well maintained.

For information and a map, contact the Supervisor, Targhee National Forest, 420 North Bridge Street, St. Anthony, Idaho 83445.

Caribou National Forest

The 1,088,000 acres of this forest in southeastern Idaho are divided among several units and extend partly into Utah and Wyoming. It is an area of stark mountain ranges divided by beautiful valleys. About half the area is forested with aspen, pine, and fir. Most peaks are in the 8,000-foot range, although some are much higher. Elk, deer, black bear, moose, bobcat, smaller animals and game birds, and stream and lake fishing are found here. There is an excellent system of trails in the northern portion of the largest unit, which, along with the moderate elevations, makes for a comfortable backpacking area.

For information and a map of the forest, contact the Supervisor, Caribou National Forest, 250 South Fourth, Federal Building, Pocatello, Idaho 83201.

There is one other major backpacking opportunity in the state outside of a national forest:

Craters of the Moon National Monument

This monument, located west of Idaho Falls near the town of Arco in south-central Idaho, offers a different sort of wilderness experience. In trailless, cinder-cone-studded lava fields, the backpacker can wander at will in a 44,000-acre igneous environment that he is unlikely to find elsewhere. Although austere, it is home for an association of hardy plants and animals, including elk, antelope, deer, cougar, coyote, bobcat, red fox, marmot, and pika. Special precautions should be taken when traveling alien terrain, so check with the superintendent of the monument first. Wood fires are not permitted in the monument and a backcountry travel permit is required.

For information and a map of the monument, contact the Superintendent, Craters of the Moon National Monument, P.O. Box 29, Arco, Idaho 83213.

Hell's Canyon National Recreation Area

See Oregon, below.

Other Public Lands

For the adventurous who like desolate, arid, and sometimes difficult terrain to roam and camp at will, there are many millions of acres of public land managed by the Bureau of Land Management in the southwest and south-central portions of the state. For example, St. Anthony Sand Dunes in Fremont County northwest of St. Anthony is a strip of wind-driven sand dunes, 10 to 100 feet high, a mile wide, and 30 miles long. Or there is Bruneau-Jarbridge Canyons in Owyhee County, southeast of Bruneau, one of the deepest, narrowest canyons in the world—67 miles long with sheer 2,000-foot cliffs and unusual rock formations. There is also the Silent City of Rocks in Cassia County, near Almo, a 24-square-mile area of weird rock formations.

For the adventurous who enjoy wild and primitive rivers as part of the scenic backdrop, numerous camp sites are located along the Salmon, Bruneau, and Jarbridge rivers. There are no dams on these rivers. They flow freely through remote wilderness areas and rural landscapes with shorelines that are largely primitive and undeveloped, providing a varied scenic panorama for backpackers. These rivers snake through rolling hills, meander through meadows, and roar through steep arid canyons.

For information on these and other public lands, contact the Bureau of Land Management, Idaho State Office, Box 042, Boise, Idaho 83724.

OREGON

This is a backpacker's paradise with thousands of miles of trails and a variety of environments—seacoast, forests, mountains, deserts, plateaus, and canyons. Thirteen national forests and many designated wildernesses constitute the bulk of its backpacking resource. The state is about three-fourths mountains and valleys, with a high desert in the southeast quarter. The western half of the state rises abruptly out of the ocean along the Coast Range, with the Cascade Range behind it about one-third of the way inland. The northeast quarter of the state is made equally rugged by the Blue Mountains. Mountains, interspersed with valleys, basins, deserts, and plateaus, comprise the scenery that Oregon is famous for. Perhaps just as important is the state's environmental ethic, which preserves it that way.

The national forests fall into 3 groups. They are described in a generally north-to-south order, beginning with the Coast Range, then the Cascades, and finally those in the northeast portion of the state. The Pacific Crest National Scenic Trail crosses Oregon. See California (chapter 6) for a discussion of this trail.

Forest recreation maps (50¢) for forests in Oregon can be obtained from the U.S. Forest Service, Pacific Northwest Regional Office, P.O. Box 3623, 319 S.W. Pine Street, Portland, Oregon 97208, as well as from the addresses given below.

A wilderness permit system is in effect in the state, and a permit is required for visitation of some of the wildernesses. Wildernesses that require permits vary from year to year. For up-to-date information on what areas require permits and how to obtain them, contact the same address as above for areas in Oregon and Washington.

General tourism information is available from the State Highway Division, Travel Information Section, State Highway Building, Salem, Oregon 97301.

Coast Range National Forests

SIUSLAW NATIONAL FOREST

This 625,000-acre forest is divided into several units along the Oregon coast, the largest of which is west of Eugene. It is an area of verdant mountains with elevations to about 4,000 feet. (Mary's Peak, at 4,097 feet, is the highest.) The wet, moderate climate supports a rain forest community of Sitka spruce, hemlock, cedar, Douglas fir, azaleas, rhododendron, and the carnivorous pitcher plant. This is the only national forest with significant ocean shoreline—45 miles of public beaches and sand dunes. Wildlife includes deer, black bear, cougar, and migratory birds, and there is good ocean, lake, and stream fishing. In addition to clamming and crabbing, you can also observe the migration of gray whales along the coast. This forest is not very remote with its many roads, and few trails are available for the backpacker. A few roadless areas provide cross-country travel for the experienced. Otherwise, a trip wandering along the coastal dunes is an experience unique to this forest (53 percent of the area is closed to motorized use).

For information and a map of the forest, contact the Supervisor, Siuslaw National Forest, P.O. Box 1148, 545 S.W. Second, Corvalis, Oregon 97330.

SISKIYOU NATIONAL FOREST

This 1,158,000-acre forest of low mountains in the southwest corner of the state is a botanist's dream, with many species of conifers, some quite rare, wild lilac, rhododendron, azaleas, pitcher plants, and the rare Kalmiopsis heath. The many streams and the beautiful Rogue River contain trout and salmon, and the mountains are home for deer, black bear, elk, cougar, bobcat, and coyote. While many good trails make this forest accessible to the average backpacker, the experienced may wish to travel the Kalmiopsis Wilderness Area.

This 77,000-acre wilderness area is a unique area of brush-covered rocky hills and low elevation canyons. Many species of conifers, hardwoods, and shrubs are found here. Some are extremely rare. Access is difficult, via a few primitive trails. Also, rattlesnakes are common, as are yellowjackets and hornets. However, the backpacker who braves these difficulties will be rewarded by solitude in an environment that has no equal.

For information and maps of the forest and wilderness area, contact the Supervisor, Siskiyou National Forest, P.O. Box 440, 1504 N.W. Sixth Street, Grants Pass, Oregon 97526.

Cascade Range Forests

MOUNT HOOD NATIONAL FOREST

This 1,060,000-acre forest is northernmost along the Cascades in the state, about 50 miles east of Portland. Snow-capped Mount Hood, at 11,235 feet, towers over the forest where most other peaks are in the 5,000-foot range. Mount Hood itself is an active volcano and still emits gases, though no major volcanic activity has occurred for hundreds of years. Surrounding the mountain is a dense, well-watered coniferous forest with scattered huckleberry fields, home for deer, black bear, and smaller mammals and birds. The many lakes and streams provide good fishing, and mushroom and huckleberry picking is also popular.

Good backpacking areas with well-maintained trails are found throughout the forest, but many of the areas are well laced with roads. The forest receives heavy visitation of more than 4 million annually, and while the trails in and around the Mount Hood Wilderness provide the best backpacking opportunities, these are heavily used. The 47,000-acre wilderness is a rugged area of live glaciers and snowfields, with several loop trips from 4 to 38 miles in length providing a range of difficulty. Mountain climbing trips to the summit are also possible.

For information and maps of the forest and wilderness, contact the Supervisor, Mount Hood National Forest, 2440 S.E. 195th Avenue, Portland, Oregon 97233.

WILLAMETTE NATIONAL FOREST

The Willamette is one of the nation's outstanding forests, just south of the Mount Hood and east of Eugene. Its 1,677,000 acres make it the second largest in the state and it is often the top timber producer of any of the nation's forests. Well managed for multiple use, this forest also offers excellent recreation opportunities, including more than 300,000 acres of designated wilderness. The densely forested mountain slopes of Douglas fir are

pierced by barren, jagged peaks and symmetrical volcanic mountains. Extensive areas in the eastern portion of the forest are
geologically recent lava flows. The varied forest environments
are home for deer, elk, black bear, wolverine, cougar, coyote, fox,
and various smaller animals, and the many lakes and streams
support several kinds of trout.

Although many roads serving the clear-cutting timber operations penetrate the forest, there are many large areas outside the
designated wilderness areas with excellent trails. Some of these
areas have particular biological or geological significance. The
forest receives moderately heavy use, but is not overcrowded,
and these areas, apparent on the forest map, provide an alternative
to the four designated wilderness areas. These wilderness areas
provide excellent backpacking opportunities, especially during
the slack shoulder season of early and late summer. Like all
wildernesses, motorized vehicles are prohibited. Permits may be
required for entry.

Covering 35,000 acres, partly in the Deschutes National Forest,
the Diamond Peak Wilderness is of moderate size. It is a cluster
of volcanic peaks with Diamond Peak rising to 8,744 feet. Almost
the entire area is covered with pine, fir, hemlock, and meadows
of wildflowers. The glaciers that have carved this wilderness are
long gone, leaving behind many lakes. These are stocked with
trout, and the forest supports deer, elk, black bear, and a variety
of smaller mammals and birds, including the pine marten and fox.
Fifty miles of trails provide access to the wilderness, but this is
an especially good area to practice your wilderness cross-country
travel skills since the terrain is not very steep. Most of the wilderness, including Diamond Peak itself, is accessible only by cross-
country travel.

The Mount Jefferson Wilderness is a 100,000-acre area extending partly into the Deschutes and Mount Hood national forests.
Like the Diamond Peak, it has volcanic origins, with Mount
Jefferson, an extinct, glacier-shrouded volcano, towering over
the wilderness at 10,497 feet. About one-eighth of the area is
bare rock, lava flows, glaciers, and snowfields. The remaining area
is covered by alpine meadows and forests of pine, spruce, hem-

lock, and cedar. Fifty lakes dot the area, many stocked with trout. Deer and elk are among the somewhat sparse wildlife population. This is rugged terrain between 3,000 feet to over 10,000 feet, with most elevations in the 6,000-foot range. Over 160 miles of trails provide access, and steep, but passable terrain makes for challenging cross-country travel.

Encompassing 247,000 acres, the Three Sisters Wilderness is by far the largest wilderness in Willamette National Forest. It is located in the part of the Cascades that has had the most recent volcanic activity, resulting in large lava flows and interesting expanses of basalt and obsidian. Most of the forest is vegetated with pine, spruce, fir, and cedar forests, wildflower meadows, and alpine tundra, all dotted by over 300 lakes. While the Sisters themselves are over 10,000 feet, much of the area is under 5,000 feet and the climate is correspondingly moderate with a snow-free season of 4 to 5 months. Wildlife is abundant with trout in many of the lakes. Numerous black bear, elk, and deer, a variety of fur-bearers, bobcat, coyote, and an occasional cougar make the forest their home. The 160 miles of trails and many trailless areas provide abundant backpacking possibilities. Although the trails around the Sisters are steep, many trails, especially in the south of the wilderness, are of only moderate difficulty.

Partly in Deschutes National Forest, the Mount Washington Wilderness comprises 47,000 acres. A large part of the wilderness is a barren, geologically recent lava flow. The stark basalt has earned it the name "Black Wilderness." Several cinder cones and other impressive volcanic formations are particularly interesting. This area is relatively flat as far as wildernesses go, and except for a few peaks, gentle grades at elevations of 3,000 to 6,000 feet are the rule. Timber covers most of the area not already covered by lava, which supports a fair-sized deer population, a few elk, and, rarely, cougar. Smaller mammals and birds are more common. Water is not abundant, with only 28 lakes and ponds. The moderate terrain makes this a good hiking area, and backpacking opportunities offered by the limited trail mileage can be increased by cross-country travel, especially easy along the edge of the lava flows and the forest.

For information and maps of the forest and wildernesses, contact the Supervisor, Willamette National Forest, 210 East Seventh Avenue, P.O. Box 10607, Eugene, Oregon 97401.

DESCHUTES NATIONAL FOREST

This 1,588,000-acre forest borders the Willamette on the east and is environmentally similar to it, except that as one travels east, the climate becomes drier. Like the Willamette, this area had volcanic origins and lava flows are still evident. The area is mostly timbered with many hundreds of miles of streams and over 300 lakes. About half of these lakes contain trout and one contains salmon. Of the approximately 250 species of birds and mammals that inhabit the forest, four birds are endangered species: the American osprey, the bald eagle, and greater sandhill crane, and the prairie falcon.

Each of this forest's four wildernesses are shared with the Willamette and are discussed above. Some of the forest's 400 miles of trails are not in these areas, but nevertheless provide good backpacking opportunities. These trails, mostly along the western edge of the forest, are often less crowded than those in the wildernesses and are usually just as good. Motorized use is allowed only on certain trails.

For information and a map of the forest, contact the Supervisor, Deschutes National Forest, 211 N.E. Revere Street, Bend, Oregon 97701.

UMPQUA NATIONAL FOREST

This 984,000-acre forest is located south of Willamette National Forest, due east of Roseburg. The forest is densely timbered. Lakes are not abundant, though creeks and streams are plentiful and contain trout. The low mountains mostly in the 5,000-foot range are inhabited by deer, black bear, and a few cougar, as well as smaller animals.

This forest has no particular distinctions as a backpacking area. There are no designated wildernesses or primitive areas, and many roads. However, 367 miles of trails are to be found in the

forest, many in large roadless areas. The lack of openness of much
of the forest does not invite cross-country travel. The most rugged
part of the forest is along the eastern boundary where elevations
are over 8,000 feet and where the forest is crossed by the Pacific
Crest Trail discussed later. Perhaps the most attractive feature of
this forest is that it is little known and little used by backpackers,
where one can find solitude during a season that can be as long as
from March to November.

For information and a map of the forest, contact the Supervisor,
Umpqua National Forest, Federal Office Building, 704 S.E. Cass
Street, P.O. Box 1008, Roseburg, Oregon 97470.

ROGUE RIVER NATIONAL FOREST

Located south of the Umpqua National Forest, this relatively
small 621,000-acre forest is environmentally similar to the Umpqua. Most of the elevations are below the 5,000-foot level, except
in the eastern portion of the forest in the vicinity of the Pacific
Crest Trail where the elevation is as high as 9,495 feet on Mount
McLoughlin. The moderately dense to open forest stands are
home for black bear, deer, elk, and an occasional cougar. Bobcat,
coyote, beaver, and other smaller mammals and birds are frequently seen.

By far, the best part of the forest for backpacking is in the Sky
Lakes area south of Crater Lake National Park in the eastern
portion of the forest extending into adjacent Winema National
Forest and covering an area of 5 miles by 25 miles. While there
are trails elsewhere, motorized use is officially condoned on
them. Motorized use is prohibited in the northern two-thirds of
the Sky Lakes area, and fortunately, this is the most attractive
portion of the forest with its high peaks, abundant mountain
lakes, and many miles of good, relatively easy trails, including
the Pacific Crest Trail. This is a particularly good family backpacking area with only moderate use.

For information and a map of the forest, contact the Supervisor,
Rogue River National Forest, P.O. Box 520, 333 West Eighth
Street, Medford, Oregon 97501.

WINEMA NATIONAL FOREST

The 909,000 acres of this national forest are divided into several units, all east of the Rogue River National Forest, and environmentally similar to it. While there are a few fair backpacking opportunities in the forest proper, the best areas are the Sky Lakes area, discussed under the Rogue River National Forest, and the 23,000-acre (6 miles by 6 miles) Mountain Lakes Wilderness. This wilderness is a high peak area of glacial topography with many lakes and an excellent loop trail system. Although fairly small, the wilderness is not well known, is relatively remote, and is not heavily used.

For information and a map of the forest, including the wilderness, contact the Supervisor, Winema National Forest, P.O. Box 1390, Post Office Building, Klamath Falls, Oregon 97601.

FREMONT NATIONAL FOREST

The southeasternmost forest in the Oregon Cascades, this forest encompasses 1,195,000 acres in south-central Oregon, northeast of Klamath Falls. It differs from the other forests along the Cascades in that, being farther inland, it is drier and generally sparsely forested. Vertical faults, buttes, and geologically recent lava flows are interesting features, as is the protected antelope herd. The higher elevations receive more moisture and many of the lakes and streams contain trout.

Outside the Gearhart Mountain Wilderness, opportunities for trail hiking are limited to only a few trails. The aridity of this forest makes cross-country travel in many of the roadless areas relatively easy, though. While there is enough water available to preclude any special preparations, normal cross-country travel precautions should be taken. The 19,000-acre Gearhart Wilderness itself provides good trail hiking in an interesting geological area with peaks to over 8,000 feet, as well as buttes, domes, and palisades. Use is light. Wildlife is not abundant, but deer, black bear, bobcat, coyote, cougar, and grouse are found here.

For information and a map of the forest and wilderness area, contact the Supervisor, Fremont National Forest, P.O. Box 551, 34 North D Street, Lakeview, Oregon 97630.

Forests in Northeastern Orgeon

UMATILLA NATIONAL FOREST

The 1,390,000 acres of this forest are divided among several large units in northeastern Oregon, extending into Washington. The low mountains mostly under 6,000 feet are covered by ponderosa pine, spruce, larch, and fir, with open meadows, parklands, and barren outcrops. Rainfall is adequate, but not heavy, forming many streams, and the forest supports a large concentration of elk, with mule deer, bighorn sheep, and upland game birds, as well as bobcat and smaller animals.

Many large roadless areas and over 900 miles of moderate-grade trails make this an excellent backpacking area. Many of these trails are open to motorized use, however. Cross-country travel in the many roadless areas of open forest is possible. The 180,000 Wenaha-Tucannon Wilderness on the crest of the northern Blue Mountains is closed to motorized traffic on all of its more than 150 miles of trails. The area boasts rugged basaltic ridges and steep canyons, and scattered timber stands, good for trail and cross-country travel. Although there are no lakes, fishing in the many streams is good. Because of its remoteness and obscurity, this area receives extremely light use, making it particularly attractive.

For information and a map of the forest, contact the Supervisor, Umatilla National Forest, 2517 S.W. Haily Avenue, Pendleton, Oregon 97801.

WALLOWA-WHITMAN NATIONAL FORESTS

These two forests east of Umatilla National Forest are administered jointly, and together total 2,238,000 acres. They are rugged and remote, similar to many of the mountain areas of Idaho. Although trails are found throughout the forests, they are mostly open to motorized use. The best backpacking areas are the Eagle Cap Wilderness, and the Hell's Canyon Wilderness (see below).

The large 294,000-acre Eagle Cap Wilderness is a mosaic of glaciated peaks almost 10,000 feet high, moraines, hanging and U-shaped valleys. About half the area is timbered and dotted with over 50 lakes. Fir, spruce, and a few pine, as well as meadows and tundra support abundant wildlife—deer, elk, black bear, mountain goat, beaver, badger, bobcat, and occasionally cougar, marten, fisher, mink, and fox may be seen. Fishing for trout is good to excellent. The many hundred miles of sometimes rugged trails and the remoteness make this a particularly good area for the solitude seeker. The higher passes may be closed by snow as late as mid-July and as early as October.

For information and maps of the forest and wilderness, contact the Supervisor, Wallowa-Whitman National Forest, P.O. Box 907, Federal Office Building, Baker, Oregon 97814.

MALHEUR NATIONAL FOREST

Located south of Umatilla and the Wallowa-Whitman National Forest, this 1,470,000-acre forest is similar to them. Its rolling forests of ponderosa pine thin to juniper and sagebrush in the arid low fringes. The forests, parklands, and grasslands support elk, deer, upland gamebirds and small mammals, and a few black bear, bobcat, and cougar. Unusual rocks, fossils, and geological formations are of particular interest.

The forest is penetrated by thousands of miles of roads and over 450 miles of trails, most open to motorized vehicles. However, the backpacker often can find fairly easy cross-country travel in the open parklands.

The best backpacking opportunities are found in the 33,000-acre Strawberry Mountain Wilderness. Impressive 9,044-foot Strawberry Mountain dominates this landscape of glacial lakes, barren peaks, and pine-fir forests and meadows. The trailless west end of the wilderness provides real challenge and rewards for the experienced cross-country traveler. Snowpack limits access until well into summer.

For information and a map of the forest and wilderness, contact the Supervisor, Malheur National Forest, 139 N.E. Dayton Street, John Day, Oregon 97845.

OCHOCO NATIONAL FOREST AND CROOKED RIVER NATIONAL GRASSLAND

These are both administered as one jurisdiction; the Ochoco is 846,000 acres and the Crooked River is 106,000 acres. Both are in central Oregon near Prineville. The environment varies from rolling prairie to the open parkland of ponderosa pine, fir, and aspen on low mountains generally lower than 6,000 feet in the national forest. This area is famed for its rockhounding and has many interesting geological features. Trout fishing is good in the many rivers and streams and in the few lakes and reservoirs. Deer are abundant, and elk, antelope, badger, bobcat, coyote, and other smaller animals may also be seen.

Backpacking is only fair in this forest and grassland. Many roads lace the forest and grassland and the trails are limited to only the northern unit of the forest. While these trails follow many attractive valleys and ridges, they are open to motorized use. The best thing the forest has going for it is that use is very light, especially if one heads cross-country through the open ponderosa parklands in one of the many roadless areas. The season is long, spring through fall, with the aspen providing brilliant fall colors.

For information and a map of the forest and grassland, contact the Supervisor, Ochoco National Forest, P.O. Box 490, Federal Building, Prineville, Oregon 97754.

Crater Lake National Park

Named after Crater Lake, the seventh deepest in the world, this 160,000-acre park is covered by dense coniferous forest and beautiful carpets of wildflowers. Crater Lake, the drowned crater of an extinct volcano, is circled by variegated lava cliffs 500 to 2,000 feet high, reflected in the deep aqua blue of the lake. Black bear, elk, deer, bobcat, bald and golden eagles, and diving water ouzel inhabit the park. Thirty-five miles of trails ring the lake, but the trails are well used. Also, water must be carried. It would be best to combine a trip here with a visit to the adjacent Rogue River and Winema national forests.

For information and a map of the park, contact the Superintendent, Crater Lake National Park, P.O. Box 7, Crater Lake, Oregon 97604.

HELL'S CANYON NATIONAL RECREATION AREA

This recently established area includes 662,000 acres astride the Snake Canyon and is part of three national forests: the Nezperce and Payette in Idaho and the Wallowa-Whitman in Oregon. Of most interest to the backpacker is the 194,000-acre portion designated as the Hell's Canyon Wilderness. This canyon is rimmed by basaltic rock on the west and the Seven Devils Mountains on the east. A depth of 5,500 feet makes it the deepest gorge in North America. Numerous trails traverse the wilderness and a trail on the Idaho side runs the length of the canyon. The volcanic Seven Devils Mountains soar violently upwards, in places gaining several thousand feet of elevation for every horizontal mile. Since canyon temperatures reach 105° F in the summer, spring and fall are the more popular seasons.

For additional information and maps, contact the Supervisor, Wallowa-Whitman National Forest, P.O. Box 907, Baker, California 97814.

Hart Mountain National Antelope Refuge

This 275,000-acre refuge in south-central Oregon northeast of Lakeview is one of the best refuges for backpacking in the country. While many refuges are swampy lowlands, this refuge is on a fault block ridge, Hart Mountain, rising above the surrounding plains to 8,065 feet. The west side of the ridge is a steep and rugged series of cliffs dropping 3,600 feet. The east side is a more gentle series of hills and ridges. This mountain is a well-watered oasis in the desert with scattered mixed timber stands and a composite of several life zones, from the hot Upper Sonoran to the cool Canadian, with a correspondingly diverse animal population. In the sagebrush and aspen of the higher elevations live bighorn sheep and mule deer, while the lower, semidesert environment is inhabited by antelope, kangaroo rat, burrowing owl, and various reptiles, including rattlesnake. Bobcat, coyote, and a variety of birds and small animals are also found throughout the refuge.

Cross-country hiking in the remote parts of the refuge is excellent, and overnight wilderness camping is officially permitted. A special permit must be obtained at the refuge headquarters.

For a map and information on the refuge, contact the Refuge Manager, Sheldon-Hart Mountain National Antelope Refuges, P.O. Box 111, Lakeview, Oregon 97630.

Other Public Lands

The entire southeast quarter of the state is public land, over 15,000,000 acres, mostly managed by the Bureau of Land Management. Grasslands, barren lava flows, buttes, canyons, lakes, reservoirs and rivers comprise this mostly arid environment. Sturgeon, trout, bass, perch, and catfish are found in the rivers and reservoirs, while deer, elk, black bear, and upland birds inhabit the arid uplands. Population is extremely sparse in this region, though cowboys and sheepherders graze their livestock here.

This region is generally not developed for backpacking, and it will be of interest to mostly those experienced in cross-country travel. Hiking along lakes, reservoirs, and river canyons is particularly attractive. Lake Owyhee, for example, has 150 miles of shoreline. The Malheur National Wildlife Refuge contains over 180,000 acres of marshes, meadows, shallow lakes, and sagebrush and juniper uplands, but there are no backpacking trails. Waterbirds, upland gamebirds, deer, and antelope inhabit the refuge. Other interesting backpacking areas include the public lands along the scenic John Day and Deschutes rivers in north-central Oregon and the Rogue River Trail along this famous river in southwest Oregon. Other good cross-country possibilities exist in the Steens Mountain area in southeast Oregon by the Malheur and Hart Mountain refuges.

For a map and information on public lands, contact the Oregon State office, Bureau of Land Management, P.O. Box 2965, Portland, Oregon 97208.

WASHINGTON

This state is the smallest state west of Iowa, but what it lacks in size it makes up for in backpacking potential. Beginning on the coast, the Olympic Mountains and several nearby islands represent a wilderness temperate rain forest. Farther inland, the Cascade Range and a string of national forests run north and south, cutting the state in half with peaks soaring to over 14,000 feet. The state flattens out to the east of the Cascades, where many ranches and farms are found, though there are many backpacking opportunities even in this part of the state. The western half of the state, where most backpacking opportunities are found, has cool summers and mild winters. In some areas the growing season can be year-round. This is a wet region, but only 20 percent of the yearly rainfall occurs from May 15 to October 15. Eastern Washington has a more continental climate with colder winters and warmer summers. This is a region of grasslands, wheat fields, canyons, and pockets of desert with rocky outcrops. Bordering this region on the north and south borders of the state are higher-elevation forests.

The many national parks, forests, and recreation areas provide the bulk of the backpacking opportunities in the state. Refer to the above section on Oregon for the discussion of wilderness permits, and see California for the discussion of the Pacific Crest National Scenic Trail, which runs through this state.

General tourism information is available from the State Department of Commerce and Economic Development, Tourist Promotion Division, Olympia, Washington 98501.

Olympic National Park and Olympic National Forest

The 901,000 acres of the park and the additional 622,000 acres of national forest that surround it comprise one of the best backpacking areas in the country. Located on the Olympic Peninsula west of Seattle in extreme northwest Washington, this area receives more rain than anywhere else in the 48 states, over 140 inches a year in some places. Other areas in the peninsula are relatively dry. The glacier-covered peaks, some to almost 8,000 feet, are surrounded by coniferous rain forest, lakes, and streams, including a 50-mile-long seacoast that is part of the park. The mountains themselves are uplifted sedimentary rock, mostly with elevations in the 5,000 to 6,000-foot range. The rain forest is an extraordinary environment of huge spruce, western hemlock, Douglas fir, and western red cedar, ferns, mosses, rhododendron, and wildflowers. The coastline, too, is an interesting environment of cliffs, beaches, offshore rocks, and islands. Sea birds, marine mammals, and other abundant sea life inhabit this near-primitive coast. Salmon, trout, elk, mountain goat, deer, black bear, wolf, cougar, bobcat, and smaller mammals and birds are found inland.

There are 600 miles of trails in the park and 180 more in the surrounding forest. The park, with its few interior roads, provides an excellent backcountry experience. Many of the trails in the park originate in the surrounding forest. Shelters are provided for those interested, and of course, no motorized vehicles are allowed on the trails in the park. The seacoast is also an excellent place for the backpacker to roam. There are a few trails here, but none are really needed. For backcountry camping, all the traveler needs is a backcountry use permit. Season is year-round on the coast and in lower elevations. Use is moderately heavy.

For a descriptive brochure of the park, contact the Superintendent, 600 East Park Avenue, Port Angeles, Washington 98362. For information on the forest and a good map (50¢) of both the park and forest, contact the Supervisor, Olympic National Forest, Federal Building, Olympia, Washington 98507.

North Cascades National Park and Lake Chelan and Ross Lake National Recreation Areas

These 3 jurisdictions total 674,000 acres of forests and lakes in the northernmost portion of the Cascade Range in north-central Washington east of Bellingham. Jagged, glacier-covered peaks rise to almost 9,000 feet above heavily forested valleys and slopes with many lakes and rivers. The variety of environments includes alpine tundra, coniferous forest and rain forest, and the dry shrublands of the lower elevations on the eastern slopes. The inhabitants are similarly varied, including mountain goat, deer, moose, grizzly and black bears, wolverine, marten, fisher, cougar, lynx, coyote, beaver, and bald eagle.

This is one of the wildest areas remaining in the continental United States. The trails, 360 miles in the park complex, provide good access, with only 12 miles open to motorized use. Cross-country travel is permitted and reasonably easy near the timberline. Use of the trails is light to moderately heavy, with some trails being quite steep and difficult. The high trails are snow-covered until summer. The adjacent Glacier Peak Wilderness, discussed later under the Mount Baker National Forest, provides additional trip possibilities.

For information and a map of the park and recreation areas, contact the Superintendent, North Cascades National Park, 800 State Street, Sedro Woolley, Washington 98284.

Mount Rainier National Park

This 235,000-acre park astride the Cascades southeast of Tacoma is dominated by the glacier-clad 14,410-foot Mount Rainier. This dormant volcano is surrounded by smaller peaks clothed with alpine meadows becoming lush forests in the lower elevations. Wildlife is particularly abundant, with elk, deer, black bear, mountain goat, red fox, coyote, bobcat, cougar, and smaller mammals and birds. Lake and stream fishing for trout is fair to good.

It is unfortunate that the state's smallest national park is also the most accessible to the population. The 290 miles of trails are well used by the nearby urban dwellers and it is difficult getting away from them because camping is permitted only in established backcountry sites. A fire permit is also required. While many of the trails are short, long trips are also possible. The diehard solitude seeker may be disappointed with this park, but the view of Mount Rainier alone is almost worth a visit.

For information and a map of the park, contact the Superintendent, Mount Rainier National Park, Longmire, Washington 98397.

Mount Baker-Snoqualmie National Forest

Mount Baker and Snoqualmie national forests were recently
combined to make this 2,505,000-acre forest that covers the northern two-thirds of the west slope of the Cascades. Rising to 10,778
feet, Mount Baker is classified as a dormant volcano, though it
still emits sulfurous fumes. It, like many of the surrounding peaks,
is clad by snowfields and glaciers, studded with hundreds of
alpine lakes, and laced with icy streams coursing down slopes
thickly clothed with Douglas fir, western hemlock, and western
red cedar on the wetter west side of the crest, and through open
ponderosa pine parklands on the east side. Wildlife includes deer,
elk, mountain goat, black bear, and trout.

Backpacking opportunities are abundant and excellent in the
forest proper, in the Glacier Peak Wilderness in the north, and
the Goat Rocks Wilderness in the south. (The Goat Rocks Wilderness is discussed below under the Gifford Pinchot National Forest.)
The forest itself has many hundreds of miles of trails, the great
majority of which are closed to motorized use. There are a few
camping restrictions, but generally the forest is open and excellent
for backpacking. Two outstanding areas are the Glacier Ranger
District in the extreme north portion of the forest and the Alpine
Lakes Area farther south, which extends into adjacent Wenatchee
National Forest (discussed below under the Wenatchee).

Perhaps the best area for the wilderness seeker is the 464,000-
acre Glacier Peak Wilderness located in the northern half of the
forest northeast of Seattle and extending into the adjacent Wenatchee National Forest. This 20- by 35-mile wilderness is punctuated
by more than 30 jagged, glacier-clad peaks of volcanic origin soaring to 10,528 feet on Glacier Peak itself. Many of the other peaks
rise 5,000 to 8,000 feet above the intervening valleys and are covered with clumps of alpine conifers, such as the whitebark pine
and rare Luall larch among the tundra, with hemlock and firs
interspersed with meadows and deciduous shrubs farther down

the slopes and in the U-shaped glaciated valleys. Trout is plentiful in the abundant meltwater-fed lakes and streams, and black bear, mountain goat, deer, marmot, cony, and ptarmigan are often spotted.

Many miles of excellent, though steep, trails, including a portion of the Pacific Crest National Scenic Trail, and good cross-country possibilities make the area a backpacker's paradise. Use is moderate on some trails, but seldom becomes a problem (remember to inquire about a wilderness-use permit). Snow can block the high passes as late as early August, but then they remain open through October.

For information and maps of the forest and wilderness area, contact the Supervisor, Mount Baker-Snoqualmie National Forest, 1601 Second Avenue Building, Seattle, Washington 98101.

Okanogan National Forest

To the east of the crest of the Cascades and adjacent to the North Cascades National Park and Ross Lake and Lake Chelan national recreation areas, this 1,521,000-acre forest comprises one of the more remote areas of the Cascades. Here erosion has been a little slower, resulting in more barren peaks and jagged spires. The reason for this is that rainfall is much less on the east side of the Cascades than on the west, because the moist winds from the ocean drop much of their precipitation during the climb up the west slope. The vegetation is correspondingly more sparse—mostly open parklands of ponderosa pine and grassy meadows. There still are over 100 lakes and many streams. Trout fishing is good, and deer, elk, and bear, though not plentiful, can be spotted.

One-third of this forest, 506,000 acres, is within the Pasayten Wilderness on the Canadian border. This area of alpine meadows, peaks to over 9,000 feet, scattered coniferous stands, and more than 500 miles of trails is one of the finest places in the forest for the backpacker. The Pacific Crest National Scenic Trail begins in this wilderness and winds its way through it. Of course, no motorized vehicles are allowed. Many more hundreds of miles of trails and few roads are found in the forest proper, so the back-packer need not limit himself to the wilderness area. Neither the forest nor wilderness is heavily used, and most of the trails are of moderate grades. The open character of the landscape lends itself to cross-country travel, insuring the backpacker solitude and a little adventure.

For information and a map of the forest and wilderness, contact the Supervisor, Okanogan National Forest, P.O. Box 950, Okanogan, Washington 98840.

Wenatchee National Forest

This large forest of nearly 2 million acres is located south of the Okanogan and east of the Mount Baker-Snoqualmie national forests in central Washington. Like the Okanogan, this forest is located on the eastern slopes of the Cascades, and precipitation is less than on the other side of the crest. However, water is one of the big attractions of the forest. From the alpine areas along the crest to the semiarid hills bordering the Columbia River on the east, this forest is laced with streams and studded with many small and several large lakes nestled between peaks in the 6,000 to 8,000-foot range. Of particular interest is Lake Chelan, winding for 55 miles between forested slopes on both sides. The forests and ponderosa pine parklands, lakes, and streams provide a habitat for trout and salmon, deer, elk, mountain goat, black bear, cougar, bobcat, coyote, smaller mammals and birds.

With 2,500 miles of forest trails and good cross-country travel possibilities, backpacking opportunities are abundant. Many of the trails are closed to motorized use, including all those in the Glacier Peak Wilderness, particularly fine in this forest and discussed under the Mount Baker-Snoqualmie National Forest above. Roads only penetrate the forest in a few places, leaving many roadless and motorless areas for the backpacker to explore. Particularly good is the Alpine Lakes Wilderness in the southwest portion of the forest extending into the adjacent Mount Baker-Snoqualmie Na-tional Forest. This is a particularly high concentration of alpine lakes, many not reached by trails, just waiting for the cross-country traveler.

Use of this wilderness is one of the heaviest in the west. A third wilderness in the forest, Goat Rocks, is discussed under the Gifford Pinchot National Forest, below.

For information and a map of the forest, contact the Supervisor, Wenatchee National Forest, P.O. Box 811, Wenatchee, Washington 98801.

Gifford Pinchot National Forest

This 1,330,000-acre forest is located on the west side of the Cascade Range along the southernmost portion of the range in Washington, adjacent to the Mount Baker-Snoqualmie National Forest on the south. Two extinct volcanic peaks dominate the forest, the 9,677-foot Mount St. Helens, reputedly the most beautiful volcanic peak of the Cascades, and the towering 12,326-foot Mount Adams. Most peaks are in the humbler range of 5,000 feet and covered with thick forests of Douglas fir, hemlock, true fir, cedar, spruce, larch, and scattered hardwoods. Hundreds of miles of streams and 310 small lakes punctuate the forest as well as do several extensive lava flows. Elk, deer, black bear, bobcat, cougar, and coyote, as well as smaller furbearers and birds inhabit the forest, and trout and salmon are found in the lakes and streams.

The forest boasts 1,300 miles of trails, some of which are open for motorized use. The forest is moderately covered by roads, but there are a few large roadless areas that might appeal to the backpacker. The best backpacking opportunities, though, are found in the two wildernesses in the forest, the Goat Rocks and Mount Adams wildernesses which require permits for those staying overnight between June 15–November 15.

The 83,000-acre Goat Rocks Wilderness is located in the northeast corner of the forest. The mountainous volcanic terrain varies in elevation from about 3,000 feet to the 8,201-foot Gilbert Peak. Fir, cedar, and pine cover the lower slopes, while in the higher elevations meadows of wildflowers, alpine tundra, glaciers, and snowfields prevail. Elk, mountain goat, deer, black bear, coyote, and an occasional cougar may be spotted. Trout inhabit many of the several lakes and streams. Hiking on the 95 miles of trails is excellent and use is moderate. Cross-country travel possibilities are good, especially since almost half of the terrain is above the timberline.

The Mount Adams Wilderness, smallish at 32,000 acres, is located on the east-central border of the forest. This area consists almost entirely of the slopes of 12,326-foot Mount Adams, the second tallest peak in the state. This volcano has left a legacy of interesting craters, cones, and lava formations throughout the wilderness. Most of the wilderness is above timberline, and much of it is covered by glaciers. Wildlife is not abundant, but occasionally one will see elk, black bear, ptarmigan, and marmot on the slopes and in the valleys. Trout have been planted in some of the larger lakes. Hiking opportunities include the portion of the Pacific Crest National Scenic Trail which crosses the wilderness and a few other access trails up the slopes of Mount Adams. Obviously, this is a good area for the backpacker partial to mountain climbing. Two fairly easy trails lead to the summit of the mountain providing a spectacular panorama.

For information and maps (50¢) of the forest and wilderness areas, contact the Supervisor, Gifford Pinchot National Forest, 500 West Twelfth Street, Vancouver, Washington 98660.

Colville National Forest

Encompassing 944,000 acres, this forest, located by the town of Colville in northeast Washington is not as rugged as most of the other forests in the state. What it lacks in spectacular volcanic peaks and glaciers it makes up for with its peaceful green valleys winding through rolling timbered slopes, dotted with lakes and laced with rivers and streams. Few peaks exceed 7,000 feet, with most in the 5,000 to 7,000-foot range. In addition to the stands of mixed conifers and deciduous trees, huckleberries and mushrooms attract eager pickers. Black bear and a variety of smaller mammals and birds are found here, and there is good trout fishing in the many lakes and streams. Mule deer are abundant and grow especially large in this environment.

This area should be of interest to the backpacker for 3 reasons. First, the forest is in a remote part of the state. Second, it is a little-known backpacking area with no designated wilderness or primitive area to draw attention to it. These first two characteristics make for a forest that receives light use on its hundreds of miles of excellent trails, many in large roadless areas. Finally, the moderate terrain makes hiking relatively easy. Cross-country travel is also possible in the more open areas.

For information and a map of the forest, contact the Supervisor, Colville National Forest, Federal Building, Colville, Washington 98114.

Kaniksu National Forest

See Idaho, above.

Umatilla National Forest

See Oregon, above.

Other Public Lands

There are no developed backpacking areas as such on the Bureau of Land Management lands, but BLM ownership is extensive and good for the adventuresome cross-country traveler. An interesting trip for history buffs would be along the Lewis and Clark Trail along the Columbia and Snake rivers in southern Washington where much of the trail is on public land. Good rockhounding and interesting geologic areas are found in the southeast portion of the state, with lands along the Yakima River being especially good for petrified wood.

A variety of maps of the state are available from the Bureau of Land Management, and any of the quadrangle maps (northeast, southeast, southwest, and northwest) showing BLM ownership can be obtained for 25¢ each from the Bureau of Land Management, Oregon State Office, P.O. Box 2965, 729 N.E. Oregon Street, Portland, Oregon 97208. (Be sure to ask for the *Washington* maps.)

Another source of information on public land suitable for backpacking is available from the Department of Game, 600 North Capitol Way, Olympia, Washington 98504. Some of the wildlife recreation areas administered by this department are good for backpacking. For example, the Desert and Potholes wildlife recreation areas around the Potholes Reservoir in central Washington provide a desolate desert environment that is most hospitable in the spring and fall. It receives extremely light use, there are no dveloped trails, and motorized vehicles are not permitted off the roads.

6

The West and Southwest: Arizona, California, Hawaii, Nevada, New Mexico, and Utah

This region has an excellent and varied backpacking resource, from deserts to tropical mountains. Arizona, Nevada, New Mexico, and Utah are mosaics of deserts, canyons, and forested mountains. Some of the country's most impressive scenery is found in these states. California is touted as having the greatest abundance of backpacking opportunities, as well as a high visibility with regard to the sport. Indeed, the word "Sierras" is synonomous with backpacking. These Southwestern states receive widely varying levels of usage, with areas in California having very heavy use while most of Nevada enjoys extremely light use. Hawaii, of course, provides a backpacking experience different from that offered by any other state. The thought of backpacking in this state does not occur to most people, but the unique backpacking areas found here are attracting more users each year.

ARIZONA

Not surprisingly, Arizona is mostly desert, but it is very interesting desert. The variety of plants, animals, and landforms is astonishing. The state is punctuated by a variety of landscapes in addition to deserts—forests, lakes, rivers, mountains, and, of course, the Grand Canyon. Some of the best backpacking opportunities are found along a corridor extending from the northwest to the southwest corners of the state. In this area, as well as in some of the remainder of the state, trail and cross-country travel opportunities are excellent. Of course, caution should be exercised in this climate. The weather varies with the elevation. In the Sonoran Desert Zone beneath 2,000 feet, normal winter lows are in the high 30s and normal summer highs can top 100°F with only a few inches of rain a year. The mountain ranges, which can reach over 12,000 feet, are the coolest with winter lows in the teens and summer highs in the 70s with about 20 inches of annual rainfall. The state's profile is lowest in the Sonoran Desert in the southwest, sloping up the foothills to the mountain region in the center of the state, then drops and levels off on the Colorado Plateau in the north.

General tourism information is available from the Arizona State Office of Economics Development and Planning, 1645 West Jefferson Street, Phoenix, Arizona 85007.

Grand Canyon National Park and Monument

Together, these areas equal 872,000 acres of canyonlands in the northwest corner of the state. The immensity of scale is the first impression upon the visitor—9 miles wide, 217 miles long, and 1 mile deep, with a total drop of 7,000 feet from the 9,000-foot elevation of the north rim to the 2,000-foot elevation of the river below. The geology of the area then catches the visitor's attention. As the Colorado Plateau slowly began to rise 7 million years ago, the Colorado River began to slice its way through successively older rocks, cutting back many hundreds of millions of years. Along with this geologic history book, the river has created a grandiose work of art. Many animals inhabit the sculptured landscape, including deer, pronghorn, bighorn, ringtail, coyote, cougar, bobcat, prairie dog, black bear, turkey, burrowing owl, roadrunner, bald and golden eagle, and chuckwalla.

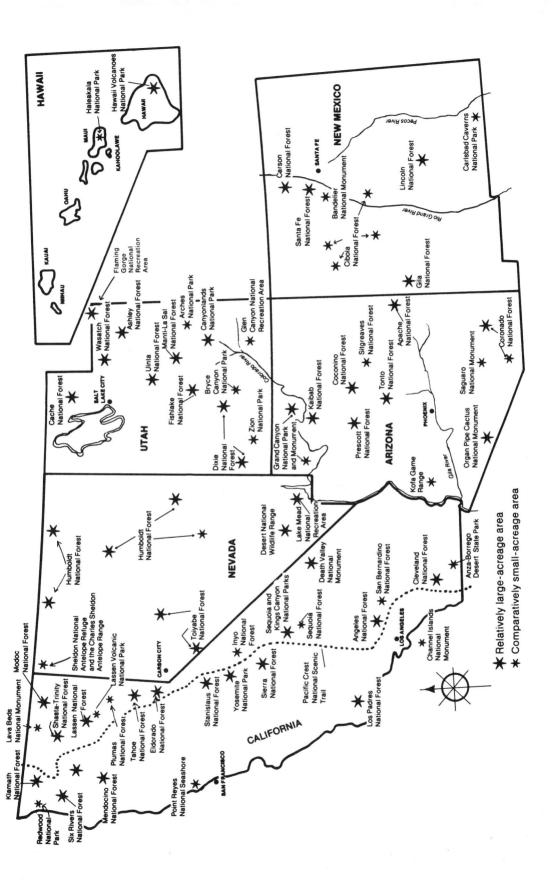

HAWAII

Haleakala National Park
Hawaii Volcanoes National Park
MAUI
KAHOOLAWE
HAWAII
OAHU
KAUAI
NIIHAU

Flaming Gorge National Recreation Area

Wasatch National Forest
Ashley National Forest
Uinta National Forest
Manti-La Sal National Forest
Arches National Park
Canyonlands National Park
Glen Canyon National Recreation Area

Cache National Forest
SALT LAKE CITY
UTAH
Fishlake National Forest
Bryce Canyon National Park
Zion National Park
Dixie National Forest
Grand Canyon National Park and Monument
Colorado River
Kaibab National Forest

Carson National Forest
SANTA FE
NEW MEXICO
Pecos River
Santa Fe National Forest
Bandelier National Monument
Cibola National Forest
Rio Grande River
Lincoln National Forest
Gila National Forest
Carlsbad Caverns National Park

Sitgreaves National Forest
Apache National Forest
Coronado National Forest
Coconino National Forest
Tonto National Forest
Saguaro National Monument
ARIZONA
PHOENIX
Prescott National Forest
Organ Pipe Cactus National Monument
Gila River
Kofa Game Range

Humboldt National Forest
Humboldt National Forest
NEVADA
Desert National Wildlife Range
Lake Mead National Recreation Area

Sheldon National Antelope Refuge and the Charles Sheldon Antelope Range
Toiyabe National Forest
CARSON CITY

Modoc National Forest
Lava Beds National Monument
Lassen Volcanic National Park
Shasta-Trinity National Forest
Lassen National Forest
Klamath National Forest
Plumas National Forest
Tahoe National Forest
Eldorado National Forest
Mendocino National Forest
Stanislaus National Forest
Yosemite National Park
Sierra National Forest
Inyo National Forest
Sequoia and Kings Canyon National Parks
Sequoia National Forest
Death Valley National Monument
San Bernardino National Forest
Cleveland National Forest
Angeles National Forest
LOS ANGELES
Anza-Borrego Desert State Park
Pacific Crest National Scenic Trail
Los Padres National Forest
Channel Islands National Monument
CALIFORNIA
SAN FRANCISCO
Point Reyes National Seashore
Redwood National Park
Six Rivers National Forest

★ Relatively large-acreage area
✳ Comparatively small-acreage area

The 239 miles of trails provide access to the park and monument backcountry, but they are increasing in popularity and many of the trails become crowded, as well as hot and dusty, during the summer. Conditions are more pleasant during the off-season, though many of the trails aré very steep. For those experienced in canyonland cross-country travel, there are challenging cross-country opportunities. A permit is required.

For information and a map of the park and monument, contact the Superintendent, Grand Canyon National Park and Monument, P.O. Box 129, Grand Canyon, Arizona 86023.

Kaibab National Forest

The 1,720,000 acres of this forest are divided into three main units: one lying north and two south of the Grand Canyon. The north unit includes the North Kaibab Plateau high country, a land of pine, spruce, and alpine forests interspersed with meadows extending to the subalpine zone. The other units are more desert-like with parts extending into the Sonoran Zone. There are only 6 trout lakes and one live stream in the forest. Deer are especially abundant on the North Kaibab, and wild turkey, the distinctive Kaibab squirrel, and a remnant herd of American bison are also found here. The southern units of the forest are inhabited by elk, black bear, antelope, and cougar.

Designated trails are few, but many dirt roads provide access. In this open environment, trails are really unnecessary if one is careful not to become lost. The experienced cross-country traveler who chooses to strike out through the open forests, parklands, and deserts should exercise caution. Obtaining water won't be a problem if planned for. A particularly rugged area, the Sycamore Canyon Wilderness on the southern boundary of the forest is discussed below under the Prescott National Forest. Other good areas include the Kanab Creek, south of Freedonia, and Saddle Mountain, in the southeast corner of the north unit.

For information and a map (50¢) of the forest, contact the Regional Forester, Southwestern Region, 517 Gold Avenue, S.W., Albuquerque, New Mexico 87102.

Coconino National Forest

This forest, totaling 1,814,000 acres, is located southeast of the Kaibab in central Arizona surrounding Flagstaff. A variety of environments comprise this area—pine, fir, and aspen forests, grasslands, mountain peaks over 12,000 feet, mesas, canyons, craters, lakes, and streams. The moderate precipitation supports a generally good vegetation cover inhabited by deer, elk, antelope, black bear, javelina, cougar, bobcat, coyote, and other animals. Trout, bass, and catfish are found in the lakes and streams.

As in the Kaibab, trails are virtually nonexistent. Access to the many wild roadless areas is provided by dirt roads. Here one can wander at will through the varied scenery with little likelihood of meeting a fellow traveler. Cross-country travel is generally unencumbered by vegetation. The Mogollon Rim on the southern border of the forest is an escarpment providing exceptional views of the forest to the north. Other good areas include Secret Mountain-Red Rock, north and west of Sedonia, and the Sycamore Canyon Wilderness discussed below under Prescott National Forest.

For information and a map (50¢) of the forest, contact the Regional Forester, Southwestern Region, same address as above.

Prescott National Forest

The 1,249,000 acres of this forest are divided between two units on either side of the city of Prescott west of the Coconino National Forest. This forest is drier than the other forests in the area, with cactus in the lower elevations of about 3,000 feet and pine and fir forests near the higher elevations of about 8,000 feet. Low mountains, rock outcrops, and a few small lakes and intermittent streams complete the environment. Deer, antelope, javelina, black bear, fur-bearers, turkey, quail, and other animals inhabit the forest.

Many good trails are found in the forest proper, especially in the western unit. The eastern unit, though, includes part of the

Sycamore Canyon and Pine Mountain Wildernesses. The Sycamore Canyon Wilderness is 48,000 acres of sparsely vegetated
canyonlands in the northeast corner of the forest. Only a limited
number of miles of trails serve the wilderness, but cross-country
travel provides unlimited opportunities. The Pine Mountain Wilderness consists of 16,000 acres on the high Verde River Rim, a
timbered island amidst a surrounding desert of canyons and
mesas. Trails are few here also, but neither of these wildernesses
is heavily used, though the forest proper receives moderate use
from nearby Phoenix. Two other good areas include Castle Creek,
3 miles west of Bumblebee, and Granite Mountain, 10 miles northwest of Prescott.

For information and a map of the forest, contact the Regional
Forester, Southwestern Region, same address as above.

Sitgreaves National Forest

The 814,000 acres of this long, narrow forest stretch eastward
from central Arizona, nearly reaching the New Mexico border
and is administered as part of the Apache-Sitgreaves National
Forests. The low mountains are a mosaic of cactus in the lowlands,
becoming grasslands, parklands, and forests of ponderosa pine
as the elevation increases. With up to 30 inches of rain in certain
areas, there are several lakes and live streams. The different
environments provide habitat for elk, deer, antelope, coyote, fox,
badger, bobcat, a few beaver, and smaller animals, with trout
in some of the lakes and streams. A few black bear and cougar
may also be spotted.

Backpacking opportunities are limited in the forest because of
the relatively numerous roads, heavy visitation, and absence of
trails. However, cross-country travel opportunities are good with
the openness and moderate relief of the forests and grasslands.
Dirt roads provide access and water is available. It is unlikely
that one will meet other backpackers in the backcountry.

For information and a map (50¢) of the Apache-Sitgreaves
National Forests, contact the Regional Forester, Southwestern
Region, same address as above.

Tonto National Forest

At 2,885,000 acres, this is the largest national forest in the state, located northeast of Phoenix in central Arizona. The semidesert environment of the low 1,500-foot elevations transforms into pine and fir forest in the higher 7,000-foot elevations. Many large man-made lakes, natural lakes, and streams in the high country, and interesting geological formations, including the Mogollon Rim, are the goal of many visitors. Deer, elk, black bear, javelina, and a few cougar are among the animals inhabiting the forest.

All of three and part of a fourth wilderness area are included in the forest, providing the best backpacking opportunities. The largest, 205,000-acre Mazatzal Wilderness, is a land of precipitous desert mountains and canyons, especially in the central and eastern portions, with elevations ranging from 2,500 feet to 7,800 feet. Desert shrubs, grassland, piñon and ponderosa pine, and even a few stands of Douglas fir are found in the higher elevations. The 180 miles of trail vary from good to very poor, and water should be carried.

Farther south in the forest is the 21,000-acre Sierra Ancha Wilderness. This scenic, rugged, and in many places inaccessible wilderness is a maze of box canyons, desert mountains, vertical cliffs, and chaparral with elevations to 8,000 feet. While the terrain prohibits much cross-country travel, the area is so remote that the trails receive light use and solitude is easy to find. Water should be carried.

The 124,000-acre Superstition Wilderness farthest south in the forest is only 40 miles from Phoenix, but inhospitable conditions turn many would-be visitors away. The scenic, barren mountains rise out of the desert floor, baking in the hot summer sun and battered by winter blizzards. This is a land of mystery—lost gold mines and Indian legends. For the backpacker it is a land of challenge. Although there is a good trail system, water must be carried, and previous experience in desert travel is valuable.

The fourth wilderness, Pine Mountain, is discussed under the Prescott National Forest above.

For information and maps (50¢) of the forest and wildernesses, contact the Regional Forester, same address as above.

Apache National Forest

The 1,189,000 acres of this portion of the Apache-Sitgreaves National Forests extend to the east-central border of the state and partly into Mexico. Water distinguishes the forest— 15 lakes and reservoirs and 250 miles of trout streams as well as four major rivers make it one of the best watered of the southwestern forests. Semidesert conditions nevertheless exist in the lower elevations, with grasslands, parklands, forests of pine, fir, spruce, and aspen, and finally timberline conditions at the highest elevations. Mount Baldy, at 11,590 feet, is the second tallest point in the state. In the forests, meadows, and around the rock outcrops and lakes roam deer, elk, javelina, antelope, black bear, cougar, bobcat, coyote, and a variety of smaller animals and birds.

Roads are not very plentiful in the forest, and cross-country opportunities are good. Most of the trails are in the small 7,000-acre Mount Baldy Wilderness in the northwest section of the forest and in the larger 175,000-acre Blue Range Primitive Area on the east side of the forest extending into New Mexico. Mount Baldy Wilderness is a high area between 8,700 feet and 11,000 feet, with gentle to severe terrain covered with subalpine vegetation flourishing in the cool climate. Two short trails following creek beds penetrate the area. The Blue Range Primitive Area has many more trails and much trailless backcountry for the cross-country traveler. The area lies at the edge of the Colorado Plateau and is bisected by the Mogollon Rim. The ridges, canyons, and other interesting geologic features are covered by spruce and fir in the higher elevations and by ponderosa parklands in the lower elevations. Use of the entire forest is generally light, but heaviest above the Mogollon Rim Area.

For information and a map of the forest, wilderness, and primitive areas in the Apache-Sitgreaves National Forests, contact the Regional Forester, Southwestern Region, 517 Gold Avenue, S.W., Albuquerque, New Mexico 87101. Same address as above.

Coronado National Forest

This southernmost forest in the state, on and near the Mexican border east of Tucson has 1,791,000 acres divided among a dozen scattered units, one of which is in New Mexico. These units lie on mountain ranges that rise to elevations over 10,000 feet like islands in the desert, supporting a variety of environments— Sonoran desert, chaparral, grasslands, and conifer forests and parklands. Geologically interesting landscapes are common, and there are a few lakes and streams. The forest is a haven for desert wildlife, including deer, javelina, black bear, bighorn, cougar, wolf, fox, coyote, bobcat, turkey, quail, and the unusual coati- mundi. Occasionally a jaguar or ocelot wanders in from Mexico.

Some of the units are suitable for cross-country travel. In some units, roads peter out into foot trails which provide access. Three designated wildernesses offer good trail-hiking opportunities. The 53,000-acre Galiuro Wilderness is a rough, brushy desert mountain range with steep grades and scenic cliffs and outcrops. A few trails penetrate the wilderness, but going is difficult due to the rugged terrain and heavy brush. Water should be carried and summer travel is best avoided. The 18,000-acre Chiricahua Wilderness lies astride the Chiricahua Mountains, rising out of the desert floor to create environments that vary with the elevation, culminating in conifer forests on the summits. The climate is a bit kinder than that of the Galiuro Wilderness, and the trails are better. Neither wilderness is heavily used.

For information and a map (50¢) of the forest and wilderness areas, contact the Regional Forester, same address as above.

The 56,430-acre Pusch Ridge Wilderness was newly created in 1978. It is located on the southwest edge of the Catalina Mountain Range and is characterized by rugged, rocky, steep canyons, where the elevation ranges from 3,200 feet at the desert floor to 8,000 feet on the slopes of Mt. Lemmon. This scenic wilderness provides a spectacular backdrop to the city of Tucson.

Lake Mead National Recreation Area

See Nevada, below.

Organ Pipe Cactus National Monument

This 331,000-acre monument is located in south-central Arizona on the Mexican border, a Sonoran Desert wilderness containing many examples of plant life found nowhere else in the country. Among the barren mountains, cactus and creosote bush flats, and canyons are found coyote, gray and kit foxes, ringtail, coatimundi, javelina, bobcat, deer, antelope, bighorn, and a few cougar.

Special precautions must be taken while traveling in the monument. There is little water and only 3 miles of trails. Cross-country travel, with permits, is allowed, but preparations must be made carefully to avoid becoming lost. Fall-through-spring travel avoids the high temperatures of summer. Few backpackers use this area and motorized use is prohibited off the roads, so those inclined to tackle this wilderness will be rewarded by solitude that is hard to match.

For information and a map of the monument, contact the Superintendent, Organ Pipe Cactus National Monument, P.O. Box 28, Ajo, Arizona 85321.

Saguaro National Monument

This 84,000-acre monument is divided into two units, one on either side of Tucson in southeastern Arizona. Over 71,000 acres of the monument is designated wilderness. Like the Organ Pipe Cactus National Monument, it is a Sonoran Desert wilderness. The giant cactus, saguaro, characterizes this monument, though a variety of life zones are found here also. The lowest elevations below 3,000 feet support a creosote bush desert like that found in Organ Pipe Cactus National Monument. Higher up is found the saguaro desert, then oak, piñon, and juniper woodlands, and finally oak, pine, Douglas fir, and other species up to about 8,660 feet.

Almost 200 species of birds, more than 50 species of reptiles, javelina, mule deer, coyote, and a variety of bats and rodents are found in the monument.

Seventy-eight miles of trails and good cross-country travel opportunities make this an excellent area for the desert buff. Water must be carried. Summer temperatures are tolerable in the higher elevations, but this area receives considerable use from nearby Tucson. No camping is allowed in the smaller unit just west of the city.

For information and a map, contact the Superintendent, Saguaro National Monument, P.O. Box 17210, Tucson, Arizona 85710.

Kofa National Wildlife Refuge

This 660,000-acre refuge is located in the southwest corner of the state, northeast of Yuma. Its several units comprise a starkly beautiful desertscape of austere, low mountains (under 5,000 feet) and flat valley floors. Since the area receives only about 5 inches of precipitation annually, vegetation is sparsely scattered and consists of various cacti, ocotilla, paloverde, short-lived wild-flowers, and other specialized desert plants. The desert animal community includes wild burro, bighorn, deer, cougar, bobcat, peccary, ringtail, badger, coyote, various smaller mammals, reptiles, and over 150 species of birds.

Backpackers visiting this area will experience one of the wildest environments in the state. No official trails are provided, and while parts of the refuge are impenetrably rugged, most areas are accessible to the cross-country traveler. Motorized vehicles are not permitted off roads. The two greatest constraints on the visitor are the heat and limited availability of water. Summer temperatures frequently hit 110°F, making late fall to early spring a much more attractive time (highs in January average in the 50s). Water should be carried even though scattered sources are present in the backcountry. Camping is permitted just about everywhere. Firewood is scarce, as are visitors. A high profile vehicle is desired for access.

For information and a map of the range, contact the Manager, Kofa National Wildlife Refuge, P.O. Box 1032, Yuma, Arizona 85364.

Other Public Lands

While public land is abundant throughout most of the state, several outstanding areas are especially good for backpacking and information on these areas is readily available. The Paria Canyon Primitive Area, administered by the Bureau of Land Management is located on the north-central border of the state extending into Utah. It provides a unique backpacking experience. Paria Canyon and adjacent Kaibab Gulch vary from a narrow sandstone canyon just wide enough to walk through to open valleys. Everywhere are interesting geologic features such as arches, spires, and caves. Evidence of native American, as well as white settlers, can still be found. Wildlife includes deer, bobcat, fox, raccoon, eagles, and other birds and animals. Paria Canyon is 40 miles long, with Kaibab Gulch an additional 17, and all of it can be backpacked, though much of it involves sloshing through water. Spring is the best season, summers are hot and prone to flash flooding ("If you get caught in the narrows in a flash flood it will probably be fatal"—Bureau of Land Management). No vehicles allowed.

Another good backpacking area is the Safford District of the Bureau of Land Management in the southeastern corner of the state. This area contains 1,317,000 acres of BLM land, all of it open to camping. The district is typical desert country with eroded mountains, outwash plains, canyons, and a variety of desert flora, including many varieties of cactus, yucca, with cottonwoods and sycamores in the river valleys. Wildlife is also varied, with small mammals, deer, javelina, cougar, quail, bobwhite, just about every songbird found in the desert, and bass and catfish in the rivers. Two areas are especially good for backpacking. A 3- or 4-day journey can be taken through the 11-mile-long Gila River Box, a beautiful gorge several hundred feet deep. The Aravaipa Canyon Primitive Area in this district also provides a good one- or two-day backpacking trip through stream bottoms flanked by high cliffs, cottonwood, sycamore, and cactus. Vehicles are prohibited in this area. Both provide an excellent opportunity to observe desert ecosystems in fascinating settings. Hikers should apply in advance for permits.

For information, maps and permits, contact the Bureau of Land Management, Arizona State Office, 2400 Valley Bank Center, Phoenix, Arizona 85073.

CALIFORNIA

This state has the most national forests with the second-greatest total forest acreage, and more parks, monuments, and recreation areas suitable for backpacking than any other state. The major physiographic features of the state include two mountain systems, the coast ranges running the entire length of the coast, and the Sierra Nevada in the northern two-thirds of the eastern half of the state. The southern third of the eastern half of the state is part of the Great Desert. Generally, the climate becomes cooler and wetter as one moves north. This long state covers a variety of climates and environments from Death Valley to the cathedral redwoods of the north California coast.

Backpacking opportunities are equally varied. The state offers a backpacking trip for every taste on its thousands of miles of trails and great expanses of backcountry. Unfortunately, this state also contains a large backpacking population and attracts many visitors. The result is overuse that transforms places like Yosemite National Park into a backpacker ghetto in the peak summer months. Most areas receive only moderate use and many are only lightly used where the solitude-seeker, with careful planning, can achieve his goal.

A permit is required for travel in any of the wilderness and primitive areas in the state. These can be obtained at ranger stations and field offices, or they can be obtained from the U.S. Forest Service, California Region, Office of Information, 630 Sansome Street, San Francisco, California 94111. Also, an entire set of forest maps for the state can be obtained from this address, at 50¢ each. Maps of individual forests are also available from the forest supervisor listed after each forest discussed below.

General tourism information is unavailable from the state.

Pacific Crest National Scenic Trail

This proposed trail when completed will extend for about 2,500 miles, mostly along the crest of mountain ranges in Washington, Oregon, and California from Canada to Mexico. The environments are varied along the trail—desert, forest, and alpine tundra covered with snow most of the year—as it passes through 23 national forests (and several wildernesses), 7 national parks, and other public and private land. Much of the trail is yet uncompleted, and even the completed sections are often high, rough mountain trails snowbound for much of the summer. This trail is by no means as tame as its eastern counterpart, the Appalachian Trail (see West Virginia, chapter 9), but at least one person has hiked its entire length in one summer.

The Pacific Crest Trail will probably never see the heavy use that the Appalachian Trail has received. The main reason is that other backpacking areas are abundant along most of its length, drawing users away from the trail. In addition, the population is not as heavy along the route of the trail as it is along the Appalachian Trail in the East. While the Pacific Crest Trail may never achieve the fame and following of the Appalachian Trail, it provides good backpacking opportunities, especially if combined with trips along its side trails to form loop journeys. Of course, there will always be those who accept the challenge of hiking the entire trail, either all at once or in a lifetime.

For information on the 1,660 miles of the trail in California, contact the U.S. Forest Service, California Region, Office of Information, 630 Sansome Street, San Francisco, California 94111. For information on the remaining portion in Washington and Oregon, contact the U.S. Forest Service, Pacific Northwest Region, P.O. Box 3623, Portland, Oregon 97208.

Beginning in the northern coast ranges, backpacking opportunities from north to south are as follows:

Six Rivers National Forest

This 1,120,000-acre forest extends for 135 miles south from the Oregon border along the west slopes of the northern coast ranges east of Eureka. These mountains, mostly under 6,000 feet, are covered with dense fir forests, and are cut by six major rivers. Deer, black bear, cougar, antelope, as well as smaller animals are found here. Lake and stream trout fishing is good, with excellent salmon and steelhead running in the fall and winter.

While there are no designated wilderness or primitive areas, several lightly used trails in the rugged back country, provide abundant backpacking opportunities. Loop trips of varying lengths can be planned, with the more remote trails found in the northern portion of the forest and along its eastern edge. Large roadless areas can be found throughout. Cross-country travel is very difficult in the thick forest. The climate is cool and wet in the winter with high dry summers.

For information and a map (50¢) of the forest, contact the Supervisor, Six Rivers National Forest, 507F Street, Eureka, California 95501.

Klamath National Forest

This forest is one of California's most outstanding for backpacking, located just east of Six Rivers National Forest and east and west of Yreka. Its 1,695,000 acres are about two-thirds covered with big timber—pine, fir, cedar, and hemlock. The remainder is mountain meadows, reforesting areas, and brush fields. The mountains are in the 4,000–8,000-foot range, with many large, powerful rivers flowing through the canyons and valleys. Cougar, black bear, antelope, deer, and various smaller animals are among the inhabitants, as well as rainbow and eastern brook trout and salmon.

The forest proper has hundreds of miles of good trails and many vast roadless areas. The terrain is only moderately steep, and many of the trails are relatively easy going. Use is light to moderate. The forest also offers about a quarter of a million acres of prime backpacking wilderness. The Salmon-Trinity Alps Primitive Area is discussed under the Shasta-Trinity National Forest. The other area is the 215,000-acre Marble Mountain Wilderness.

The Marble Mountain Wilderness is a rugged area of fir and pine forests, alpine meadows, peaks to about 8,300 feet, fast, icy streams, and about 80 lakes. Marble Mountain itself is composed of marble that gleams in the sun, giving the impression of perpetual snow cover. Several rare species of plants and all of California's conifer species are present, as is 93,000 acres of timber. The wilderness has a good system of trails, but they are often steep, and the secondary spur trails may be substandard, though passable. Cross-country travel is difficult because of dense vegetation and steep terrain. The good trail system and only moderate use makes cross-country travel unnecessary anyway.

For information and maps (50¢) of the forest and wilderness areas, contact the Supervisor, Klamath National Forest, 1215 South Main Street, Yreka, California 96097.

Mendocino National Forest

This 1,000,000-acre forest is south of the Trinity National Forest on the North Coastal Mountain Range about 100 miles north of San Francisco. The elevations are from about 1,000 feet to over 8,000 feet in the Yolla Bolly Mountains in the northern portion of the forest. These higher elevations resemble the middle elevations of the Sierras: rugged ridges and canyons, and open valleys with scattered stands of bitter cherry and brewer oak. Many lakes of various sizes and 650 miles of fishing streams are scattered throughout the forest. The environment of the slopes varies with the direction they face. Cool, north-facing slopes are heavily forested with mixed hardwoods and conifer, with south-facing slopes correspondingly warmer, drier, and less densely forested. The west slopes have brush-covered summits with Garry oak and Douglas fir lower down. The eastern slopes, in the mountains' rain shadow, are dry and warm with ponderosa pine and Douglas fir on the summits and open grasslands on the foothills. The variety of environments supports an equally varied animal population: black bear, deer, cougar, coyote, bobcat, ringtail, gray and red foxes, a variety of smaller mammals and reptiles (including rattlesnakes), and over 100 species of birds, salmon, trout, and bass.

While there are many miles of trails in the forest proper, none are really remote, and most are used by motorized vehicles. Cross-country travel in the open parklands and grasslands is good, and a haven for backpackers in the 110,000-acre Yolla Bolly-Middle Eel Wilderness in the northern portion of the forest extending partly into the Shasta-Trinity National Forest. Elevations are from 2,700 feet to 8,083 feet, with several peaks over 7,500 feet. Fir, pine, and cedar are common, with some juniper, hemlock, and cottonwood. The forests are interspersed with "glades" (wet or dry meadows), oak woodlands, and brushlands. The extensive trail system is generally good and use is light. Cross-country travel is inadvisable in much of the wilderness where heavy vegetation makes the going difficult.

For information and a map (50¢) of the forest and wilderness, contact the Supervisor, Mendocino National Forest, P.O. Box 431, Willows, California 95988.

Beginning in the northern inland ranges, backpacking opportunities from north to south are as follows:

Modoc National Forest

This 1,651,000-acre forest is located the northeastern corner of the state by Alturas. The forest lies generally below 7,000 feet, is well laced by roads, has few trails, and is intensively lumbered. Backpacking opportunities of significance are found in the Lava Beds National Monument, discussed later, and in the 69,000-acre South Warner Wilderness.

This wilderness lies atop the Warner Mountains, an area of glacial and landslide-formed lakes, canyons, peaks, and streams coursing through mountain meadows. The tallest peak, Eagle Peak, towers to 9,906 feet. Deer is the most common large mammal, and trout fishing in the streams is good. The main backpacking trail follows the mountain crests above 9,000 feet and extends from north to south through the wilderness. While this trail provides the best alpine scenery, there are many equally good spur trails leading down the crest to lakes and meadows. The best way to travel in this wilderness is by cross-country. The open alpine environment makes travel easy, and many of the points of interest are not reached by trails.

For information and a map (50¢) of the forest and wilderness, contact the Supervisor, Modoc National Forest, P.O. Box 611, Alturas, California 96101.

Shasta-Trinity National Forest

These two forests have been combined into one jurisdiction for a total of 2,073,000 acres; the Trinity is east of Eureka and the Six Rivers National Forest, while the Shasta is northeast of the Trinity and north of Redding. The forests are topped by 14,162-foot Mount Shasta, covered by eternal snow and 5 live glaciers. Pine, fir, cedar, juniper, and meadows and oak parklands drape the slope and valleys. Other interesting features include volcanic lava flows, caves, and chimneys. There are many streams, but only a few small lakes and some very large impoundments in the lower elevations. Cougar, coyote, red fox, ringtail, bobcat, black bear, roadrunner, water ouzel, turkey, and trout are found in the forests.

Both forests have good backpacking trails, with the Trinity having fewer roads and more remote trails than the Shasta. Two areas are particularly good, though a bit more heavily used than the forest proper. One, the Yolta Bolly-Middle Eel Wilderness, is described above under the Mendocino National Forest. The other area is the 225,000-acre Salmon-Trinity Alps Primitive Area, the second largest wild area in the state. This is a land of tall peaks and deep canyons. Many of the peaks are in the 7,000–9,000-foot range, with steep, jagged peaks of bare granite with talus slopes. Many lakes and streams are reached by the over 400 miles of good trails, and use is light to moderate. Rattlesnakes are present, but not in numbers to present a problem. One of the best seasons to visit the area is in the fall after about mid-September when the maple, oak, and dogwood are ablaze with color.

A third area, the Whiskeytown Unit of the Whiskeytown-Shasta-Trinity National Recreation Area, includes 365 shoreline miles around the 3,000-acre Shasta Lake, for a total area of 42,000 acres in the southern portion of the Shasta National Forest. While there are 57 miles of good trails in this very picturesque setting, most are used by off-road vehicles. The lake also is heavily used, so even though a shoreline hike might be attractive, the backpacker is never really left to himself.

For information and maps (50¢) of the forests, wilderness, primitive and recreation areas, contact the Supervisor, Shasta-Trinity National Forest, 2400 Washington Avenue, Redding, California 96001.

Lassen National Forest and Lassen Volcanic National Park

A total of 1,155,000 acres (107,000 acres in the park and 1,048,000 acres in the forest) comprise this area east of Redding in northeast California. This is where the southernmost stretch of the Cascades merges with the Sierra Nevada, rising to 10,457 feet on Lassen Peak in the park, but are generally under 8,000 feet in the surrounding forest. Lassen Peak, a symmetrical, plug-dome volcano dominates the surrounding landscape of coniferous forests, mountains, lava beds, hot springs, fumaroles, mountain lakes, and streams. Deer, cougar, red and gray foxes, black bear, river otter, loon, pelican, water ouzel, and rubber boa are among the inhabitants.

The backpacker has 4 options in this area: the forest proper, the park, the Caribou Wilderness, and the Thousand Lakes Wilderness. While the forest proper does not have the most exciting trails, they are among the least used. The only significant trails system is in the southern portion of the forest, mostly in the southwest corner. Here most elevations are under 3,000 feet and the trails are relatively easy. Cross-country travel is difficult.

Lassen Volcanic National Park boasts 150 miles of trails linking most of the 50 wilderness lakes. This is the most spectacular area, but also has some of the steepest trails and heaviest use. Volcanic activity is most apparent here. Adjacent on the eastern boundary is the 19,000-acre Caribou Wilderness, a gently rolling, easily traversed forested plateau dotted by many glacial and volcanic lakes among barren rocky outcrops. Trails are not abundant in this small wilderness, and none link into the adjacent national park. Use is moderate, and some cross-country travel is possible above the timberline.

The 16,000-acre Thousand Lakes Wilderness north of the park is for the cross-country traveler who is not afraid of a rough climb. Elevations range from 5,000 feet to 9,000 feet with open mountainsides and ravines, lava and other rock outcrops, meadows and brushy areas, mountain lakes and streams, as well as dense stands of fir, pine, and hemlock. The extensive trail system is poorly maintained, and is rocky and steep. This is the best area for solitude, especially off the trails in the remote recesses of the wilderness.

For information and a map (50¢) of the park, contact the Superintendent, Lassen Volcanic National Park, Mineral, California 96063. For information and maps of the forest and wilderness, contact the Supervisor, Lassen National Forest, 707 Nevada Street, Susanville, California 96130.

Plumas National Forest

This 1,154,000-acre forest surrounding the town of Quincy south of Lassen National Forest has too many roads but there are a few trails of interest to the backpacker. The Pacific Crest National Scenic Trail discussed above crosses the forest, but much of the southern portion is yet uncompleted. The forest has many peaks under 8,000 feet, beautifully forested valleys, and is inhabited by deer, black bear, waterfowl, and other birds and animals. There are several challenging trails into the Middle Fork of the Feather River and the Lakes Basin has trails connecting many Alpine Lakes.

For information and a map (50¢) of the forest, contact the Supervisor, Plumas National Forest, P.O. Box 1500, Quincy, California 95971.

Tahoe National Forest

This forest is a checkerboard of public-private ownership— 803,000 acres public, and about 406,000 acres private within the forest boundary. However, recreational use of the public-private land is generally indiscriminate. The forest lies northeast of Sacramento and south of the Plumas National Forest, and includes the famous Lake Tahoe on its southeast boundary. Tahoe National Forest is in the central Sierras and is characterized by a variety of plant associations: mountain chaparral, mixed conifers, alpine plants, stands of piñon and juniper, stands of lodgepole pine, and sage bitterbrush. Many barren, jagged granite peaks soar to 9,000 feet, interspersed with glacial-formed and other lakes of various sizes. Black bear, deer, cougar, small mammals, trout, and various other animals and birds inhabit the forest.

The best backpacking opportunities are limited to a band of high peaks and mountain lakes in the central portion of the forest. Two areas along this band have been designated for nonmotorized use only and provide the best backpacking. The Granite Chief Motor Vehicle Closure Area is about 30,000 acres of high peaks, mountain streams, and a few lakes just west of Lake Tahoe. Trails generally follow the stream beds and cross-country travel is possible in the open alpine areas. Farther north, Grouse Lakes Off Road Motor Vehicle Control Area is about 18,000 acres of alpine terrain mostly closed to motorized use. One hundred twenty-five lakes are nestled in the mountain granite surrounded by open alpine meadows and scattered stands of juniper and aspen. A few trails provide access, then, for those so inclined; a little cross-country travel will allow them to claim some remote mountain lake as a campsite.

For information and a map (50¢) of the forest and motor vehicle control areas, contact the Supervisor, Tahoe National Forest, Highway 49 and Coyote Street, Nevada City, California 95959.

Eldorado National Forest

This 786,000-acre forest is east of Sacramento and south of Tahoe National Forest. The forest includes rangeland foothills, densely forested slopes, and barren granite peaks to 10,000 feet. Deer and black bear are two of the over 300 species of mammals, birds, reptiles, and fish that inhabit the forests, lakes, and 890 miles of streams. Two of these are on the endangered-species list: the peregrine falcon and southern bald eagle. The forest proper is too heavily used by tourists, including the motorized trail-users, to be of much interest to the backpacker. Cross-country travel is only feasible near and above timberline, and these environments are included in the two wildernesses in the forest that offer good backpacking opportunities.

Desolation Wilderness is 63,000 acres of glaciated granite, typical of the High Sierras. About 130 lakes are scattered through this alpine area of fir, pine, cedar, and spruce, which ranges in elevation from 6,500 feet to 10,000 feet. The trails are steep, but are nevertheless among the most heavily used in the country. Use is heavy enough to cause the Forest Service to consider limiting use. Camping by certain lakes is already forbidden. Since this is open alpine country, cross-country travel is possible, and those so inclined will escape the crowds that rob the wilderness experience. The other wilderness, Mokelumne, includes 50,000 acres, partly in Stanislaus National Forest, in the southeast part of the forest and is similar to Desolation Wilderness: granite peaks to 10,000 feet, with intersecting canyons, lakes, and eroded granite formations, served by a good trail system. Unlike the Desolation, though, use here is only moderate. Backpackers who wish to stick to the trails, but don't like backcountry overpopulation, would do better to visit this wilderness rather than Desolation.

For information and a map (50¢) of the forest and wildernesses, contact the Supervisor, Eldorado National Forest, 100 Forni Road, Placerville, California 95667.

Stanislaus National Forest

This is one of California's best backpacking forests—896,000 acres of forests and mountains, 7,000 acres of lakes, 810 miles of streams, and 750 miles of good trails to take you there. The forest is east of San Francisco and south of Eldorado National Forest. Elevations range from 1,100 feet to 11,570 feet on Leavitt Peak, and several large lakes have cut deep canyons in the glaciated granite. Up to about 3,000 feet, the vegetation is oak parkland, then becomes heavily forested with pine, fir, cedar, and scattered hardwoods that provide beautiful fall color. Above about 8,000 feet the wildflowers of the alpine meadows accent the granite outcrops and barren peaks and lava flows that form the backdrop. Wildlife is similar to that of Eldorado National Forest.

There are excellent wildernesses in the forest, and the forest proper offers exceptional backpacking opportunities in the large roadless northeast quadrant. Most of the many trails in this area are closed to motorized use. The trails lead up along the high-stream valleys between peaks over 9,000 feet, and receive only light use. For a real wilderness experience, one could attempt cross-country travel in the alpine regions of the area north of the Emigrant Wilderness—not only is this a roadless area, but it also lacks any trails. Obviously, it is for the very experienced only.

Emigrant Wilderness is located on the east-central boundary of the forest along Yosemite National Park and comprises 107,000 acres. Elevations range from 5,200 feet in the granite basins to over 11,000 feet on the lava-capped peaks. Many lakes dot the landscape, most not reached by trails. Cross-country travel is advisable because of the heavy use of this area. This heavy use also makes fish in many of the lakes reluctant to take a hook. The other wilderness, Mokelumne, is discussed above under the Eldorado National Forest.

For information and a map (50¢) of the forest and wildernesses, contact the Supervisor, Stanislaus National Forest, 175 Fairview Lane, Sonora, California 95370.

Toiyabe National Forest
    See Nevada, below.

Yosemite National Park

This 761,000-acre park is one of the West's most popular—and it's easy to understand why. One reason is its location on the southeast border of the Stanislaus National Forest, within easy driving of San Francisco and Los Angeles. But more importantly, it is a granite fairyland, with glacier-sculptured peaks and valleys, waterfalls tumbling from hanging valleys atop imposing cliffs, forests of oak, giant sequoias, and other conifers dotted with hundreds of wilderness lakes and trout streams. Other wildlife includes deer, black bear, cougar, bobcat, coyote, mink, wolverine, red and gray foxes, and ringtail.

Yosemite Valley, one of the most beautiful in the world, is chaos in the summer. Heavy use has made this park the epitome of overuse, requiring controls on visitation and use. The backcountry is likewise overused. One would think with 749 miles of trails there would be some trails where use is light. There aren't. John Muir and the Sierra Club he founded are inadvertently partly responsible for this park's overuse by making it so well known. The park's beauty is the other cause. A conscientious backpacker would visit the park in the offseason, plan a cross-country itinerary into a lightly used area with the help of a ranger, or at least plan to take a less used trail, entering perhaps from one of the surrounding forests. Fires are only permitted in established firesites and wood fires are not permitted above 9,000! A back country permit is required. As in all national parks, motorized use of trails is prohibited.

For information (including information on entry quotas) and a map of the park, contact the Superintendent, Yosemite National Park, P.O. Box 577, Yosemite National Park, California 95389.

Inyo National Forest

This 1,836,000-acre forest is located south of Mono Lake and is divided into two main units, one on either side of Bishop (part of this forest also extends into Nevada). Superlatives best describe it—it contains the tallest peak in the state, 14,495-foot Mount Whitney, and has many other peaks in the 12,000–14,000-foot range; it contains the oldest living things on earth, the 4,000-year-old Bristlecone Pines, part of the largest, finest, but most heavily used wilderness in the state, the John Muir Wilderness. Some large roadless and trailless areas are also in the forest. It is typical High Sierra environment—high, jagged peaks of gleaming granite, interspersed with alpine lakes, lava fields, craters, and basaltic formations. Vegetation consists of alpine communities with thick coniferous forests farther down the slopes. The eastern unit of the forest is drier with stands of juniper, piñon pine, and contains the Ancient Bristlecone Pine Forest natural area. Wildlife is varied including deer, black bear, cougar, coyote, bobcat, wolverine, and the visitor has a good chance of spotting bighorns in the California Bighorn Sheep Zoological Area. There are seasonal visitation restrictions within the zoological area.

The backpacker has 4 wilderness areas, and many trail and trailless areas in the forest proper to choose from. The John Muir Wilderness is discussed below under the Sierra National Forest. The Hoover Wilderness is mostly in the Toiyabe National Forest, which in turn is mostly in Nevada. This small 48,000-acre wilderness on the north edge of the forest is extremely rugged, with elevations from 8,000 feet to 13,000 feet. Since most of the area is above timberline, open alpine expanses, bare granite outcrops, and a few scattered stands of lodgepole pine and aspen comprise the landscape. The many lakes are stocked with trout and offer good fishing. The backpacking season is short—July and August—and the trails are steep. In one area, there is a 5,000-foot climb over a horizontal distance of only 5 miles. This discourages many visitors but is a blessing in this heavily backpacked part of the state. Cross-country travel is possible, but it, too, can be difficult over the steep terrain.

The Minarets Wilderness comprises 109,000 acres of tall, stark granite peaks and an environment similar to that of the Hoover Wilderness. Elevations range from 7,000 feet to 14,000 feet, with many peaks in the area over 12,000 feet. The several lakes in its central portion and many tributary streams offer good fishing. As in the Hoover, trails are tough and cross-country travel is difficult; solitude in this austere part of California is hard won, but well worth the effort. This wilderness extends into the Sierra National Forest discussed below.

The Golden Trout Wilderness includes 306,000 acres of the Inyo and Sequoia National Forests. Areas of extensive timber, large meadows, and outstanding scenery, are typical of this wilderness. Fishing is good. A well developed trail system leads into, and through, the area, which is mostly below 12,000 feet.

Wilderness areas are not the only backpacking havens, though. For the more adventuresome, the northern half of the eastern unit is a trackless expanse of valleys, mountains, and plateaus, including the Ancient Bristlecone Pine Forest on its southern edge. Roads around the perimeter of this unit provide access to challenging cross-country travel opportunities.

For information and a map (50¢) of the forest and wilderness areas, contact the Supervisor, Inyo National Forest, 873 N. Main Street, Bishop, California 93514.

Sierra National Forest

This 1,294,000-acre forest is one of the most heavily used in the state, being located in the Sierras about midway between San Francisco and Los Angeles, adjacent to Yosemite, Kings Canyon, and Sequoia National Parks. The landscape is typically High Sierra—forests of conifers, including giant sequoias, thinning out at the bases of imposing granite peaks rising to 13,000 feet. Most of the common large mammals are represented here, including black bear, cougar, deer, bobcat, and coyote. Trails exist throughout the forest proper and are heavily used. The best backpacking areas are in the wildernesses and primitive areas, but these are likewise crowded, even though the permit system puts a ceiling on their use. These are the Minarets Wilderness, discussed above under the Inyo National Forest, the High Sierra Primitive Area, discussed later under the Sequoia National Forest, and the John Muir Wilderness Area.

The John Muir Wilderness at 503,000 acres is the largest and best-known wilderness in the state. Accordingly, it is the most heavily used. It lies partly in the Inyo National Forest and extends almost from Yosemite to Sequois national parks along the crest of the Sierras. In the lower elevations, pine and fir forests cover the slopes, but much of the wilderness is above timberline with numerous snow-capped peaks. Thousands of lakes and hundreds of miles of streams are stocked with trout. Deer are abundant and a few bands of bighorns roam the southern portion near Mount Whitney. This would be a backpacker's paradise if it weren't so heavily used. The best way to visit this wilderness is to use the trails for access only, then head cross-country as soon as possible. In a half-million acres, you are sure to find your private niche.

For information and a map (50¢) of the forest, wilderness, and primitive areas, contact the Supervisor, Sierra National Forest, Federal Building, Room 3017, 1130 O Street, Fresno, California 93721.

Sequoia and Kings Canyon National Parks

These two adjacent parks have a combined area of 847,000 acres and are located due east of Fresno. Like Yosemite, they are High Sierra wildernesses, with granite mountains, cliffs, lakes, streams, waterfalls, valleys, and forests containing the world's largest living things, the giant sequoias. Wildlife includes deer, black bear, cougar, coyote, bobcat, ringtail, bighorn, wolverine, pine marten, fisher, golden eagle, and water ouzel.

Also like Yosemite, these parks are overused, and for the same reasons. The 773 miles of trails are crowded (with about 41,000 users in 1977), and the backpacker may want to take the same approach here as suggested for Yosemite. The backcountry of these parks is presently managed as wilderness and soon will be officially included in the wilderness system. There is currently a quota system for all trails leading into the park, and reservations are accepted until May 31. This, like Yosemite, is some of the finest Sierra high country and can be enjoyed if one plans carefully to avoid the crowds.

For information and a map of the parks, contact the Superintendents, Sequoia and Kings Canyon National Parks, Three Rivers, California 93271.

Sequoia National Forest

This 1,116,000-acre forest is located east of Porterville and lies on the southern edge of the Sierras. Elevations range from 1,000 feet to over 12,000 feet, with terrain varying from the high Sierras to the foothills of the San Joaquin Valley and the edge of the Mohave Desert. The lower valleys and ridges are timber-covered and the high granite country is dotted with trout lakes and streams. Black bear and deer are the most common large mammals. The most outstanding feature of the forest is the giant sequoia; 39 cathedral-like groves of these beautiful trees are found here. Trails are abundant and excellent in most parts of the forest, but use is fairly heavy on most of them. Three designated areas, the Dome Land Wilderness and the High Sierra Primitive Area and the Golden Trout Wilderness, are especially suited to the backpackers.

Dome Land Wilderness is a semiarid environment with elevations from 3,000 feet to 9,000 feet. It takes its name from the dome-shaped monolithic rock outcrops scattered throughout the 62,000-acre wilderness. Vegetation becomes scrubby on the lower slopes, with stands of mixed conifers. The open expanses are inviting to the cross-country traveler, especially in the trailless southern half of the wilderness where it is easy to find oneself alone. The High Sierra Primitive Area is small at 10,000 acres, but what it lacks in size, it makes up for in ruggedness and scenic splendor. This small primitive area is among the wildest in the state, and Tehipite Valley within the area is compared to Yosemite Valley. Many life zones are crossed traveling from the valley floor to the surrounding peaks. Only a few trails penetrate the area, and all are steep, a blessing for a backpacking area so close to the crowds of Kings Canyon National Park.

See, Inyo National Forest above for a discussion of the Golden Trout Wilderness.

For information and a map (50¢) of the forest, wilderness, and primitive area, contact the Supervisor, Sequoia National Forest, 900 West Grand Avenue, Porterville, California 93257.

Moving back to the coast ranges, backpacking opportunities from north to south are as follows:

Los Padres National Forest

This forest's 1,724,000 acres makes it the second largest in the state, but it is exceptional in other ways also. Its two main units provide a wilderness playground virtually in the backyard of many large population centers such as Santa Barbara and it is well managed for backpacking. Elevations range from sea level to almost 9,000 feet in the rugged mountains, which are snow-capped in the winter. Chaparral and grasslands cover the lowlands, oak parklands are in the middle slopes, and coniferous forests of pine, redwood, fir, and cypress are found in the higher elevations, which may receive up to 60 inches of precipitation a year along the coast. Deer, black bear, and peccary (a wild pig) are found here, as are many hundreds of miles of trout streams. The rare California condor is this forest's celebrity, and two sanctuaries have been established in the forest to protect the 100 or so that remain. Good trails serve most portions of the forest, and motorized use is controlled and prohibited on many trails. Special regulations control the use of fire and some areas are closed during the fall periods of high fire danger. Otherwise, the season is year-round. The Ventana and San Rafael, and Santa Lucia wildernesses provide exceptional backpacking opportunities.

The Ventana Wilderness is 159,000 acres of mountainous terrain in the northern tip of the forest. Many rare plants, as well as the coast redwood, are found here, as are the headwaters of many of the area's rivers. These unusual river canyons with their mild climate provide a year-round wilderness experience (a wilderness with a year-round season is rare). Although controlled by a permit system, use is still heavy and travelers in the off-season will avoid the crowds on the trails. Cross-country travel is also good. The San Rafael Wilderness farther south was the first designated primitive area, and contains 143,000 acres of mountainous terrain in the mid-southern portion of the forest. Elevations are from about 1,200 feet to 6,000 feet. Access is via 125 miles of good trails, and cross-country travel expands the backpacking opportunities. Use is controlled by a permit system, and a portion is closed in the summer and fall due to fire danger. Otherwise, the season is year-round. The 21,000-acre Santa Lucia Wilderness contains 13 miles of trails. Rainbow trout inhabit Lopez Creek. The season is year-round, but a permit system is in effect.

For information and a map (50¢) of the forest and wilderness areas, contact the Supervisor, Los Padres National Forest, 42 Aero Camino, Goleta, California 93017.

Angeles National Forest

This 691,000-acre forest is adjacent to the Los Angeles metropolitan area, and that in itself is probably enough to turn most backpackers away. Surprisingly, these chaparral- and pine-covered slopes with elevations to 10,064 feet on Mount Baldy offer some good cross-country travel possibilities. Water and wildlife are not abundant, though there are a few streams and the visitor might spot a bighorn among the crags. Since there are few trails in the forest, cross-country travel is the best way to backpack in the forest. Entry is limited in some areas during periods of high fire danger.

The 36,000-acre San Gabriel Wilderness in this forest offers the best backpacking opportunities. Elevations are between 1,600 feet and 8,200 feet, with chaparral to about 5,000 feet, then mixed fir and pine along the ridges. Few trails exist in the wilderness, but cross-country travel over rough terrain is rewarding and not too difficult. Fishing is good in the streams.

For information and a map (50¢) of the forest and wilderness, contact the Supervisor, Angeles National Forest, 150 South Los Robles Avenue, Suite 300, Pasadena, California 91101.

San Bernardino National Forest

This 621-000-acre forest is located near San Bernardino, and it is physically similar to the Angeles National Forest. Its mountains are a little higher with elevations to 11,485 feet on San Gorgonio with six other peaks more than 10,000 feet. Life zones vary from desert to alpine in just a few horizontal miles. Deer are found here as well as lake and stream fishing.

While there are more trails in this forest than in the Angeles, the best backpacking is found traveling cross-country, especially in the three wilderness areas. Some areas are closed during periods of high fire danger. The small 9,000-acre Cucamonga Wilderness in the north end of the forest is a very steep land of sharp peaks and pine-covered slopes, with only one fishing stream and a scarcity of water in the higher parts. Scattered small bands of bighorn may be spotted here, especially if one is traveling cross-country to the more remote areas. The 35,000-acre San Gorgonio Wilderness in the middle of the forest lies atop the tallest mountain range in southern California, and like other forests in the region, it is rather dry. The cooler north-facing slopes are covered with open stands of fir, pine, and oak. Environments from desert to alpine are represented in the wilderness, as are deer and bighorns. Fishing is fair in many of the lakes. Water is scarce and the going sometimes rough, but the best way to experience the wilderness is by cross-country travel to remote areas where one can be undisturbed for days. The third wilderness, the San Jacinto, comprises 21,000 acres divided into two units in the southern part of the forest. The northern portion of this wilderness is the best for wilderness lovers since there are no trails or public camps. This area has some of the most spectacular scenery in southern California, with many good fishing streams and picturesque waterfalls. Of course, with no trails, travel is by cross-country only, through life zones from desert to alpine.

For information and a map (50¢) of the forest and wilderness areas, contact the Supervisor, San Bernardino National Forest, 144 North Mountain View Avenue, San Bernardino, California 92408.

Cleveland National Forest

This is the southernmost forest in the state, reaching to within 5 miles of the Mexican border. The 567,000 acres of this forest are divided among several units north and east of San Diego. The forest consists of low hills and mountains in the 5,000-foot range, with chaparral-covered lower slopes and forests of pine, fir, cedar, and oak on the summits. Deer, coyote, bobcat, and a few cougar are the forest's larger inhabitants. Trail travel opportunities are very limited throughout the forest, but the cross-country travel is fairly easy. The most rugged, scenic, and remote area for the backpacker is the 26,000-acre Agua Tibia Primitive Area, a canyon and chaparral-covered land with coniferous forests on its 5,400-foot mountains. Cross-country travel is the most common mode of travel. Except for periods of high fire danger when entry is restricted, the primitive area has a year-round season.

For information and a map (50¢) of the forest and primitive area, contact the Supervisor, Cleveland National Forest, 880 Front Street, Room 6-S-5, San Diego, California 92188.

Redwood National Park

This 106,000-acre area in the extreme northwest corner of the state is one of the newer additions to the national park system, designated to preserve remnants of the magnificent redwood forest that formerly extended for hundreds of miles along the West Coast. In addition, there are beaches, dunes, marshes, and streams inhabited by black bear, gray fox, cougar, bobcat, coyote, beaver, river and sea otters, sea lion, sea elephant, gray whale, and nesting birds along the 30 coastal lines. There are only 17 miles of trails, which, of course, are very crowded. Fires are only permitted in established sites, and cross-country travel is not advisable (but it is the only way to get away from it all). Some of the land is still in private and state ownership.

For information and a map of the park, contact the Superintendent, Redwood National Park, Drawer N, Crescent City, California 95531.

Lava Beds National Monument

This monument is located south of Tulelake, in northern California and as the name suggests, is 46,000 acres of volcanic landscapes. In places where the soil is thick enough, plants gain a foothold among the cinder cones, craters, caves, and lava formations. Some of the animals living in this environment include the deer, pronghorn, cougar, coyote, bobcat, pika, and jackrabbit. Forty-four miles of trails penetrate the monument. Cross-country travel is permitted and is the best way to experience this environment. A special attraction is cave exploration.

For information and a map of the monument, contact the Super-

intendent, Lava Beds National Monument, P.O. Box 867, Tulelake, California 96134.

Point Reyes National Seashore

As a peninsula on the California coast just north of San Francisco, this 65,000-acre seashore has sand dunes, cliffs, forests,
meadows, and estuaries. About 25,000 acres have been designated
wilderness. The notable inhabitants of the seashore are the sea
mammals and shore birds: whales, dolphin, sea lion, seal, pelican,
cormorant, murre, and guillemot. Large land mammals include
cougar and deer. Needless to say, use of this seashore so close to
a metropolitan area is heavy, especially on the 75 miles of trails.
Cross-country travel is permitted but fires and camping are permitted only at established sites. While this park is an excellent example of an urban "backyard" backpacking area, its proximity to
the Bay Area and resultant use detracts from its wilderness
character.

For information and a map of the seashore, contact the Superintendent, Point Reyes National Seashore, Point Reyes, California
94956.

Death Valley National Monument

This large 1,908,000-acre monument lies west of Las Vegas
astride the California-Nevada border and extends partly into
Nevada. While parts of this desert are as inhospitable in summer
as its name would lead you to believe, the monument has a variety
of environments, including 11,000-foot mountains that are inviting to backpacking even in summer. Unlike in the lower elevations
where the temperature has hit 134°F, the mountain ranges that
ring the valley have much more comfortable temperatures. Also,
the lower elevations in the winter enjoy temperate days in the 60s
and 70s with brisk evenings. Some of the many plant species are
unique to this area, and the variety of animal life is also surprising,
including wild burro and horse, cougar, bighorn, deer, gray and
kit foxes, bobcat, kangaroo rat, desert tortoise, and a variety of

bats, birds, and lizards. With only 8 miles of trails, cross-country travel is the common mode opening almost unlimited backpacking possibilities for the experienced cross-country traveler.

For information and a map of the monument, contact the Superintendent, Death Valley National Monument, Death Valley, California 92328.

Channel Islands National Monument

The two islands, Anacapa and Santa Barbara, comprise 1,000 acres with an additional 17,000 acres of surrounding water. They are located south of L.A. off the coast and the only access is by boat. The sandy beaches, headlands, and coves are sites for rookeries of sea lion, sea elephant, sea otter, and brown pelican. The opportunities for backpacking are very limited with no trails, but cross-country travel is permitted with camping in established sites. Water must be carried.

For information and a map of the monument, contact the Superintendent, Channel Islands National Monument, 1699 Anchors Way Drive, Ventura, California 93003.

Anza-Borrego Desert State Park

This 520,000-acre park between San Diego and the Salton Sea comprises a variety of environments: canyons, washes, springs, and mountains to over 6,500 feet. Cactus, yucca, and ocotillo are found in the drier areas with willows and tamarisk around the seeps and springs. Wildlife includes bighorn, antelope, cougar, bobcat, ringtail, deer, kit and gray foxes, coyote, and over 150 species of birds, including the roadrunner. There are several good trails that, along with cross-country travel, make this a good desert backpacking area. The Santa Rose Mountains State Wilderness in the north of the park is especially good for the cross-country wilderness seeker. No open fires permitted (campstoves and the like are O.K.) and water should be carried because natural sources are undependable. The best seasons are winter and spring. Use is light for so large an area.

For information and a map of the park, contact the Manager, Anza-Borrego Desert State Park, P.O. Box 428, Borrego Springs, California 92004.

Other Public Lands

The Bureau of Land Management manages thousands of acres of de facto wilderness on public lands. While little is developed for backpacking use, much provides excellent cross-country travel possibilities on a wide variety of terrain and environments. Some of these lands are extremely rugged and remote and are for the experienced only.

The King Range National Conservation Area encompasses about 54,000 acres, most of which are in the public domain. It extends for about 35 miles along the King Range near the coast south of Eureka. Elevations are from sea level to 4,087 feet at the summit of King's Peak, with very steep slopes extending in most cases right down to the sea. One hundred to 200 inches of rain drench these mountains in the winter months, but otherwise the climate is mild and equable. The greater rainfall on the western slopes has eroded them more steeply than the eastern slopes, and both are covered with chaparral and Douglas fir in open stands. Vegetation along the stream beds is varied and dense, with the northern low portion of the conservation area a grassland. Wildlife includes seal, sea lion, marine birds, black bear, deer, river otter, mink, and upland birds. There is surf fishing and trout and salmon fishing in the streams. A good 16-mile trail serves the King's Peak area with two other trails in the southern portion of the area, and there are good hiking possibilities along the beach. Cross-country travel in the mountains is difficult because of the steep terrain, cliffs, and talus slopes. Backcountry camping is permitted on BLM lands.

Other large BLM ownerships open to public use include the Owens Valley, a desert valley with elevations from 4,500 feet to 5,000 feet at the eastern foot of the Sierra Nevada. The Alabama Hills west of Lone Pine near this valley have been used often as Hollywood backdrops. The Afton Canyon and Rodman Mountains east and south of Barstow in south-central California provide good rockhounding as well as splendid scenery. In fact, the entire Mohave Desert region of southern California is suitable for adventuresome cross-country travel if one is so inclined, but experience and preparation are a prerequisite. Winter is the best season. Two especially good areas administered by BLM in the area is the 20,000-acre Cima Dome-Joshua Tree area located west of Needles, and the Otay Mountain east of San Diego, with its 5,000 acres of Tecate Cypress.

For information and maps of BLM-managed areas in the state, contact the Bureau of Land Management, Federal Building, Room E-2820, 2800 Cottage Way, Sacramento, California 95825.

HAWAII

Few will travel to this state just to go backpacking. However, two national parks have good backpacking opportunities, as do a few forest preserves. Backpacking trail development in many of the extensive wilderness areas on the islands are just getting started, and cross-country travel is frequently difficult or impossible because of the vegetation and steep terrain. It is common knowledge that the climate is comfortable year-round. That is mostly true, but in the higher elevations it drops below freezing and there is snow on the tall peaks in the winter months. Also, while much of the island is covered with lush tropical forests, other areas are desertlike and quite dry. The temperature on the islands, however, has never exceeded 100°F.

General tourism information is available from the Hawaii Department of Planning and Economic Development, P.O. Box 2359, Honolulu, Hawaii 96804.

Hawaii Volcanoes National Park

A backpacking trip in this 220,000-acre park on the island of Hawaii is a unique experience. The park begins on the ocean shore, extends up through lush lowland jungles, past active volcanoes, lava flows, and rain-shadow deserts, reaching its highest elevation, 13,680 feet on Mauna Loa, the world's largest active volcano. Plant life is diverse, with tropical trees such as the beautifully blossoming ohia, and a variety of ferns and air plants. The most prevalent wildlife is the hundreds of species of birds, exotic as well as common ones. Mammals include wild pig, goat, and mongoose, all introduced by man. Saltwater fishing is good.

One hundred thirteen miles of back country trails penetrate the main areas of the park. One trail extends along the shore, another climbs to Mauna Loa. No special precautions need to be taken, just expect an environment excitingly unfamiliar to most backpackers. Cross-country travel is possible only in the sparsely vegetated areas. Expect rain anytime during the year-round season. Back country users must register.

For information and a map of the park, contact the Superintendent, Hawaii Volcanoes National Park, Hawaii 96718.

Haleakala National Park

This 27,000-acre park lies atop the island of Maui, and includes the 10,023-foot-high Haleakala Crater, 7½ miles long and 2½ miles wide. The volcano is now dormant, having last erupted about 200 years ago, and provides an unusual hiking experience among lava flows, black sand, and cinder cones. The most notable life form in the crater is the silversword plant, similar to the yucca with its silvery dagger-shaped leaves and flowering stalk. Other wildlife includes ferns, rushes, small shrubs, a variety of birds, and introduced wild pig, goat, and mongoose.

The 30 miles of trails and fairly easy cross-country travel provide good backpacking opportunities, though a 2- or 3-day trip is usually enough for most visitors in this bizarre environment. Camping is permitted only in designated areas and at established sites for a limit of 3 days. Fuel and water must be carried, even though it rains frequently. There are a few cabins in the crater reached only by trail which may be reserved.

For information and a map of the park, contact the Superintendent, Haleakala National Park, P.O. Box 537, Makawao, Hawaii 96768.

Other Public Lands

There are 13 state forest reserves and several large state parks within the islands. The environment varies from rain and dryland forests to steep, barren, jagged peaks and ridges impossible for the average backpacker to negotiate and often even closed to climbers. The vegetation is typically Hawaiian, unfamiliar and exotic to most, with strange-sounding names: *ohia, alani, papala,* and many, many others. A characteristic of tropical plant communities is that there are usually a great variety of species, but few and widely scattered members of each, as opposed to temperate forests where one often finds almost pure stands of a single species. Birds are likewise exotic, varied, and abundant.

While there are many existing trails, lengths are generally under 10 miles. These trails can be quite rugged and even dangerous (a few have "extreme exposure hazard," which means "possibility of falling straight down or down slope without the chance of stopping in time"). The islands of Oahu and Kauai have good backpacking opportunities; Oahu has over 100 miles of trails on state park and forest lands. Kauai has an interesting trail, the Kalalau, though it's barely over 10 miles long with additional mileage planned. The Kalalau Trail traverses ocean shores, sandy beaches, and spur trails extend up beautiful valleys to picturesque Hanakoa Falls.

For information and maps of trails in state parks, contact the Department of Land and Natural Resources Division of Forestry, 1179 Punchbowl Street, Honolulu, Hawaii 96813.

NEVADA

This is the wildest state of any of the contiguous 48. The federal government is responsible for 61 million acres of land in the state, about 87 percent of the total, and most of it is open for general recreation use by the public. However, only a small part of this land is desirable for backpacking. Nevada is what geologists call a range-and-basin province, short mountain ranges surrounded by flat desert valleys. Except for the several million acres of forest on the scattered mountains, the state is arid and semiarid desert with no developments for the backpacker. In addition, the harsh climate, lack of water, and general monotony of the environment make much of the state generally unattractive for backpacking. There are notable exceptions, discussed below.

General tourism information is available from the Nevada Department of Economic Development, Carson City, Nevada 89701.

Humboldt National Forest

This 2,523,000-acre forest is divided into many units in the north-central, east, and east-central parts of the state. These mountains of nearly 13,000 feet are not the heavily forested peaks normally associated with the West. The granite peaks are pocketed by glacial basins and cut by step-walled canyons and covered with only sparse vegetation. The sagebrush lowlands transform into alpine meadows with only scattered stands of fir, pine, cottonwood, and aspen. Wildlife is varied with antelope, deer, cougar, bobcat, coyote, mink, otter, beaver, and a variety of upland birds and waterfowl. Although vegetation is sparse, water is not scarce, with trout fishing in many of the streams.

While the 65,000-acre Jarbridge Wilderness contains perhaps the most wildly beautiful mountain range in the state and is the best for trail backpacking, the entire forest is excellent for cross-country travel. The two northern units (Santa Rosa and Humboldt divisions) are the most popular with good trail systems, but use is extremely light throughout the forest, especially if one takes advantage of the cross-country possibilities. Except for the four-wheel-drive roads, the forest is a very wild, if somewhat austere, environment. The season is year-round in the lower elevations, though temperatures may reach the 90s in the summer. The peaks are snow-covered with temperatures down to 0°F in the winter.

For information and a map of the forest and wilderness, contact the Supervisor, Humboldt National Forest, 976 Mountain City Highway, Elko, Nevada 89801.

Toiyabe National Forest

At 3,133,000 acres, this is the largest national forest in the 48 contiguous states. It is so large and spread out that it actually covers two types of regional environments. The first type is found in those units lying on the Nevada-California line in the vicinity of Lake Tahoe and Mono Lake. This is typically High Sierra environment with coniferous forests dotted with alpine lakes and cold, rushing streams, becoming drier on the lower eastern slopes. The high peaks in this area are over 10,000 feet, and those in the Hoover Wilderness are over 11,000 feet (see the Inyo National Forest in California for a discussion of this wilderness). Wildlife includes deer, black bear, bobcat, porcupine, partridge, sage grouse, and other small animals.

The units farther east—one by Las Vegas, the others in the interior of the state—are desert ranges to over 11,000 feet. The lowest zone is cactus, yucca, and creosote bush that changes to juniper and piñon pine at about 5,000 feet. From here on up the environment becomes more heavily forested, first with mountain mahogany, oakbrush, and ponderosa pine, and then with aspen and fir. Above 9,000 feet, spruce becomes apparent, as well as various mountain wildflowers. Deer, elk, antelope, wild turkey, coyote, bobcat, fox, and cougar are found in these generally remote, wild mountain ranges.

Hundreds of miles of trails extend into just about every portion of this forest. The units on the California border receive heavy use, especially near the Hoover Wilderness and Yosemite National Park. In the alpine areas and as the trees thin out in the lower eastern slopes of the units, cross-country travel is possible. The units in the interior of the state have equally good trail systems, but receive extremely light use (the unit by Las Vegas receives a bit heavier use). Since the vegetation never really becomes heavy in these units, cross-country travel is possible just about any place where the terrain permits. These desert mountain ranges provide a unique, secluded backpacking opportunity and offer breathtaking views of the surrounding desert basins. The temperature is not as extreme as one might imagine, about 0° to 100°F, and is quite temperate in the summer in the higher elevations. The season is most pleasant in the spring and fall, and is mild even in the winter in lower parts of the forest.

For information and maps of the forest and wilderness, contact the Supervisor, Toiyabe National Forest, P.O. Box 1331, Reno, Nevada 89504.

Lake Mead National Recreation Area

This is one of the outstanding national recreation areas for back-packing in the country. Its 1,497,000 acres with a 700-mile shore-line consist of sand beaches, colorful canyons, the mountainous Shivwits Plateau, Lake Mead and Lake Mohave, and the Colorado River. The recreation area lies within the northeast corner of the Mohave Desert, with its yucca, creosote bush, Joshua tree, and a variety of cacti in the lower elevations. Along the shore grow cottonwood and willow, and above 6,000 feet juniper, sagebrush, piñon, and Gambel oak are found. Wildlife includes deer, bighorn, ringtail, cougar, coyote, beaver, tortoise, gila monster, and various aquatic and upland birds.

There are no trails, but cross-country travel is encouraged, especially during the cooler months. Carry water in the mountains and canyons, register with a ranger, and exercise normal caution as in any wilderness, and this area need not be excessively hazardous. The season is year-round, but the summers are hot—up to 110°F. The best season is from September to December and from February to May. Backcountry use away from Lake Mead is light.

For information and a map of the recreation area, contact the Superintendent, Lake Mead National Recreation Area, 601 Nevada Highway, Boulder City, Nevada 89005.

Desert National Wildlife Range

Located just north of Las Vegas in southern Nevada, this 1,588,000-acre preserve is the largest outside of Alaska, with 6 mountain ranges with elevations from 2,500 feet to almost 10,000 feet. Five life zones are represented: creosote bush-salt brush, yucca-Joshua tree, piñon-juniper, ponderosa pine-fir, and bristlecone pine on the mountain peaks. Two hundred forty-five species of birds, 31 species of reptiles and amphibians, and 52 species of mammals, including bighorn, deer, cougar, bobcat, coyote, and fox, are represented here.

Certain areas are open to backpacking on a permit and reservation basis only. Very few trails, but good cross-country travel possibilities and a variety of wildlife make this an attractive area for those interested in a typical desert mountain landscape. Summers are hot, but otherwise the season is year-round. Water must be carried.

For information and a map of the range, contact the Refuge Manager, Desert National Wildlife Range, 1500 North Decatur Boulevard, Las Vegas, Nevada 89108.

Sheldon National Antelope Refuge and the Charles Sheldon Antelope Range

These two separate but adjacent areas are located in northwest Nevada. The refuge (no hunting) contains about 34,000 acres and the range contains 544,000 acres. This semidesert country is between 4,500 feet and 7,600 feet in elevation with many lakes, reservoirs, and streams, mesas and rolling hills dissected by narrow valleys and steep canyons. Rockhounding is a popular activity. The vegetation is largely sagebrush and grassland with a few juniper, mountain mahogany, and quaking aspen. Antelope and deer are the most conspicuous animals with coyote, jackrabbit, bobcat, and cougar occasionally spotted. One hundred forty-seven species of upland and aquatic birds have been recorded on the refuge and range.

Backpacking is allowed throughout the refuge and range, but camping is limited to 18 designated areas. Cross-country travel is the most common mode and most of the camping areas are in trailless areas. The season is from mid-May through September, with the weather during June and July being the most comfortable. Severe snowstorms in the winter make travel dangerous or impossible. Use is extremely light in the area, but users must obtain a permit.

For information and a map of the refuge and range, contact the Manager, Sheldon-Hart Mountain National Antelope Refuges, Federal Building, Lakeview, Oregon 97630.

NEW MEXICO

Thirty-two million acres of public land and only about 1 million residents make this state outstanding for backpacking. The western two-thirds of the state is mountainous, with Wheeler Peak the tallest at 13,161 feet. The eastern third is a high plateau with badlands, canyons, and plains. The climate is mostly semiarid and arid, but more humid in the higher elevations. The north and the higher elevations of the south have cold winters, but the remainder of the state has mild winters with year-round backpacking if extra preparations are made for the occasional cold snap in the high desert country and forests of piñon, juniper, aspen, ponderosa, spruce, and fir. Afternoon thunderstorms are common in the mountains from mid- to late summer.

The backpacker can take his choice in this state. The best wilderness experience is found in the mountains of southwest New Mexico where the forests and canyons present a variety of environments and the greatest solitude. The extensive forests, deserts, and geological areas in other parts of the state also provide excellent backpacking opportunities. There are 700,000 acres of wilderness in the nearly 9 million acres of national forests and while most developed trails are found in these forests, the backpacker is tempted by an abundance of other public land in this state, beckoning him to just roam at will. New Mexico is one of the best states for it, but climatic extremes and rough, confusing canyonscapes in some areas make this dangerous for the inexperienced and ill-prepared, and sometimes just plain uninviting.

General tourism information is available from the New Mexico Department of Development, 113 Washington Avenue, Sante Fe, New Mexico 87501. Any of the 6 forest maps mentioned below are also available for 50¢ each from the U.S. Forest Service, Office of Information, 517 Gold Avenue, S.W., Albuquerque, New Mexico 87101.

The national forests are, from north to south, as follows:

Carson National Forest

Wheeler Peak, the tallest mountain in the state, is the main attraction of this 1,411,000-acre forest. It is divided into 3 units, all near the north-central state border by Taos. Elevation is between 6,000 feet and 13,000 feet, with the forested and scenic Sangre de Cristo Mountains gracing the eastern unit of the forest. Elk, black bear, deer, cougar, bobcat, coyote, golden and bald eagles, and various other animals are found here.

This is not an outstanding forest for backpacking, but good trips can be had by traveling cross-country through the open parkland and meadows, or on the trails if you don't mind a little company. Some of the most spectacular scenery—and wildest in this rather "tame" forest—is found in the Pecos Wilderness, discussed below under the Sante Fe National Forest, and in the Wheeler Peak Wilderness. This 6,000-acre wilderness encompassing Wheeler Peak is the smallest in the West, but includes one of the few high alpine areas in the state with a few small lakes and streams. This wilderness is best enjoyed by cross-country travel. A permit is required for entry.

For a map (50¢) and information on the forest and wilderness, contact the Supervisor, Carson National Forest, Forest Service Building, P.O. Box 558, Taos, New Mexico 87571.

Sante Fe National Forest

This 1,469,000-acre forest is one of the state's best. Its two units lie on either side of Sante Fe astride the Jemez and Sangre de Cristo ranges with elevations to over 13,000 feet. Forests of aspen, fir, pine, and spruce, and hundreds of streams and about a dozen lakes provide habitat for elk, deer, black bear, cougar, coyote, bobcat, various fur-bearers, game birds, eagle, and trout.

Roads penetrate the forest thoroughly, and there are no trails except in and around the three wilderness areas which provide the best backpacking opportunities. The 41,000-acre San Pedro Parks Wilderness is a 10,000-foot high plateau of rolling topography covered with grassy and sometimes swampy meadows, and dense stands of conifers interspersed with aspen and shrub oak. Trails are relatively easy and the snow-free season is from May to November. The much larger 167,000-acre Pecos Wilderness in the eastern unit of the forest is more rugged than San Pedro Parks with elevations from about 8,000 feet to over 13,000 feet. Several fishing lakes and streams and an excellent trails system makes this a fine backpacking area, but use can be heavy. The best season is in May and in September and October after the crowds thin out. A permit is required for entry. The 48,000-acre Chama River Canyon Wilderness is a rugged canyonland lying on both sides of the Rio Chama. A corridor including the river and road penetrate the wilderness as far as the Monastery of Christ in the Desert. There are no trails. The snow-free season is May to December. No permits are required.

Information and maps (50¢) of the forest and wilderness areas are available from the Supervisor, Santa Fe National Forest, Santa Fe, New Mexico 87501.

Cibola National Forest

The 9 separate units of this forest totaling 1,661,000 acres are scattered around Albuquerque. The forest consists of mountain ranges rising from the desert throughout central New Mexico to over 11,000 feet. Environments vary with the elevation: from desert at about 5,000 feet, through juniper, pine, spruce, and fir forests, to alpine areas above the timberline. The climate is dry enough to keep the forests open and easily traversed. Rock outcrops are common. Wildlife includes antelope in the lower elevations with deer, turkey, a few elk, and bighorn higher up the slopes. The availability of surface water is limited.

The forest offers fair trail hiking, with excellent cross-country possibilities through the open forests and barren peaks. Dirt roads penetrate much of the forest, but the peaks are generally wild with beautiful vistas of the surrounding desertscape. Other attributes include a year-round season (though winters can be severe on the high peaks) and very low use by backpackers. There are two wilderness areas in the forest: the 31,000-acre Sandia Wilderness just east of Albuquerque, and the 37,000-acre Manzano Wilderness 30 miles southeast of the city. The best, though most heavily used, trails are found here.

For a set of maps ($2) and information on the forest, contact the Supervisor, Cibola National Forest, 10308 Candelaria N.E., Albuquerque, New Mexico 87112.

Apache National Forest

See Arizona, above.

Gila National Forest

This 2,702,000-acre forest in the southwest corner of New Mexico is the state's finest. Many would rank this among the best backpacking areas in the country. The variety in this forest is hard to match: mountains to almost 11,000 feet, flat mesas, deep precipitous canyons with sculptured spires, and many large rivers. The lower elevations of just above 4,000 feet is semidesert shrub and grassland, with cottonwoods, alders, and sycamores along the streams. Farther up the slopes are found piñon-juniper-oak woodlands and pine-spruce-fir forests in the higher elevations. Desert-type vegetation is often found far up the south-facing slopes. Wildlife is varied and abundant, including elk, deer, black bear, coyote, bobcat, cougar, porcupine, skunk, and various smaller mammals and birds; trout are found in the almost 200 miles of streams.

The entire forest is wild and excellent for backpacking with trails throughout, as well as almost unlimited cross-country opportunities. Almost a third of the forest is designated wilderness or primitive: Gila Wilderness, 430,000 acres (the nation's first wilderness); Gila Primitive Area, 136,000 acres; and Black Range

Primitive Area, 182,000 acres. These areas extend across the southern half of the forest. The Gila Wilderness and Primitive Area offer the most spectacular canyons and varied scenery, and the Black Range is the least used (chances are you won't meet anyone here). Throughout these areas the observant backpacker can spot ancient cliff-dwellings predating Christ. Many remain yet to be discovered. While these are protected by law from tampering by visitors, they still provide an exciting glimpse into the past for the backpacker lucky enough to chance upon one during backcountry wanderings. Another attribute of the area is its year-round season in the river valleys.

This area is not without its drawbacks, though. Many of the most popular trails cross and recross rivers, drenching hiking boots if one does not change into tennis shoes for each crossing. In any case, the water is painfully cold in the winter and spring. This area is so attractive for cross-country travel that one is drawn to wandering in the maze of canyons, heedless of the ease of becoming lost. Nevertheless, in the danger of encouraging overuse, these wilderness and primitive areas are highly recommended for anyone backpacking in the state. Use is presently low to moderate.

For a map (50¢) and information on the forest, wilderness, and primitive areas, contact the Supervisor, Gila National Forest, 2610 North Silver Street, Silver City, New Mexico 88061.

Lincoln National Forest

Along the crest of the Capitan, Guadalupe, and Sacramento mountain ranges in south-central New Mexico east of Alamogordo lies this 1,087,000-acre forest. These mountains rise out of the grassland and desert lowlands to elevations of 12,000 feet—oases of timbered slopes and trout streams. The forests are mostly ponderosa pine, with limber pine, spruce, and fir. The forests, along with the juniper- and brush-covered foothills, are home for deer, black bear, coyote, fox, badger, bobcat, cougar, raccoon, skunk, and other small animals and upland birds. There is only one lake of significance, but several live streams.

Trails are found only in the northernmost two of the three

forest units. The best trail backpacking is found in the 31,000-acre White Mountain Wilderness in the northern unit of the forest. Although this wilderness is small, the trail system is good and there is an interesting, abrupt transition of life zones as one travels from about 6,000 feet to almost 12,000 feet elevation. The trails are somewhat steep, but use is only light to moderate. For those more adventuresome and skilled in rugged cross-country travel, the mountains throughout the forest, especially the Guadalupe of the southern unit, provide an exciting wilderness challenge. The forest is penetrated mostly by dirt roads, with many roadless areas of open forest, shrub, and grassland that is negotiable. Water is not abundant, but doesn't present a problem if one inquires locally as to its availability.

For a map ($1) and information on the forest and wilderness, contact the Supervisor, Lincoln National Forest, Federal Building, Alamogordo, New Mexico 88310.

Carlsbad Caverns National Park

Most visitors visit the vast underground caverns that honeycomb the limestone bedrock, but this 47,000-acre park in extreme southeast New Mexico also provides good backpacking opportunities. Located on the northeastern slope of the Guadalupe Mountains, the park is a rugged, arid, rock-strewn jumble of ridges and canyons. In the lower elevations, desert shrubs are the dominant vegetation, while in the wetter canyon bottoms black walnut, oak, hackberry, and willow are common. Higher up the slopes, agave, yucca, sotol, ocotillo, and desert grasses predominate, with juniper, pine, madrone, and a few Douglas fir in the high elevations. Common wildlife includes ringtail, fox, porcupine, deer, various other small mammals, and over 200 species of birds. Less common animals include coyote, badger, bobcat, and cougar and rattlesnakes.

Many miles of primitive trails provide access to the park, and, armed with good maps, the backpacker has almost unlimited cross-country travel possibilities. There is no dependable water supply, so all water must be carried. Also, use of native fuels is prohibited. The season is year-round, though short-lived snowstorms can occur in the winter, and summers are quite warm. A backpacking trip combined with a visit to the caverns is the best way to become acquainted with this area.

For information and a map of the park, contact the Superintendent, Carlsbad Caverns National Park, 3225 National Parks Highway, Carlsbad, New Mexico 88220.

Bandelier National Monument

This 30,000-acre monument is located by Los Alamos in north-central New Mexico on the 7,000-foot-high Pajarito Plateau. Over 80 percent of it is designated wilderness. The tall cliffs, forested mesas, and rugged gorges stand the same as they did when this land was inhabited by Pueblo Indians almost 1,000 years ago. Remains of their dwellings can still be seen here today. Virtually all of the monument is undisturbed wildland of alternating ridges and canyons, with beautiful waterfalls and scenic vistas. There are more than 60 miles of maintained trails which provide the only access into the backcountry. Both trail and cross-country travel are rewarding, especially along the Rio Grande on the monument's southeast border. A permit is required.

For information and a map of the monument, contact the Superintendent, Bandelier National Monument, Los Alamos, New Mexico 87544.

Other Public Lands

The Bureau of Land Management manages approximately 13 million acres of public land in New Mexico, mostly in the western and southern parts of the state. The land ranges from arid deserts to 9,000-foot mountain peaks. All of this public land is open for recreation uses such as backpacking, camping, and hunting in season.

Areas of primary interest to hikers include:

RIO GRANDE GORGE RECREATION AREA AND WILD RIVER

Located about 35 miles northwest of Taos, this area of 13,780 acres of public land, includes 48 miles of the Rio Grande Wild River. The area has developed and primitive campgrounds and hiking trails from the east rim of the canyon down to the river. Fishing is permitted in season and there is a visitor center on the east rim which offers interpretive information about the area.

ORGAN MOUNTAINS RECREATION AREA

Located 15 miles east of Las Cruces, this area covers about 35,000 acres of rugged mountainous terrain including 9,200-foot Organ Peak. Included within the area is the Aguirre Spring Recreation Site (camping permitted) on the east side of the mountains and approximately 10 miles of developed hiking trails which cross the mountain.

EL MALPAIS NATURAL AREA

About 10 miles southeast of Grants is an area of 84,000 acres of public land which contains one of the most spectacular lava flows in the country. This area is as yet undeveloped with the exception of a single hiking trail east to west across the lava bed. Access is via State Highway 117. The area contains geological formations, flora and fauna unique to the lava, and outstanding photographic areas. Future development may include camp sites and additional trails.

For information and maps on all areas, contact the Bureau of Land Management, New Mexico State Office, P.O. Box 1449, Santa Fe, New Mexico 87501.

UTAH

This state is famous for its magnificent and colorful geological formations, but it has much more. For the backpacker, the biggest attraction is the state's mountainous spine with 7 national forests totaling many millions of acres. Running from north to south down the middle of the state, this section of the Rocky Mountains contains good backpacking opportunities, from the open arid foothills to the dense coniferous forests of the western slopes. The eastern and southern portions of the state contain spectacular canyons, arches, and spires, and these areas also provide good trail and cross-country backpacking opportunities. The western third of the state is the poorest, with an environment similar to the desert and range of Nevada. The season is year-round in the southern canyonlands, with the mountains and northern portion of the state receiving considerable snow and cold temperatures in the winter. Use is light in most of the areas.

General tourism information is available from the Utah Travel Council, Council Hall, Salt Lake City, Utah 84114. A set of maps for all seven of the state's forests can be obtained from the Forest Service, Federal Office Building, 324 Twenty-fifth Street, Ogden, Utah 84401.

The national forests from north to south are as follows:

Cache National Forest

Extending into Idaho, this 679,000-acre forest north of Ogden provides only a fair backpacking resource. The northern half is best, with low, arid mountains, canyons, fossil beds, a few lakes, and numerous springs, sinkholes, and streams. Elk, deer, and upland birds are common, with sightings of cougar, black bear, fox, mink, and bobcat less common. Trails are found in most of the forest, and none form loops, though cross-country travel is easy and could complete loop trips. The forest is moderately heavily used for non-backpacking recreation, but lightly used for backpacking. However, this forest ranks low among others in the state.

For information and a map (50¢) of the forest, contact the Supervisor, Wasatch National Forest, 125 South State Street, Salt Lake City, Utah 84138.

Wasatch National Forest

The 4 units of this forest, totaling 892,000 acres, are distributed around Salt Lake City. The three westernmost units are drier with sparse vegetation, but provide a soaring, frequently snow-covered backdrop to the city. The fourth and largest unit is higher with many peaks over 12,000 feet and wetter with hundreds of alpine lakes and many streams. This unit lies astride the Uinta Mountains, a curiosity among mainland U.S. mountains because they run east and west rather than north and south. The slopes of these mountains are cloaked in coniferous forests, generally open stands that locally become dense. Elk, deer, cougar, coyote, smaller fur-bearers, and birds are common, with the 500 or so moose, unique in the state, being the most notable inhabitants. Trout fishing is good in many of the lakes and streams.

Most backpackers in the forest travel the excellent High Uintas Primitive Area, discussed under the Ashley National Forest below, but the forest proper is less heavily used and also excellent. The three western units are the least used with the fewest trails, but offer challenging cross-country travel possibilities. The 30,000-acre Lone Peak Wilderness (just recently designated as such) is located here east of Salt Lake City. The eastern unit which contains part of the primitive area is more popular with many miles of good trails, forested mountainsides, lakes, and streams. Two large high mountain lake areas in this unit are especially attractive with some lakes accessible by trail. Many more can only be reached by cross-country travel of only moderate difficulty, a good opportunity for the solitude-seeker.

For information and a map of the forest, contact the Supervisor, Wasatch National Forest, 125 South State Street, Salt Lake City, Utah 84111.

Ashley National Forest

The southern slopes of the Uinta Mountains are included in this 1,337,000-acre forest just south of the Wasatch extending into Wyoming. One of the state's finest, this forest has many attractions:

several peaks over 13,000 feet, including the tallest in the state, 13,528-foot Kings Peak; Flaming Gorge National Recreation Area, discussed under Wyoming; and extensive wild high country, including the High Uintas Primitive Area, studded with lakes, rocky mountains, forests, and meadows. The lower elevations are grasslands grazed by antelope as well as livestock, with the higher elevations supporting elk, deer, a few bighorn and moose, abundant black bear, along with a variety of smaller animals and birds. Trout fishing is excellent.

More than anything else, backpackers flock to this forest with the High Uintas Primitive Area their goal, and it's no surprise that they should. Almost 323,000 acres in and near the area are managed as a wilderness. The elevation ranges from 8,000 feet to 13,528 feet with the deep red of the exposed sandstones and conglomerates covering about half the area lending a special effect. Another third is forested, with the remainder covered with meadows and grasslands. Five hundred lakes and over 400 miles of streams provide excellent trout fishing. The only drawback of the area is its moderately heavy trail use, which can be avoided if one takes advantage of the almost unlimited cross-country travel possibilities. It is not uncommon to have a pristine lake off the trail all to oneself while those lakes on the trails may be crowded and overused. Those who prefer trail hiking, but don't like the crowds, may wish to consider any of the many forest trails throughout the crest of the Uintas east of the primitive area with environments very similar to it.

For information and maps of the forest and primitive area, contact the Supervisor, Ashley National Forest, 437 East Main, Vernal, Utah 84078.

Uinta National Forest

The several units of this 813,000-acre forest are located east of Provo and border the Ashley National Forest on the west. The peaks here are lower than in the Ashley—in the 8,000-foot to 11,000-foot range—but are just as imposing as they rise out of the arid lowlands. The forest is moderately well forested, with spruce, aspen, and fir on the slopes above grasslands used for grazing. The taller mountains have alpine environments on the summits, but have few lakes. Water is not scarce, though, with over 200 miles of streams containing trout and grayling. Common animals include elk, deer, various birds, and fur-bearers such as the marten, mink, and beaver. Cougar, black bear, coyote, and bobcat are also found here, but are rare.

With over 1,000 miles of trails, backpacking opportunities are abundant, but few areas in the forest are truly remote, and it can't match the Ashley National Forest for scenic splendor. Roads and logging operations have tamed this forest almost completely. However, some of the taller peaks and their environs still retain their wilderness character, and trails here as in most of the forest are not heavily used. One of the best areas is the Mount Timpanogos Scenic Area surrounding the 11,750-foot peak of the same name. Although served by trails, cross-country travel along this range amidst the alpine lakes and glacial terrain is especially rewarding. Another good area is the 30,000-acre Lone Peak Wilderness located between Salt Lake City and Provo. This area is characterized by rugged glaciated peaks of weather-resistant granite rocks. And it is served by a good trail system.

For information and a map of the forest, contact the Supervisor, Uinta National Forest, P.O. Box 1428, Provo, Utah 84601.

Manti-La Sal National Forest

The 3 units of this forest contain a variety of environments with a total of 1,333,000 acres. The largest unit is west of Price and south of the Uinta National Forest with a moderately high mountain environment similar to it. The two other units are in the southeast with one extending into Colorado. These are more arid with interesting rock formations and mountains rising out of the surrounding desert. Farther up the slopes, fir, spruce, pine, and aspen provide habitat for introduced wild turkeys, as well as elk, deer, cougar, bobcat, small mammals, and upland birds. Some of the world's largest aspen are found in this forest.

The forest is very lightly used by recreationists, including backpackers. Many miles of trails are found in each unit, as well as large roadless areas of open forest, meadows, and rocky areas with good cross-country travel potential. Trails are generally poorly marked and in some cases have not been maintained for many years. There are many high lakes, but most are reached by road. In addition, year-round and intermittent streams are found in much of the forest, so water isn't a problem. While the forest is generally not outstanding for backpacking, the low use makes it attractive nonetheless.

For information and a map (50¢) of the forest, contact the Supervisor, Manti-La Sal National Forest, 350 East Main Street, Price, Utah 84501.

Fishlake National Forest

This 1,427,000-acre forest consists of 4 units located around Richfield in south-central Utah. While peaks in the forest reach over 12,000 feet, it is not rugged country. The forest lies upon 3 north-south running plateaus sloping off into side canyons and valleys. The plateau tops are flat or rolling hills, with only the tallest peaks presenting rugged features. Rainfall is adequate for a good timber stand of fir, spruce, pine, and aspen, with many streams and lakes, some quite large, containing trout (the large Mackinaw grows to 35 pounds in 2,600-acre Fish Lake). Other wildlife includes deer, elk, black bear, cougar, coyote, fox, badger, and smaller mammals as well as a variety of upland birds.

While the forest has many miles of trails with easy hiking on the most gently rolling terrain, this same gentle terrain precludes any truly remote areas. Roads are common in each unit, but use, especially by backpackers, is very light. The visitor will find the most interesting and scenic trail and cross-country travel on and around the taller peaks in the two largest units. Roads do not penetrate here, and there is some memorable, if not breath-taking, scenery.

For information and a map of the forest, contact the Supervisor, Fishlake National Forest, 170 North Main, Richfield, Utah 84701.

Dixie National Forest

At 1,885,000 acres, this is the largest forest in the state, located in the southwest by Cedar City. As in the Fishlake National Forest, the 4 units of this forest lie atop plateaus rising among the colorful canyons and rangelands of the surrounding desert. Elevations range from 3,000 feet to over 11,000 feet with a mostly open cover of grassland and forest parkland. This is one of the warmest and driest forests in the state, but there are still many streams and hundreds of lakes among the plateaus and mountain peaks. Wildlife is similar to that in the Fishlake, with the addition of introduced partridge and wild turkey.

Trails are not plentiful in the forest, but cross-country travel is possible, though steep terrain sometimes makes the going difficult. While roads penetrate the forest, large roadless areas are remote and still very wild. The canyonlands surrounding the bases of the plateaus are especially interesting. The season in these lower elevations is spring through fall, and the higher elevations are snow-free from about June to October. Use is very light throughout the forest. The rolling hills and forest on the easternmost unit of the forest, one of the highest and tallest plateaus in the country, is an excellent and challenging cross-country travel area.

For information and a map of the forest, contact the Supervisor, Dixie National Forest, 500 South Main Street, Cedar City, Utah 84720.

Zion National Park

Located in the southwest corner of the state by St. George, this 147,000-acre park is canyon and mesa country with natural arches and other sandstone formations, box canyons, streams and waterfalls, and a variety of animals, including deer, cougar, bobcat, red and gray foxes, coyote, and badger. The climate is semiarid with mostly desert-type vegetation such as yucca and cactus, but deciduous and coniferous trees are found in some of the wetter spots in canyon bottoms and by seeps. Like the Grand Canyon, the landscape was mostly carved by the rivers as they cut through the slowly rising Colorado Plateau, on the edge of which this park lies.

Visitation of the park is moderate, but use of the 155 miles of backpacking trails is light and cross-country travel possibilities are almost limitless. Water should be carried, but more importantly, extreme care should be taken when traveling cross-country—the canyons and mesas can become a deadly maze for the inexperienced and ill-prepared. The snow-free season is spring through fall, with very warm, dry summers and considerable snow in the winter.

For information and a map of the park, contact the Superintendent, Zion National Park, Springdale, Utah 84767.

Canyonlands National Park

This 258,000-acre park is located in southeast Utah southwest of Moab. As its name suggests, it is a fantastic canyon environment at the junction of both the Green River and Colorado River canyon systems. Like much of this part of the state, it is a product of erosion by wind and water which has carved arches and sliced canyons, creating a landscape similar to that of Zion National Park and the Grand Canyon. Bighorn, deer, cougar, bobcat, beaver, and ringtail are among the inhabitants. The climate is warm and arid, and vegetation is sparse, generally confined to scattered, oasislike stands. The 84 miles of trails and the backcountry in general are only lightly used. Water must be carried, and spring and fall are the most comfortable seasons.

For information and a map of the park, contact the Superintendent, Canyonlands National Park, First Western Building, 72 South Main, Moab, Utah 84532.

Bryce Canyon National Park

This 36,000-acre park in southwest Utah between units of the Dixie National Forest is one of the country's most active areas of erosion. In some places, this erosion causes cliffs to retreat at the rate of 1 foot per 50 years, very fast in geological time. What this erosion leaves behind are deep canyons and steep cliff faces with wave after wave of pinnacles, turrets, and amphitheaters of multicolored rock, giving the impression of fantastic medieval castle battlements. In the difference of 2,500 feet of elevation, 3 major plant communities are found, beginning with piñon-juniper associations at about 6,500 feet, then ponderosa parklands, and finally spruce-fir associations up to the highest elevations at 9,100 feet. Small mammals, marmot, badger, bobcat, porcupine, deer, and various birds and reptiles are fairly common. Coyote and cougar are rare.

Backcountry camping is allowed along only one trail, 29 miles long, through two-thirds of the length of the park. It generally follows the valley floor, but has many steep stretches that switchback up and down the dissected plateau. It's a fantastic route and the best way to really experience the park. No dependable water source is found along the trail. The climate is pleasant from April to October, but winters are severe. Few backpackers use the park, though day hikers will be met on parts of the trail.

For information and a map of the park, contact the Superintendent, Bryce Canyon National Park, Bryce Canyon, Utah 84717.

Glen Canyon National Recreation Area

This is the biggest chunk of canyon environment in the state with a total of 1,197,000 acres, extending south from Canyonlands National Park all the way into Arizona. The main feature of this area is Lake Powell, created by the damming of the Colorado River at Page, Arizona. When full, the lake will extend for 180 miles with 1,800 miles of shoreline. This is typical arid canyon country with colorful canyons and impressively eroded landforms. Unfortunately, the greatest natural beauty of the area is now under water. The lake provides access to the many canyons of the Colorado's tributaries, inhabited by coyote, bighorn, deer, bobcat, chuckwalla, white pelican, beaver, and bald and golden eagles. Fishing is good.

There are no trails in the area, but there are also no restrictions on backcountry travel. A combined backpacking and boating trip is the easiest way to travel in the area. Spring and fall are most comfortable, with yearly temperatures ranging from below 0° to over 100°F. Water must be carried, and extra caution should be exercised in this area as in any extreme environment.

For information and a map of the area, contact the Superintendent, Glen Canyon National Recreation Area, P.O. Box 1507, Page, Arizona 86040.

Arches National Park

This park lies just north of Moab in southeast Utah. It includes about 64,000 acres of the most densely clustered collection of arches, pinnacles, and spires known in the country. In addition, the sandstone here has been eroded into a variety of weird forms and coves that lend an eerie air to the landscape. Although quite arid with relatively little vegetation, there is a population of deer, coyote, fox, small rodents, reptiles, and many species of birds inhabiting the park. Wildflowers bloom in the moist stream beds during most summers.

This is one of the least developed of our national parks. Few visit the park, there are no facilities, and only a few miles of trails penetrate the backcountry. Cross-country travel and backcountry camping is permitted. Since there is only sparse vegetation, the only obstacle to cross-country travel is the terrain, which is moderately easy to traverse but very easy to get lost in. A few days alone in this backcountry is like a visit to another uninhabited world. The climate is pleasant spring through fall, but there is a danger of flashfloods during this period. Water must be carried at all times of the year.

For information and a map of the forest, contact the Superintendent, Arches National Park, c/o Canyonlands National Park, First Western Building, 72 South Main, Moab, Utah 84532.

Dinosaur National Monument

See Colorado, chapter 7.

Flaming Gorge National Recreation Area

See Wyoming, chapter 7.

Other Public Lands

Most of the arid land in the east, south, and west of the state is administered by the Bureau of Land Management and is open to the public. However, there are few recreational developments on this land. Four areas administered by the BLM are exceptions, offering excellent mountain and canyon trail and cross-country travel opportunities.

The Grand Gulch Primitive Area is a large area enclosed by state routes 263, 95, and 261, and the San Juan River in the southeast corner of the state. This colorful gorge contains over 100 miles of the main gulch and side canyons, with scattered stands of piñon and juniper among the cactus, yucca, and other desert-type vegetation. Wildlife includes deer, smaller mammals and lizards, eagles and songbirds, rattlesnakes, and scorpions. There are few established trails, but cross-country travel through the canyons is possible. Flashfloods should be watched for. The season is March through November. In some areas water is available, in others it must be carried. Specific information on this area is available from the Bureau of Land Management, San Juan Area Office, P.O. Box 1327, Monticello, Utah 84535.

The Escalante River, located in south-central Utah south of the Dixie National Forest, offers about 50 miles of trails and many more miles of cross-country travel along the Escalante Gorge beginning at an arm of Lake Powell in the Glen Canyon National Recreation Area and extending northward. The gorge is physically similar to Grand Gulch, perhaps a little less rugged. Hiking in the gorge itself entails occasionally wading through ankle-to-waist-high water, making canvas shoes advisable. Good, lightly used campsites are available along the canyon, as are springs. The season is from April to October, with flashfloods occurring throughout this period. Specific information on the river is available from the Bureau of Land Management, Kanab Field Office, 320

North First Street, Kanab, Utah 84741. Information can also be obtained from this address for the Paria Canyon Primitive Area which extends into Arizona and is described under the heading "Other Public Lands" in Arizona, above.

A forest-parkland environment is found in the Henry Mountains nestled between Capitol Reef National Park and Glen Canyon National Recreation Area. This is a very primitive, trailless forested area where the only access is by rough dirt road. A herd of about 100 bison roams throughout the area. Cross-country travel is not too difficult, with good campsites. For information on this area contact the Bureau of Land Management, Henry Mountain Resource Area Office, P.O. Box 11, Hanksville, Utah 84734.

7

The Midcontinent: Colorado, Kansas, Montana, Nebraska, North Dakota, South Dakota, and Wyoming

There can be no objective judgment as to which region or state offers the best backpacking opportunities. Some prefer the lowland backpacking of Minnesota to the mountains of Montana, or the dry summers of the Sierras to the temperate rain forests of Washington. The Midcontinent region, with the northern and midmountain states of Montana, Wyoming, and Colorado, though, ranks among the best for backpacking opportunities in the country.

Colorado offers environmental diversity; Wyoming and Montana encompass outstanding wilderness areas and have less backpacking use. A backpacking trip in the wilderness of one of these three states becomes a yardstick for measuring all other experiences. Summer days are warm and dry, except for brief afternoon thunderstorms, and evenings are cool. The abundant yearly precipitation in the mountains keeps them green throughout the summer and there are plentiful cold, clear lakes and streams. The

144]

mountains have retained most of their wilderness character, except for the few roads and fine trail systems that provide access for the backpackers who enjoy them. Wildlife in these mountains also has remained much as before the civilization of the country.

The other 4 states in this region have not been so lucky. The forests and prairies of Kansas, Nebraska, North Dakota, and South Dakota have succumbed to the ranchers and farmers and very little wilderness remains. The few patches of natural areas that have escaped the worst of civilization's onslaught barely warrant a brief stopover on the way to the real wilderness of the Rocky Mountain states found beyond.

COLORADO

For alpine backpacking, this state is one of the finest. The mountains here are among the most beautiful in the world. Rugged, snow-capped peaks and slopes lush with vegetation are laced with cold rushing mountain streams connecting a myriad of mountain lakes and meadows. Be prepared for severe terrain and weather, though. Most trails roller-coaster up and down the mountains, and being caught in afternoon summer thundershowers, snow, and hailstorms is common. Snow blocks the higher passes into July and again in early fall. Needless to say, the high country winters are very severe.

While the mountains are the state's greatest asset, much of the state is prairie and canyonland. The eastern third is an extension of the Kansas-Nebraska grasslands. Then, along a north-south line where the largest cities are found, the mountains rise out of the prairie, range after range. The northern mountains are cool and lush, becoming drier and warmer in the south, with fingers of the arid southwest extending around them. West of the state's mountainous backbone, the mountains subside, the climate becomes drier, and precipitous river canyons become the attraction. Fortunately for the backpacker, most of the land in the state is in public ownership.

General tourism information is available from the Director of Travel Development, State Capitol, Denver, Colorado 80203.

Rocky Mountain National Park

This is one of the country's most beautiful parks, covering 264,000 acres of mountain wilderness 70 miles northwest of Denver in north-central Colorado. Most of the park is in the 8,000- to 12,000-foot elevation range, with rugged, glaciated peaks and gorges, alpine lakes and meadows, forested uplands, and alpine tundra. Pockets of snow remain throughout the year. Forest zones change with the elevation. Ponderosa and lodgepole pine are in the lower altitudes and Engelmann spruce and subalpine fir occur up to the treeline. Wildflowers are especially abundant on the alpine tundra above the treeline. This variety of environments supports a corresponding variety of wildlife. Large mammals include cougar, black bear, deer, elk, and bighorn. Beaver, coyote, bobcat, red fox, whistling swan, and white-tailed ptarmigan also inhabit the park. Trout fishing is good.

Three hundred thirty miles of trails crisscross the park. Most traverse steep terrain. Cross-country travel is allowed, and everyone camping overnight in the backcountry is required to have a permit. Most visit the park during the summer. Although many of the trails are heavily used during this time, use of the backcountry is not as great as one might expect. The bulk of visitors at national parks are car travelers who, except for a short nature hike, seldom venture into the backcountry. This leaves the trails available for those who have learned that many of the national parks provide excellent backpacking opportunities. Cross-country travel above the treeline is especially rewarding.

For maps and information on the park, contact the Superintendent, Rocky Mountain National Park, Estes Park, Colorado 80517.

The national forests in Colorado are its greatest asset. About one-fourth of the state is national forest (there are 11 national forests all together), and a wide choice is available to the backpacker. The forested areas generally follow the Continental Divide and run north and south in the central and western portions of the state. The following discussion of the national forests

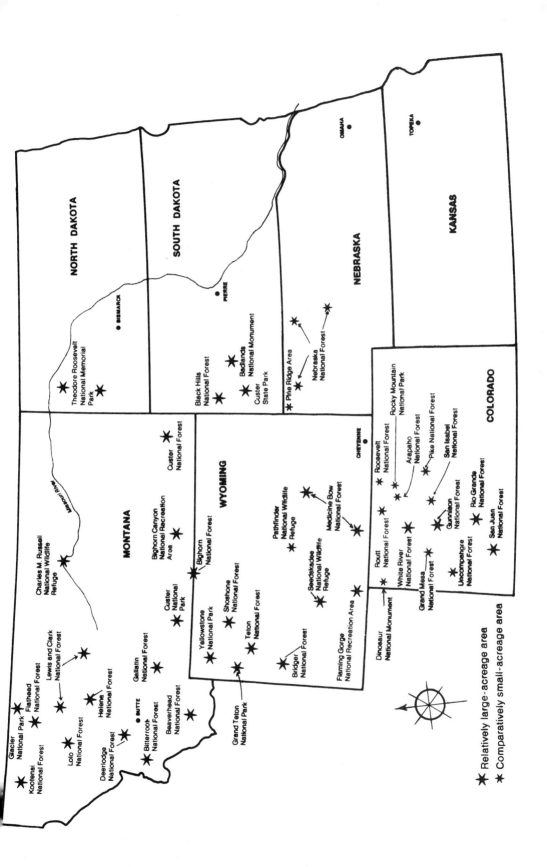

★ Relatively large-acreage area
★ Comparatively small-acreage area

NORTH DAKOTA

• BISMARCK

Theodore Roosevelt
National Memorial
Park ★

SOUTH DAKOTA

• PIERRE

Black Hills
National Forest ★

Badlands
National Monument ★
Custer
State Park ★

Pine Ridge Area ★

Nebraska
National Forest ★

NEBRASKA

• OMAHA

KANSAS

• TOPEKA

Kootenai
National Forest ★

Glacier
National Park ★
Flathead
National Forest ★

Lolo
National Forest ★

Helena
National Forest ★

Lewis and Clark
National Forest ★

Charles M. Russell
National Wildlife
Refuge ★

Deerlodge
National Forest ★

• BUTTE
Bitterroot ★
National Forest ★

Beaverhead
National Forest ★

Gallatin
National Forest ★

MONTANA

Bighorn Canyon
National Recreation
Area ★

Custer
National Forest ★

Custer
National
Park ★

Grand Teton
National Park ★

Yellowstone
National Park ★

Teton
National Forest ★

Shoshone
National Forest ★

Bighorn
National Forest ★

Bridger
National Forest ★

Flaming Gorge
National Recreation Area ★

Seedskadee
National Wildlife
Refuge ★

Pathfinder
National Wildlife
Refuge ★

Medicine Bow
National Forest ★

WYOMING

• CHEYENNE

Dinosaur
National Monument ★

Routt
National Forest ★

White River
National Forest ★

Grand Mesa
National Forest ★

Uncompahgre
National Forest ★

San Juan
National Forest ★

Roosevelt
National Forest ★

Rocky Mountain
National Park ★

Arapaho
National Forest ★

Pike National Forest ★

San Isabel
National Forest ★

Gunnison
National Forest ★

Rio Grande
National Forest ★

COLORADO

Missouri River

begins in the north and proceeds southward. Many of the forests are adjacent and have common boundaries.

Roosevelt National Forest

This 790,000-acre forest (and the 71,000-acre adjacent Colorado State Forest) lies north and east of Rocky Mountain National Park in north-central Colorado abutting the Continental Divide. High peaks, glaciers, alpine lakes and streams, and dense coniferous forests typify this area. The larger mammals include abundant elk and deer, a few black bear, bighorn, and cougar.

Good trails are found throughout the forest proper. One area popular for backpacking is the east slope of the Continental Divide south of Rocky Mountain National Park just northwest of Denver. The scenery is exceptional, but so is the use, especially on weekends. The best area in the forest is the 27,000-acre Rawah Wilderness. Though small, it is extremely rugged, with breathtaking alpine scenery. The trails are also quite breathtaking for those not in shape. Cross-country travel above the timberline is good, with peaks to over 12,500 feet, with about 11,000 feet the average.

For information and a map of the forest and wilderness, contact the Supervisor, Arapaho and Roosevelt National Forests, P.O. Box 1366, Fort Collins, Colorado 80521.

Routt National Forest

This forest, encompassing 1,125,000 acres, lies astride the Continental Divide to the west of the Roosevelt National Forest in north-central Colorado near the town of Steamboat Springs. Its high altitude makes parts of this forest perpetually ice- and snow-covered, supplying the many alpine lakes and trout streams. The rugged Continental Divide provides a breath-taking backdrop and strenuous hiking even for those in good shape. Elk, deer, black bear, various small mammals, and birds are common.

The forest is well supplied with trails, and use is moderate. Motorized use is permitted on many of the trails. One way to get away from it all is by traveling cross-country. Due to the elevation, much of the forest is upland meadow and alpine tundra, which makes for good cross-country travel. Off-trail travel will give the best opportunity of seeing shy wildlife and will take you to the best fishing. Good trail and cross-country backpacking opportunities are also found in the Mount Zirkel Wilderness Area. This area comprises about 72,000 acres astride the Continental Divide in the northern part of the forest. Many alpine lakes surrounded by lodgepole pine and Englemann spruce provide good fishing, and the area is the summer range for elk. With elevations of up to 12,200 feet, cold, stormy weather is a possibility at any time. The trails are rugged, but the scenery, especially the Sawtooth Range, is awesome. For a discussion of the Flat Tops Primitive Area, see the White River National Forest.

For information and maps of the forest and wildernesses, contact the Supervisor, Routt National Forest, Hunt Building, Steamboat Springs, Colorado 80477.

Arapaho National Forest

Adjacent to and south of both Routt and Roosevelt National forests, the Arapaho lies due west of Denver. Its 1,004,000 acres are laced with streams and dotted with mountain lakes and ponds. The area just south of Rocky Mountain National Park along the Continental Divide is especially scenic. Elk, deer, and black bear are often spotted, and fishing is good.

The forest is well developed for recreation, almost too well developed, and as it is close to Denver, it is heavily used. The highest auto road in the United States is here at the crest of 14,260-foot Mount Evans, and skiing developments have provided chairlifts to many peaks. But don't be discouraged; many miles of trails lead off into the wilderness. The best backpacking areas are the trails to the Continental Divide just south of the Rocky Mountain National Park and the Gore Range-Eagles Nest Primitive Area described under the White River National Forest.

For information and maps of the forest and primitive area, contact the Supervisor, Arapaho and Roosevelt National Forests, P.O. Box 1366, Fort Collins, Colorado 80521.

White River National Forest

This large forest, covering 1,960,000 acres in central Colorado, is divided into two units. The northern unit is by the town of Glenwood Springs, the southern unit by Aspen adjacent to the Arapaho National Forest. In addition to its mountainous forests and alpine lakes, this forest also contains hot mineral springs, caverns, waterfalls, and beautiful Glenwood Canyon along the Colorado River. Wildlife includes elk, deer, black bear, bighorn sheep, and many smaller mammals and birds. Fishing for trout is good in the many lakes and streams.

Four wilderness areas provide good backpacking opportunities in the forest, but the area is heavily used. The Maroon Bells-Snowmass Wilderness, 71,000 acres in the southern unit of the forest, is one of the most popular in Colorado, and for good reason. Covered with Englemann spruce and aspen, sprinkled with alpine lakes, and topped by several peaks over 14,000 feet, this is one of the most beautiful parts of the Rockies. The largest of the lakes, Snowmass, is the goal of many backpackers and tends to become a little cramped. Expect rugged terrain and cold temperatures in any season. The nearly 74,000-acre Hunter-Frying Pan Wilderness is a similar environment, but not as heavily used. This area was designated as wilderness in 1978.

The larger Flat Tops Wilderness, 102,000 acres in the northern unit of the forest, is an undulating plateau with elevations remaining under 12,000 feet, bordered by precipitous escarpments and plunging cataracts. Once covered by spruce-fir forest, much of the area is now grassland and dead timber left in the wake of an insect epidemic; about 55 percent is forested. The recovering landscape is nevertheless still wild and beautiful. Large herds of deer and elk, capitalizing on the grassland and open forests, use this area as a summer and fall range. The rolling terrain of this area is kinder to the backpacker than most wild Rocky Mountain areas, but the weather can still be cold.

In contrast to this relatively gentle terrain, the 61,000-acre Gore Range-Eagle Nest Wilderness which overlaps the eastern edge of this forest and the western edge of the adjacent Arapaho National Forest is one of the most rugged areas in the Rockies. That hasn't stopped this from being one of the most popular areas in Colorado, though. The environment is similar to that of the Rawah Wilderness Area and contains many spectacular mountain vistas, forested valleys, and glaciers. Due to the severity of the terrain, trails are not plentiful and some areas are virtually inaccessible to the backpacker.

Backpacking opportunities are excellent throughout the White River National Forest. There are numerous small lakes, streams, canyons, and mountain peaks away from the most popular attractions in the forest. Many of the general forest areas provide good opportunities for backpacking under conditions which are often less crowded than many of the most popular wilderness trails.

For information and maps of the forest, wilderness, and primitive areas, contact the Supervisor, White River National Forest, Federal Building, Ninth and Grand Aves., Glenwood Springs, Colorado 81601.

Pike National Forest

This forest is also adjacent to the Arapaho National Forest and is located southwest of Denver extending down to Colorado Springs. Its 1,105,000 acres are well used by residents of nearby Denver and Colorado Springs. Fortunately, many of them are content to only visit those areas reached by auto. This forest is more arid than those found to the north, but the higher elevations are nevertheless covered with thick stands of timber, including the famed long-lived bristlecone pine. Elk, deer, bighorn, antelope, and black bear inhabit the forest, and Pike's Peak is one of the major bighorn habitats in the state.

For the backpacker, there is an extensive trail system throughout the forest. The western portion is the least used. Two scenic areas are of particular interest. The Lost Creek Scenic Area in the center of the forest is rugged alpine scenery managed to preserve the beautiful vistas. The trails are not too steep, and stream trout fishing is good. The Abyss Lake Scenic Area in the northern tip of the forest is smaller and more heavily used, with trails leading to Abyss Lake through well-timbered mountain slopes.

For information and maps (50¢) of the forest, contact the Supervisor, Pike and San Isabel National Forests, 910 Highway 50 West, Pueblo, Colorado 81008.

Grand Mesa National Forest

In west-central Colorado, east of Grand Junction, this forest is adjacent to both the White River and Gunnison national forests. Although a small national forest by Colorado's standards, its 368,000 acres provide a high-quality recreational resource. The Mesa itself is an imposing 10,000-foot table mountain, the largest in the United States, covered with spruce forest, aspen groves, and meadows of wildflowers. Perhaps this area's biggest attraction is its lakes—about 300 of them, many accessible only by trail. The lakes are home for native, brook, brown, and rainbow trout, and the forests and meadows provide forage for deer and elk.

This forest is intensively managed for recreation, with abundant campgrounds and roads. Fortunately, it is not well known and is fairly remote. If the backpacker plans his trip wisely and chooses the less developed areas in the eastern and southwestern portions of the forest, he will be rewarded by an excellent wilderness experience. Don't expect imposing mountain vistas, but by the same token there are no steep, exhausting grades. The deep snowpack lingers on until May, and good backpacking weather extends into fall.

Information and a map (50¢) of the forest can be obtained from the Supervisor, Grand Mesa-Uncompahgre and Gunnison National Forests, P.O. Box 138, Delta, Colorado 81416.

Gunnison National Forest

This crescent-shaped forest, covering 1,663,000 acres near the town of Gunnison, borders the Grand Mesa National Forest on the southeast. It is one of the wilder national forests in Colorado. As in much of southwest Colorado, the lower elevations are semiarid with corresponding desertlike vegetation. As one moves up in altitude the environments progress as if one were traveling north: from desert, through pine forest, then dense spruce-fir-aspen stands (including the world's largest blue spruce), and then finally into the alpine zone. Deep canyons and tall, eroded spires add geological interest, with many meadows and open grassy areas supporting the large population of deer and elk.

Hundreds of miles of trails penetrate this forest, and some are quite rugged and steep. Prepare yourself accordingly, and take appropriate gear, especially footwear. Rock slides are frequently encountered on the trails. Be thankful—such terrain discourages motorized use.

For a particularly rugged and wild experience, guaranteed free from motorized intrusions, visit the West Elk Wild Area in the northwest part of the forest. Although only 61,000 acres, this area contains the best wilderness attributes of the forest, including the finest examples of badland erosion and the tallest peak, West Elk, at almost 13,000 feet. Also in this forest is part of the La Garita Wild Area, discussed under the Rio Grande National Forest.

For maps and information on the forest and wild areas, contact the Supervisor, Grand Mesa, Uncompahgre, and Gunnison National Forests, P.O. Box 138, Delta, Colorado 81416.

San Isabel National Forest

Adjacent along the eastern boundary of the Gunnison National Forest, west of the town of Pueblo, this forest strings out along 1,106,000 acres of mountain ranges to the southeast. It is divided into 3 units and all are typified by mountains—tall mountains. This forest has the highest elevation of any national forest, with 21 peaks over 14,000 feet. Needless to say, the scenery is spectacular. Spruce forests extend to the timberline, there dissolving into the fragile alpine tundra. Bighorn and mountain goats frequent the rocky slopes, and trout are found in the many cold alpine lakes and streams. Deer, elk, and black bear are also found in the lower elevations.

Hundreds of miles of trails extend into all 3 units of the forest. Some of the best backpacking found in the forest is around Mount Elbert, the highest peak in Colorado at 14,433 feet, in the northwestern portion of the forest, and also along the east face of the Sangre de Cristo Range farther south. This range, also discussed below under the Rio Grande National Forest, has many trails leading up the rugged mountainsides, but few passing over the crest. The spectacular scenery this forest has to offer is not easily won. The rarefied air combined with steep grades make backpacking in this country a challenge. The temperature ranges from below freezing to the 50s, and afternoon rain and lightning storms are common. The season is generally May through October, with pockets of snow year-round. Be prepared for bright sunlight in this high altitude.

For maps and information of the forest, contact the Supervisor, Pike and San Isabel National Forests, 910 Highway 50 West, Pueblo, Colorado 81008.

Rio Grande National Forest

At 1,800,000 acres, this forest is the state's third largest. It borders the San Juan, the San Isabel, and Gunnison national forests and is divided into two units, both in south-central Colorado near the town of Monte Vista. The forest is well supplied with trails and dirt roads. Like the Gunnison, it contains some rather arid lower regions. Overall, the forest cover is about half forested, with a variety of ecozones from semiarid to alpine. Since this forest is some distance from population centers, it is not heavily used but use is increasing yearly. It is all fairly wild, but 3 areas, the Weminuche Wilderness Area, the La Garita Wilderness Area, and the Sangre de Cristo Range, are of particular interest.

The Weminuche Wilderness is located in the western tip of this forest extending into the neighboring San Juan National Forest. At 401,000 acres, this is the largest designated wilderness in the state. This is high country with elevations up to 14,000 feet, and is home for several large mammals, including elk, deer, cougar, bighorn, and black bear. There are a few lakes in the area with trails leading to them. Trails are not plentiful, but cross-country travel is possible.

The 48,000-acre La Garita Wilderness Area, half lying in the Gunnison and half in the Rio Grande National Forest, has an environment similar to the Weminuche Wilderness Area, but although the elevation is high, the terrain is not particularly rugged. There are a few lakes in the area, and trails generally follow the stream courses.

The Sangre de Cristo Range forms the eastern unit of this forest and also part of the San Isabel National Forest. This area has many lakes and trails, and some quite spectacular peaks and canyons. Because it has not been designated either a wilderness or primitive area, its use is moderate. Unfortunately, some of the use includes motorized vehicles, including jeeps. Request a travel map for areas closed to vehicles.

For information and maps on the forest and wilderness areas, contact the Supervisor, Rio Grande National Forest, 1803 W. Highway 160, Monte Vista, Colorado 81144.

Uncompahgre National Forest

This forest encompasses 926,000 acres and is located in southwest Colorado near the towns of Montrose and Delta. It is divided into two main units. The northern unit is atop the Uncompahgre Plateau, a high tableland broken by rugged canyons, with the spruce, pine, and alpine stands of the Plateau merging with the piñon and juniper of the foothills below. The southern unit is an area of high peaks, with several over 14,000 feet, deep canyons, and alpine meadows and beautiful waterfalls. Trout are found in the lakes and streams and wildlife is abundant. Elk, deer, black bear, bighorn, cougar, lynx, bobcat, and coyote may be spotted, as well as smaller mammals such as fox, marten, mink, weasel, beaver, and badger.

Two primitive areas, both in the southern unit, are of particular interest to the backpacker. The Uncompahgre Primitive Area surrounding the town of Ouray is a unit of about 53,000 acres, but it is cut in two by U.S. 550. The area is marred by many roads and mining sites, and opportunities for extended trips are limited. To the west is the Wilson Mountains Primitive Area. This small area of 27,000 acres spills over into the adjacent San Juan National Forest. It has fewer civilized intrusions than the Uncompahgre Primitive Area, and although trail mileage is not great, good short trail trips and cross-country travel are possible.

Many other good trails are found in the northern unit and the southeast portion of the southern unit of the forest. These areas are generally surrounded by Bureau of Land Management lands onto which the trails extend. All total, there are many hundreds of miles of trails, providing opportunities for trips of varying lengths and environments.

For information and a map (50¢) of the forest, primitive areas, and surrounding BLM land, contact the Supervisor, Grand Mesa, Uncompahgre and Gunnison National Forests, P.O. Box 138, Delta, Colorado 81416.

San Juan National Forest

This forest, located in extreme southwestern Colorado just north of Durango, is the second largest in the state with 1,866,000 acres. Elevations range from about 7,000 feet to more than 14,000 feet. The climate is somewhat arid and the spruce-fir-aspen forest cover is limited to the lower slopes of the mountains just below timberline, changing into meadows and grasslands and pine near the mountain base. Numerous canyons and waterfalls are also part of the setting.

Of greatest interest to the backpacker is the 401,000-acre Weminuche Wilderness Area with the best scenery, trails, fishing, and wildlife. Motor vehicles of course are not allowed. This area is located in the northeast part of the forest extending into the Rio Grande National Forest. Many excellent trails, mostly along stream beds, lead to the many lakes in the area. The mountain-canyon scenery is spectacular, there is good fishing, and elk, deer, and bighorn are found in the area. Use is heavy in some areas. Part of the Wilson Mountains Primitive Area, discussed under the Uncompahgre National Forest, is also in this forest.

For a map (50¢) of the forest, wilderness, primitive areas, and a travel map which shows areas where motor vehicles are prohibited, contact the Supervisor, San Juan National Forest, 701 Camino Del Rio, Durango, Colorado 81301.

Dinosaur National Monument

The 206,000 acres that comprise this monument are in the extreme northwest corner of the state. Although intended as a monument for the extensive dinosaur fossil beds it contains, it also protects the fantastic canyons of the Green and Yampa rivers. This is the main attraction of the backcountry along with the mule deer, prairie dog, bighorn, antelope, coyote, cougar, and golden eagle. Fishing is only fair. The climate is arid and can become quite hot in the summer.

Only 8 miles of trails suitable for backpacking exist in the monument, though 30 more miles of jeep trails could also be used. The best way to experience the park is to travel cross-country, but the climate and terrain increase the dangers of cross-country travel. One should first write for general information on what to expect and how to prepare for it, and then stop in at the ranger station to register before heading out.

For a map and information, contact the Superintendent, Dinosaur National Monument, P.O. Box 201, Dinosaur, Colorado 81610.

Other Public Lands

The Bureau of Land Management administers 8.5 million acres of public land in Colorado—12 percent of the entire state. Most of this land lies at lower elevations on the western slope. It consists of a variety of topographic and vegetative diversity, but the more arid rimrock and sagebrush-covered landscapes are characteristic. Smaller parcels of these public lands occur at higher elevations adjacent to lands of the national forests, and some sizable areas lie adjacent to some of the state's major rivers. The greatest recreational use of these lands is for hunting, fishing, river running, off-road vehicle use, and for general dispersed recreation use such as hiking, picnicking, and pleasure driving.

Though much of the land is suitable for cross-country travel, and back-country camping is permitted most places, you should check with BLM's field offices to be sure. Regulations for issuing permits and fees for certain types of generalized outdoor recreation use on the public lands recently were signed into effect. Also be aware that proposed off-road vehicle regulations are soon to be written; these will also affect the type of cross-country use of these lands that is permissible; so you will need to contact these field offices for these reasons also. Improvements, for the most part, consist only of dirt roads. The experienced outdoor recreation user should ready himself with land status (ownership) maps and USGS topographic maps to be prepared for using these lands. Of course, all users should use discretion in exercising their right to use these public lands to protect these often fragile resources and to provide for their own as well as other's safety.

For additional information and for maps, contact the Bureau of Land Management, Colorado State Office, Room 700, Colorado State Bank Building, 1600 Broadway, Denver, Colorado 80202.

KANSAS

This state has no backpacking opportunities. However, if you are passing through and looking for a place to visit, the 10,800-acre Kirwin National Wildlife Refuge near the city of Kirwin in north-central Kansas provides camping in developed campgrounds. Hiking is permitted throughout the refuge, but back-country camping is not allowed. (There is no backcountry anyway). In Kansas, this is the best you will be able to do.

MONTANA

Montana has rugged, wild environments and few people—a combination that makes it an excellent state for backpacking. The prairies in the eastern two-thirds slope up to the spectacular mountains of the west. This mountainous western third of the state provides most of the backpacking opportunities the state is famous for. The Montana Rocky Mountains are rugged, frequently snow-covered, with extensive forests and glaciers. The area is particularly rich in wilderness and in wildlife, including the grizzly bear. These bears are a temperamental animal and have long been at odds with man. Before the advent of the white man and firearms, the grizzly was a match for man, and the Indians had great respect for him. The gun has all but eliminated the grizzly, but the grizzly is still a match for the backpacker. The vendetta between man and grizzly continues to this day in the backcountry and every year there are deaths on both sides. Before entering a grizzly bear area, check with local rangers or officials. They can tell you if there have been any local bear problems, what areas to avoid, and how to cope with the bears if you decide to go anyway.

Most of the best backpacking opportunities in the state are found in the wilderness and primitive areas. There are also excellent trails and wilderness environments in the Glacier National Park backcountry. Though Montana is quite distant from the bulk of the U.S. population, the quality of its backpacking areas draws backpackers from all over the country. If its public lands weren't so extensive, they might even become crowded. In this high northern state, snow can be expected anytime in the high country and can block high passes as late as July and as early as September.

General tourism information is available from the Montana State Highway Commission, Helena, Montana 59601.

Glacier National Park

This 1,013,000-acre park is found in the northwest corner of the state by the town of West Glacier. The park encompasses the most breath-taking scenery in Montana, with jagged mountains thrusting up from glaciated valley meadows. The park's glaciers, after which it was named, are its most notable feature. These glaciers and their predecessors have honed the mountains to sharp peaks and gouged out U-shaped valleys and lakes, and they are still at work today changing the face of the park. Many live glaciers can be visited by the backpacker. The wildlife is also notable. Mountain goat, bighorn, moose, elk, grizzly and black bear, beaver, pika (a rock-inhabiting rodent), and an unusual bird, the diving water ouzel, inhabit the park. The hundreds of miles of streams and the nearly 14,000 acres of lakes provide excellent trout fishing.

Glacier National Park is particularly appealing to the backpacker because although it receives heavy visitation, most people never leave the roads. The park has retained its wilderness character, and 700 miles of well-kept trails lead the hiker up through the forested lake and stream-filled valleys. The northern section of the park is the wildest and provides the most solitude. Cross-country travel above the timberline is possible, but difficult over the steep terrain and talus slopes. Warm days and cold nights are the rule during summer. There are no restrictions on backcountry travel except that a backcountry camping permit is required and issued no sooner than a day before departure.

For information and a map of the park, contact the Superintendent, Glacier National Park, West Glacier, Montana 59936.

The national forests lying astride the Rocky Mountains provide the bulk of the backpacking opportunities. Generally proceeding from north to south, they measure up as follows.

Kootenai National Forest

This forest is particularly remote with its 1,820,000 acres filling the northwest corner of the state and extending partly into Idaho. Elevations are in the 3,000- to 8,000-foot range and are cloaked in thick coniferous forests. There is lake and stream fishing, and animal inhabitants include a population of black bear, a few grizzly, deer, and many other fur-bearers and birds.

Although there are many hundreds of miles of trails throughout the forest, the best hiking and scenery are found in the Cabinet Mountains Wilderness where there are no motorized intrusions or logging operations. These 94,000 acres along the backbone of the national forest provide scenic vistas without too long a climb. The tallest mountain, Snowshoe Peak, is 8,712 feet. It and other peaks above 7,000 feet are barren, jagged, and snow-clad much of the year in contrast to the rest of the forest. The area is not very well known and use is light. Cross-country travel is encouraged, with many lakes accessible only by leaving the trail.

For maps and information about the forest and wilderness, contact the Supervisor, Kootenai National Forest, P.O. Box AS, 418 Mineral Avenue, Libby, Montana 59923.

Kaniksu National Forest

See Idaho, chapter 5.

Lolo National Forest

Just south of Kootenai and surrounding Missoula, this large national forest of 2,087,000 acres extends in 3 segments to the northwest, northeast, and southeast along the Bitterroot, Swan, and Sapphire mountains respectively. The mountains are well timbered with elevations up to about 9,000 feet. The huge Selway-Bitterroot Wilderness Area is partly in this forest and is discussed under the Nezperce National Forest in Idaho. The Scapegoat Wilderness Area, also partly in the Lolo, is discussed with the Lewis and Clark National Forest, below. Black and grizzly bear, deer, elk, and mountain goat are found here as are trout in the lakes and streams.

Most backpackers visiting the area will choose one of several excellent wilderness and primitive areas nearby, but the forest itself offers good backpacking also. While motorized use is allowed on many of the trails, the size and remoteness of the forest makes use relatively light. Many trails climb to hundreds of lakes and peaks, many of which you can have all to yourself. Missoula is conveniently located to supply those last-minute needs and to provide a place to stay for that first night you return to civilization.

For information and a map of the forest and wildernesses, contact the Supervisor, Lolo National Forest, Fort Missoula, Building 24, Missoula, Montana 59801.

Flathead National Forest

Between Missoula and Glacier National Park, north and east of the Lolo National Forest, lies the Flathead. This forest of 2,346,000 acres is the largest in Montana and includes some spectacular glacial mountain scenery, with hanging valleys, glaciers and glacial lakes, and dense forested slopes. Large mammals include grizzly and black bear, moose, elk, deer, bighorn, mountain goat, lynx, bobcat, wolverine, cougar, and timber wolf. Trout are plentiful in lakes and streams.

This forest can be divided into 3 geographical areas: the forest proper to the north abutting Glacier National Park, the large Bob Marshall Wilderness to the southeast, and the Mission Mountains Wilderness to the southwest. Since these wildernesses attract many of the backpackers, the forest lands to the north are sparsely used. North Fork of the Flathead drains the area and roads and trails follow this river and its tributaries. The relatively low elevations of under 8,000 feet make for generally moderate hiking even though the country traversed is quite rugged. The western part of this area is typical Rocky Mountain alpine setting complete with lakes, streams, meadows, and trails to get you there. Many of the access trails through this forest leading to the wildernesses and primitive areas are closed to motorized traffic. The area constitutes the proposed Great Bear Wilderness.

The Bob Marshall Wilderness is a large 950,000-acre area containing a wide variety of environments, including dense forests, barren rocky mountain tops, alpine meadows, lakes, streams, geological formations, and 60 miles of the Continental Divide. Hundreds of miles of trails lead through the area, making it a popular and well-known wilderness to backpackers and pack-train users alike. However, the size of the area lessens the impact of the thousands who use it. This is prime grizzly, moose, and elk country and is one of the last strongholds of the black-spotted native cutthroat trout. Fossils, minerals, and the geology of the area are interesting, particularly the spectacular 20-mile-long, 1,000-foot-high, overthrust escarpment known as the Chinese Wall.

The much smaller Mission Mountains Wilderness, 79,000 acres, makes up for what it lacks in size by its ruggedness. Mostly above timberline, this area is characterized by alpine tundra and snowfields. Trails are not abundant, making this a good area for the experienced, rugged-wilderness-loving cross-country enthusiast. Extra care should be taken when traveling in this area because it is favorite grizzly country. Many lakes are found in the southern portions of this area and in the Flathead Indian Reservation which adjoins the wilderness to the west.

For maps and information on the forest, wilderness, and primitive areas, contact the Supervisor, Flathead National Forest, P.O. Box 147, 290 North Main, Kalispell, Montana 59901.

Lewis and Clark National Forest

Just east of the Flathead and on either side of Great Falls lie the several units of this 1,835,000-acre forest. Its open timber stands and grassy meadows lie beneath limestone peaks that range from 5,000 to 9,000 feet. There are only a few lakes, but many cold streams. This is a particularly good area for spotting mountain goat, especially on Scapegoat Mountain. Other wildlife include grizzly and black bear, elk, deer, bighorn, cougar, wolverine, coyote, bald eagle, and ptarmigan.

Backpacking is good in 3 of the units. The northwest unit contains part of the Bob Marshall Wilderness (discussed above) as well as part of the Scapegoat Wilderness. The 239,000-acre Scapegoat was established in 1972 and is contiguous to the Bob Marshall and is environmentally similar to it though less heavily used. It consists of rock ridges, limestone cliffs, scattered forests, parklands, and alpine lakes and meadows, with good trails. Elsewhere in the forest, the two largest units southeast of Great Falls both have several trails, but the experience is not quite as wild as in Bob Marshall and Scapegoat. In all of the units, cross-country travel is possible throughout the parklands and grassy meadows of this slightly drier environment.

For information and a map of the forest and wildernesses, contact the Supervisor, Lewis and Clark National Forest, P.O. Box 871, Great Falls, Montana 59403.

Helena National Forest

The 969,000 acres of this forest are distributed in several units around the city of Helena in west-central Montana. It's a rugged area with bare rock mountains, scattered timber stands, several alpine lake areas, and precipitous banks of the Missouri River. All the large Rocky Mountain mammals are represented here, including antelope and grizzlies. The rare osprey and bald eagle also inhabit the forest.

The best areas for the backpacker are the Scapegoat Wilderness, discussed previously under the Lewis and Clark National Forest, and the Gates of the Mountains Wilderness Area. Although the area is small at only 29,000 acres, it is little known and little used. Limestone cliffs and narrow canyons are reached by trails and cross-country travel. There are few trails outside these wildernesses in the forest, but good cross-country trips can be taken in many of the alpine areas.

For information and maps of the forest and wildernesses, contact the Supervisor, Helena National Forest, Federal Building, 301 S. Park, Helena, Montana 59601.

Deerlodge National Forest

The several units of this 1,358,000-acre forest are distributed around the city of Butte in southwestern Montana. Rolling sage and juniper-covered foothills rise to granite mountains of over 10,000 feet, broken by narrow gorges and canyons. Over 100 high mountain lakes and almost 300 miles of streams provide good fishing. Elk, moose, deer, grizzly and black bear, mountain goat, lynx, bobcat, coyote, and a variety of smaller mammals and birds dwell in the fir-spruce-pine forests of the lower elevations and in the alpine meadows higher up.

The excellent Anaconda-Pintlar Primitive Area found in this forest is discussed later under the Beaverhead National Forest. There are good backpacking opportunities outside the primitive area in both of the larger units. The western unit has the best trail system and good cross-country possibilities to many of the backcountry lakes. While this forest is a popular forest, well used by residents of nearby Butte, the many hundreds of miles of trails and remoteness of the backpacking areas make for light use outside the primitive area.

For information and maps of the forest and primitive area, contact the Supervisor, Deerlodge National Forest, P.O. Box 400, Butte, Montana 59701.

Bitterroot National Forest

Just west of the Deerlodge National Forest extending south from Missoula into Idaho is the 1,576,000 acres of the Bitterroot. The mountainous areas are steep and rocky with elevations from about 3,000 feet to over 10,000 feet, with warmer, drier river bottoms along the Selway, Salmon, and East Fork of the Bitterroot rivers. The forested lowlands and alpine areas around the bases of the bare rock peaks are home for mountain goat, moose, deer, black bear, and rare cougar. Rattlesnakes are found along the river bottoms. The summer months are generally dry and warm.

One-third of this forest is wilderness and primitive areas. The Selway-Bitterroot Wilderness and the Salmon River Breaks Primitive Area are described under the Nezperce Forest in Idaho (see chapter 5) and the Anaconda-Pintlar Wilderness is described below in the Beaverhead National Forest. The forest outside these areas also has hundreds of miles of good trails and many backcountry lakes throughout. It is very wild and remote with few roads, making this forest one of the best backpacking areas in the state. Use is light even though Missoula is so close.

For information and maps of the forest, wildlerness, and primitive areas, contact the Supervisor, Bitterroot National Forest, 316 North Third Street, Hamilton, Montana 59840.

Beaverhead National Forest

Just southeast of the Bitterroot, in the southwest corner of the state, lie the many units of the Beaverhead National Forest, for a total of 2,115,000 acres. The units on the western border of the state along the Continental Divide and the large unit just east of them are typified by tall peaks with spruce, fir, and pine-covered slopes, mountain lakes, and meadows. The large unit just west of Yellowstone National Park is mostly grassland and river canyon with scattered timber stands becoming mostly timbered in the Snowcrest Range. The forest is especially wild in the higher elevations in the above-mentioned units. Wildlife includes deer, elk, moose, mountain goat, black bear, cougar, coyote, bobcat, smaller mammals and birds, with antelope in the lower elevations.

This forest does not attract many backpackers, but the trails are plentiful, good, and range widely in difficulty. The season can start as early as May in the lower elevations in the area west of Yellowstone. One of the best, though most crowded, areas is the 158,000-acre Anaconda-Pintlar Wilderness. This rugged, barren wilderness with elevations from 5,000 to over 10,000 feet is similar to the Sierras of California with its jagged granite peaks, glaciated valleys and cirques, and many alpine lakes, forests, meadows, and streams. The excellent trail system is heavily used and the solitude seeker may want to head out cross-country to one of the many lakes that are not reached by trail. Additional backpacking opportunities are found in the East Pioneers northwest of Dillon, in the Bitterroot Range west of Jackson, and in the Tobacco Root Range east of Sheridan.

For information and maps of the forest and wilderness, contact the Supervisor, Beaverhead National Forest, P.O. Box 1258, Skihi Street and Highway 91, Dillon, Montana 59725.

Gallatin National Forest

This 1,711,000-acre forest is divided into several units, the largest of which borders Yellowstone National Park on the north. This is one of Montana's most outstanding national forests, from both the scenic and recreational standpoints. Elevations range from 5,000 to 10,000 feet, culminating in snow-covered peaks above forested, grassy, and rocky slopes, canyons, and plateaus. There are more than 200 lakes, 11 outstanding waterfalls, and thousands of miles of trout streams. The forest is particularly attractive because of this variety of environments. Wildlife includes grizzly and black bear, moose, elk, deer, bighorn, and mountain goat, with trout, perch, and bass fishing in the lakes, streams, and rivers. Each unit of the forest has an excellent trail system with good opportunities for mountain climbing and cross-country travel (the terrain is rugged, though). Two wildernesses attract the backpacker; they are rugged, and the trails are steep. Absaroka-Beartooth Wilderness is described under the Custer National Forest, which follows. A good long-distance trip could originate in adjacent Yellowstone National Park, loop through this wilderness, and return. The season may be limited by snow blocking the trails on surrounding ridges, but they are usually passable by mid-summer. Along the western edge of the forest is found the 51,000-acre Spanish Peaks Wilderness Area. Like the Absaroka, the area is small but rugged with elevations ranging from 6,000 feet in the valleys to 11,015 feet on Gallatin Peak. Over 60 lakes provide fine trout fishing among the glaciated peaks.

For information and maps of the forest and wildernesses, contact the Supervisor, Gallatin National Forest, P.O. Box 130, Federal Building, Bozeman, Montana 59715.

Custer National Forest

The 1,186,000 acres of this national forest are divided among several units, some of which are in South Dakota. Granite peaks, glaciers, plateaus, lakes, streams, waterfalls, and perpetual snow-fields make this one of the state's most attractive and varied forests. As one moves east off the jagged summits, dense coniferous forests and then the grasslands and buttes of eastern Montana are encountered. Hundreds of lakes provide excellent trout fishing, and black bear, grizzly bear, moose, deer, bighorn, mountain goat, and antelope are also present.

The unit of most interest to the backpacker is southwest of Billings in south-central Montana. In this unit, extending into the adjacent Gallatin National Forest, is the outstanding Absaroka-

Beartooth Wilderness. This 905,000-acre area is the most primitive of any in the state, encompassing the most rugged mountain country, most of it above 9,000 feet, including the state's tallest mountain, 12,799-foot Granite Peak, the objective of many mountaineers. There are only a few trails in the entire area, making this a good place to exercise your cross-country skills. The great majority of lakes are only accessible by cross-country travel. The rewards are towering peaks, plunging canyons, timbered valleys, tundra plateaus, waterfalls, and alpine meadows and lakes, some still waiting to be discovered.

In another unit of Custer National Forest south of Billings are the Pryor Mountains. This is a different type of environment, an arid and semiarid prairie and canyon landscape. Mule deer are the most common large mammal. Eagles may also be seen. Many miles of trails originating in the surrounding Bureau of Land Management lands extend into the forest, and plenty of water should be carried. As when traveling in any arid country, experience and caution are especially important.

For information and maps of the forest and primitive area, contact the Supervisor, Custer National Forest, PO. Box 2556, 2601 First Avenue North, Billings, Montana 59103.

Bighorn Canyon National Recreation Area

This 123,000-acre area in south-central Montana is an arid region bisected by a 71-mile-long reservoir extending into Wyoming. The taller peaks are timbered and fall off into steep-walled canyons. Cliffs and rock outcrops contain fossils. Wildlife includes beaver, waterfowl, wild horse, mule deer, black bear, and elk.

There are no trails in the area, but cross-country travel is encouraged. Only a fire permit is required for backcountry travel. Caution should be exercised when traveling in arid areas like this, so discuss your plans with the ranger when you obtain your fire permit, especially if you are inexperienced in this type of climate.

For maps and information on backcountry travel in the area, contact the Superintendent, Bighorn Canyon National Recreation Area, P.O. Box 458, Y.R.S., Hardin, Montana 59035.

Charles M. Russell National Wildlife Refuge

This refuge of approximately 1 million acres extends along the Missouri River for about 125 miles in an area northeast of Lewistown. Here the river is dammed, creating the large Fort Peck Reservior, flanked by badlands, native sagebrush-grasslands, pine-forested coulees, and cottonwood bottoms. Wildlife is abundant and varied, including deer, bighorn, elk, pronghorn, prairie dog, possibly the rare black-footed ferret, and great concentrations of birds resting here during seasonal migrations.

While there are no designated backpacking trails as such on the refuge, backpacking and camping are allowed. The semiarid, undulating landscape has only sparse vegetative cover and is excellent for cross-country travel. Water is not abundant, but is available in most areas. Use is extremely light, but motorized vehicles are allowed on established roads and trails in the refuge. This is an outstanding area for the cross-country traveler looking for wild terrain that is moderately easy to traverse but at the same time is lightly used.

For information and a map of the refuge, contact the Manager, Charles M. Russell National Wildlife Refuge, P.O. Box 110, Lewistown, Montana 59457.

Other Public Lands

There are 6 state forests that are associated with a nearby national forest and do not offer significant additional backpacking opportunities to warrant special mention. The Bureau of Land Management administers about 8 million acres of public land open for backpacking and backcountry camping. BLM designates two areas in the state as primitive areas. The Humbug Spires Primitive Area, located about 25 miles south of Butte, consists of 7,000 acres of rolling hills, ponderosa pine, and hundreds of white granite spires, some over 600 feet tall. There are no trails, but it is an excellent place to roam and camp at backcountry sites. The Beartrap Canyon Primitive Area is 4,000 acres along the 9-

mile, 1,500-foot-deep gorge of the Madison River about 30 miles west of Bozemen in southwestern Montana. A 9-mile trail extends through the length of the area, and good side trips are also possible.

BLM ownership is scattered throughout the state, with an average of about 10 percent timbered. One of the largest areas is around the Fort Peck Reservoir, with an especially attractive area of wooded hills emerging from the surrounding prairies called the Little Rockies. The Garnet Range east of Missoula is another good backpacking area. Other areas of large BLM ownership are in the intermountain valleys of the southwest and in the prairies of the southeast. This is all generally tractless wild land for the experienced cross-country traveler only.

For information on the above-mentioned primitive areas and other BLM land in the state, contact the Bureau of Land Management, P.O. Box 30157, Billings, Montana 59107.

NEBRASKA

Although not outstanding for its backpacking opportunities, Nebraska is not entirely covered by wheat and corn fields. The northwest part is an interesting amalgam of physical geography, and plentiful public land invites the backpacker. Of course, don't expect rugged mountains and rushing streams, but in its own way, the state offers a different sort of backpacking experience. Rainfall is about 15 to 20 inches a year, with warm, dry summers. The season is spring through fall, although winter backpacking is possible for those so inclined.

General tourism information is available from the Nebraska Game and Parks Commission, P.O. Box 30370, Lincoln, Nebraska 68503.

Pine Ridge Area

Comprising the northwest corner of the state, this large area is a combination of environments under several state and local jurisdictions. The high plains of the Oglala National Grasslands, the timbered Pine Ridge, and the bizarre Badlands support a variety of plant and animal life. Ponderosa pine cloaks the ridges with poplar, ash, elm, and other broadleaf trees along the stream bottoms, while yucca and other desert plants intermingle with prairie grasses and shrubs on the uplands. The animal life is equally diverse. Deer, bobcat, skunk, badger, and porcupine are found here as well as the poisonous prairie rattler. More than 180 species of birds have been spotted in the area including golden and bald eagles and wild turkeys. Water is scarce in some areas, but there are trout in some streams.

Throughout all these public lands there are only 24 miles of trails developed for the backpacker. However, the countryside is open and the cross-country backpacker should have no trouble keeping from getting lost. The best guide to this area is the Recreation Guide Map of the Nebraska Pine Ridge Area, available from the Nebraska Game and Parks Commission, P.O. Box 30370, Lincoln, Nebraska 68503, or the Supervisor, Nebraska National Forest, 270 Pine Street, Chadron, Nebraska 69337.

Nebraska National Forest

The 255,000 acres of these forests are divided among 3 units. One unit is along the Pine Ridge described above, another is in north-central Nebraska south of the town of Nenzel, and the third is in the central part of the state southwest of the town of Halsey. These last two units are mostly rolling grass-covered sand hills with extensive forest plantations. The unit by Halsey is adjacent to a state recreation area around the Merritt Reservoir. Antelope, deer, coyote, bobcat, skunk, badger, rabbit, grouse, prairie chicken, and wild turkey are among the inhabitants of the forests.

The forests are by no means wilderness, but the rolling, grassy sand hills have a certain mystique. The limited forest areas are trees planted in neat, unnatural rows. There are no trails or other developments for backpacking. However, one can wander at will through many thousands of acres of roadless, public land over the sand hills and around the reservoir.

A map of the forest is available from the Supervisor, Nebraska National Forests, 270 Pine Street, Chadron, Nebraska 69337.

Other Public Lands

One other area provides backpacking opportunities. The Sand Hills Lakes area of about 24,000 acres is located in northwest Nebraska between the towns of Rushville and Lakeside. This area is grass-covered sand hills dotted with marshes and lakes. Wildlife, especially birds, is particularly abundant here. There are no back-packing trails, but abundant opportunities for the cross-country backpacker to observe a variety of wildlife in a softly interesting environment. The most popular season is from spring to fall, with bird populations peaking during the fall migrations in about October.

For information on the Sand Hills, contact the Nebraska Game and Parks Commission, P.O. Box 30370, Lincoln, Nebraska 68503.

NORTH DAKOTA

This state has little to offer the backpacker, with few good areas. Since many travelers pass through North Dakota on their way to places elsewhere, an overnight hike in the state may provide a good break in the trip.

General tourism information is available from the North Dakota Travel Division, State Highway Department, Bismarck, North Dakota 58501.

Theodore Roosevelt National Memorial Park

This 70,000-acre park is divided into two units, one in the north by Watford City, the other by Medora. Both encompass badland topography along the Little Missouri River with ravines, hills, ridges, and prairie. One of the most interesting features of the park was a burning vein of lignite ignited by a lightning-caused prairie fire in 1951. It only recently burned out. Scoria, one of the most erosion-resistant rocks in this area, is caused by these underground fires baking sand and clay into natural brick. The relationship of the plant communities to the terrain is also interesting. Most areas are grass prairie, except along wetter stream bottoms where cottonwoods are found, and on north- and south-facing slopes. North slopes, because of their more oblique relation to the sun, are cooler and consequently damper. They support ash and juniper trees. Conversely, south-facing slopes receive more direct sunlight and are warmer and drier and support yucca, cactus, and other desert-type species. These varied environments support a varied animal population, including bighorn, bison, pronghorn, beaver, prairie dog, and other small mammals, coyote, fox, bobcat, and many species of birds and reptiles.

There are 70 miles of trails in the park, and more are planned. The southern unit has a better trail system, but cross-country travel is excellent in both units. The footing is precarious in some areas, and the terrain is generally rugged. No open fires are permitted and water should be carried. Topographic maps are valuable for exploring and can be purchased at the park. May to October is the best season, though there is no need to worry about crowds at any time of the year in this little-known park.

For information and a map of the park, contact the Superintendent, Theodore Roosevelt National Memorial Park, Medora, North Dakota 58645.

SOUTH DAKOTA

This state is below average in what it has to offer the backpacker. However, there are a few backpacking opportunities. Generally, the state is a flat grassland bisected by the impounded Missouri River running north and south. The southwest corner is the exception. Here, piled on the earth, are the Black Hills and dug into the earth are the Badlands.

General tourism information is available from the South Dakota State Division of Tourism, Pierre, South Dakota 57501.

Black Hills National Forest and Custer State Park

This national forest, located just west of Rapid City, is about 70 by 110 miles, encompassing 1,233,000 acres. The Black Hills themselves are a huge dome of granite pushed up and then eroded into hills and valleys. Their black appearance comes from the mantle of ponderosa pine which cloaks them. Deer, turkey, coyote, and even mountain goat make their home here. Unfortunately, this area has been almost totally subjugated to the whim of the tourist, even to the extent that a whole mountainside has been chiseled into the likeness of huge human heads. The forest is fairly well saturated with roads, and livestock graze in much of it. Nevertheless, it is a national forest and the public is allowed to use it. Backcountry camping is permitted unless posted otherwise. A backpacker armed with topo maps and a little imagination could do quite well in this area. One small area around Harney Peak has several good trails and some spectacular vistas that make you forget you're in a plains state. Open fires are not permitted in the backcountry unless a permit is obtained.

In a 72,000-acre pocket on the east edge of the forest is the Custer State Park. This is a more arid area of rolling prairie interspersed with pine groves. The wildlife includes mountain goat, bighorn, elk, deer, buffalo, and wild burros. Bisecting the park east and west is the French Creek, which has created a 5-mile-long roadless gorge southeast of Mount Coolidge that is quite inviting to the backpacker. The season is spring through fall.

For information and a map (50¢) of the national forest, contact the Supervisor, Black Hills National Forest, P.O. Box 792, Custer, South Dakota 57730. For information on the Custer State Park, contact the South Dakota Game, Fish, and Parks Department, State Office Building, Pierre, South Dakota 57501.

Badlands National Monument

On a low plateau of soft sedimentary rock east of the Black Hills, erosion has created this 244,000-acre monument of ridges, gullies, canyons, knobs, and scattered stands of cottonwood, yucca, and juniper, laced with fossils of prehistoric mammals that have long since vanished with the marsh that used to be here. The Badlands are home today for prairie dog, coyote, badger, jackrabbit, pronghorn, antelope, deer, and golden eagle. All this makes for an environment that is unique in this country and easily accessible to the backpacker. There are no trails and water must be carried. Nevertheless foot travel is surprisingly easy through the low hills. Backcountry camping is permitted, but one should register with officials and inquire as to what are the best routes. Open fires are not permitted, so bring a camp stove. There is generally little use of the backcountry, though some horsemen may be encountered. Be prepared for temperature extremes, aridity, and sudden storms.

For information and a map of the monument, contact the Superintendent, Badlands National Monument, P.O. Box 72, Interior, South Dakota 57750.

Other Public Lands

These include rolling grasslands mostly in the northwestern part of the state containing pronghorn, deer, grouse, prairie chicken, wild turkey, rabbit, prairie dog, skunk, badger, coyote, and bobcat. The South Dakota unit of the Custer National Forest (see Montana), 3 national grasslands, and Bureau of Land Management lands equal about 1,226,000 acres. These lands are not developed for backpacking and there are no official trails. However, a set of 9 maps has been prepared that shows public ownership. If you are interested in a different sort of cross-country backpacking, these will indicate what's available in the state. Called the Recreation Guide Maps, these maps are available from the State Director, Bureau of Land Management, P.O. Box 30157, Billings, Montana 59107. Maps 1 and 8 show the Custer National Forest and the Grand River National Grassland which are probably the best areas for this type of backpacking. These two maps are also available from the Supervisor, Custer National Forest, P.O. Box 2556, 2601 First Avenue North, Billings, Montana 59103.

WYOMING

This state has a wide variety of environments to offer the backpacker. It boasts the first national park, Yellowstone, the first national forest, Shoshone, and the first national monument, Devils Tower. The lower elevations (which in this state are still over

5,000 feet) are generally grasslands and deserts, but varied terrain can be found throughout the state. In the northwest is a large mountainous area with several national parks and forests. Several mountain chains run north and south about mid-state, and rugged terrain also rises out of the prairie in the northeast by the Black Hills. Trails in the high country are blocked by snow in all but the summer months. The state's population is low, and most backpackers who use the state's resources come from elsewhere. However, overuse is rarely a problem because of the vast acreage of public land suitable for backpacking.

The state caters to tourists, even backpackers, and has excellent literature available. The Wyoming Travel Commission, 2320 Capitol Avenue, Cheyenne, Wyoming 82001, can supply general tourism information.

Yellowstone National Park

This most famous of the national parks, located in the northwest corner of the state, probably brings to mind those very things the backpacker tries to get away from—crowded campgrounds, overused natural areas, obnoxious tourists, tame wild animals, traffic jams, and commercialization. This image is entirely correct for the 1 percent of the park abused by crowd-loving visitors. The remaining 99 percent of the park's 2,222,000 acres contains the most varied wilderness environment a backpacker can find under one jurisdiction.

The center of the park is a volcanic plateau of about 8,000-foot elevation, almost entirely surrounded by mountains, some rising to over 11,000 feet. Nestled in these mountains is 88,960-acre Yellowstone Lake, and throughout the park is found a mosaic of forests, meadows, thermal displays, fossils, canyons, rivers, lakes, and perhaps the greatest concentration of wildlife in the country. Grizzly and black bear, bison, elk, pronghorn, bighorn, coyote, lynx, bobcat, deer, moose, whistling and trumpeter swan, white pelican, and other wildlife are found here. The lakes and streams provide good trout fishing.

For the backpacker, there are 1,100 miles of trails. Use is not as heavy as one might suspect, because Yellowstone, like many national parks, does not receive much publicity as a backpacking area. It is not unusual to be on the Yellowstone backcountry trails for a week without seeing anyone. The park is notorious grizzly country, though, and there are some areas where backpacking is not recommended because of them. The park officials can tell you stories of backpackers who ignored their advice and were treed by grizzlies for the night. They probably won't tell you the more violent tales to avoid upsetting you excessively. You will need to stop in for a fire permit, so ask about bears. The backpacking season is generally May to October, with May, September, and October sometimes becoming quite cold. Winters are among the coldest in the nation. Temperatures generally range from the 50s at night to the 70s during the day in summer with freezing temperatures occurring year-round.

Yellowstone probably has more written about it than any other recreation area in the country. To start with, contact the Superintendent, Yellowstone National Park, Wyoming 82190, to obtain maps and information.

Grand Teton National Park

This 310,000-acre park is located just south of Yellowstone. The Teton Mountains, the central feature of the park, are remarkable, rising 7,000 feet above the surrounding plain. Grand Teton, the tallest, reaches 13,770 feet. The mountains are jagged products of glaciation, with many existing glaciers and snowfields. At the base of the mountains is Jackson Hole, famed as one of the most scenic areas in the country. Pine, spruce, fir, cottonwood, and aspen cover the valleys and mountainsides, and streams and lakes of varying sizes are scattered throughout the park. Like Yellowstone, this park contains much wildlife including the nation's largest herd of elk as well as pronghorn, bighorn, deer, moose, pika, marmot, grizzly and black bear, cougar, lynx, bobcat, beaver, bald and golden eagle, trumpeter swan, and white pelican.

There are 175 miles of trails in the park, which is not much considering the number of tourists using them. Expect company along

the trails. The least-used trails are in the northwest portion of the
park. Also, cross-country travel is permitted, but backpackers are
required to register. There is an extremely rugged, trailless section
of the park just west of Jackson Lake that would be a challenge to
any backpacker. The season is the same as in Yellowstone. All
campfires above the valley floor are banned.

For information and a map of the park, contact the Superintendent, Grand Teton National Park, Moose, Wyoming 83012.

Shoshone National Forest

This 2,431,000-acre forest, located just east of the Yellowstone
and Grand Teton National Parks, was the country's first national
forest established as a forest preserve in 1891. The forest is rug-
gedly magnificent with bare rock peaks interspersed with meadows and forests of pine, spruce, fir, juniper, cottonwood, and aspen.
It generally follows the Continental Divide, with elevations ranging from 4,600 feet to 13,785 feet at Gannett Peak, the highest
point in the state. Wildlife includes deer, bighorn, mountain goat,
antelope, moose, black and grizzly bear, bald and golden eagle,
coyote, a variety of waterfowl and songbirds, and wolves (yes,
wolves, but very few).

The forest is well served by many hundreds of miles of good
trails, but the most attractive areas for the backpacker are the 3
wildernesses and one primitive area covering about half of the
forest. Beginning in the north is the North Absaroka Wilderness
Area with its 351,000 acres of precipitous peaks and canyons.
There are several long trails through the wilderness leading up the
Continental Divide to areas untouched by humans. Glaciers, a
natural bridge, and standing petrified trees are among its interesting features. A few miles south across the North Fork of the
Shoshone River valley begins the vast 687,000-acre Washakie
Wilderness Area. The South Absaroka Wilderness and the Stratified
Primitive Area were combined to create this wilderness in 1972. It
is similar to the North Absaroka Wilderness, with its long trails,
petrified plant remains, and wild, rugged terrain with many lakes
and streams. This is a popular hunting area.

In the south, the Fitzpatrick Wilderness is 191,000 acres of high country. Many of the largest glaciers in the 48 states are found here, as well as numerous alpine lakes. Bare granite peaks seem to be everywhere. Farther south is the Popo Agie Primitive Area, somewhat small at 71,000 acres, but containing more than 200 lakes. It is surrounded by the national forest where many of its trails begin. Like the Fitzpatrick, it has many alpine lakes, canyons, and peaks along its 7 major trails, and as throughout the forest, use is not heavy. Cross-country travel through this open alpine area is possible, but rugged. The high country opens about mid-July.

For information and maps of the forest, wildernesses, and primitive areas, contact the Supervisor, Shoshone National Forest, P.O. Box 961, Cody, Wyoming 82414.

Teton National Forest

Just east and south of the Grand Teton National Park in northwestern Wyoming are the 1,701,000 acres of this national forest. The forest is largely unspoiled forested backcountry with several mountain ranges and the Continental Divide with peaks in the 9,000- to 12,000-foot range. Wildlife includes moose, elk, deer, bighorn, and grizzly bear. While the entire forest is suitable for backpacking with many hundreds of miles of trails, the northern portion is wildest. None of the trails is particularly difficult and cross-country travel is possible in the large alpine areas.

Especially attractive to backpackers is the 557,000-acre Teton Wilderness Area along the eastern boundary abutting the Washakie Wilderness Area in the Shoshone. Over 400 miles of trails are within this area alone, so it seldom gets crowded. The eastern portion of the wilderness has the greatest relief, with high plateaus, mountains, narrow canyons, and river valley meadows with elevations of about 8,000 feet to more than 12,000 feet. The trails are less steep and the terrain is less rugged in the western half of the wilderness where timbered ridges and grassy slopes and meadows are in the 7,500-foot to 10,000-foot elevation range. The heavy-use period is during the hunting season, when excellent hunting attracts thousands of hunters to the high country, but then, as during the regular season, the alpine plateaus of the eastern part provide good cross-country travel opportunities in little-used areas.

For maps and information on the forest and wilderness area, contact the Supervisor, Bridger-Teton National Forests, P.O. Box 1888, Jackson, Wyoming 83001.

Bridger National Forest

The 1,712,000 acres of this forest are divided between two units. One unit extends directly south of the Teton National Forest along the Wyoming Mountain Range. The other extends southeast along the Wind River Range. The forest is mostly high country with many barren high peaks and remote areas. Black and grizzly bear, moose, elk, bighorn, deer, and cougar are found here, as well as excellent lake and stream fishing in the 1,379 lakes and 800 miles of streams.

The southeast unit along the Wind River Range is a backpacker's paradise. Abutting both the Glacier and Popo Agie primitive areas is the 90-mile-long, 392,000-acre Bridger Wilderness Area. This is a wilderness of snowy peaks and granite outcrops, but more than anything, it is an area of lakes, more than 1,300 of them. There are nearly 600 miles of trails reaching these lakes originating from 6 main trailheads, making this one of the most accessible wildernesses in the country. It is possible to be deep in the wilderness in very few miles of hiking. For a real adventure in solitude, the backpacker can take off cross-country to any of the many lakes not reached by trails. You can be sure the fishing will be excellent and you won't meet up with weekend hikers. High passes are open only from mid-July to mid-September, and afternoon rain is common.

The wilderness is divided into 5 units, each with its own wilderness map. There is also a map for the entire forest. For a set of these maps and information on the forest and wilderness area, contact the Supervisor, Bridger-Teton National Forests, P.O. Box 1888, Jackson, Wyoming 83001.

Bighorn National Forest

In north-central Wyoming there is an island of mountains amidst the prairie called the Bighorn National Forest. This 1,114,000-acre forest south of Sheridan contains more than 300 lakes, snow-capped peaks, and glaciers. Forests, open parklands and meadows, and rocky outcrops in elevations to 13,165 feet make for interesting hiking. The pine, spruce, fir, cedar, aspen, and cottonwood forest provide homes for deer, moose, elk, black bear, bighorn, fox, and coyote.

While trails are found throughout the forest, so are many roads. The backpacker looking for solitude should try the 137,000-acre Cloud Peak Primitive Area in the center of the forest. This is high country between 8,500 and 13,165 feet, and the season runs only about mid-June to mid-September. Tall vertical walls of granite from 1,000 to 5,000 feet, 256 lakes, and 50 miles of streams greet the backpacker. There are 81 miles of maintained trails and 10 backcountry campsites, but much of this wilderness is trailless and provides an excellent opportunity for cross-country travel, especially in the open alpine areas.

For information and maps of the forest and primitive area, contact the Supervisor, Bighorn National Forest, P.O. Box 2046, Sheridan, Wyoming 82801.

Medicine Bow National Forest

On the other side of the state, the 1,092,000 acres of this forest are divided among 4 forest units. Two are located in the south-central part of the state west of Laramie and abut the Routt and Roosevelt national forests in Colorado. Another unit is between Laramie and Cheyenne, with the fourth unit farther north extending southeast of Casper. The Thunder Basin National Grassland, administered as a unit of this forest, consists of scattered holdings for a total of about a half-million acres in the northeast part of the state. It does not offer significant backpacking opportunities. See the following discussion of other public lands in the state for reference to it.

The forest lies along several mountain ranges with varying degrees of forest cover. Most peaks are in the 8,000- to 10,000-foot range, with the tallest, Medicine Bow Peak, at 12,013 feet. The 3 southern units are more humid and hence have greater vegetation cover, but in all units interesting rock formations are often found where the pine, spruce, meadows, and grasslands disappear. Black bear, elk, deer, antelope, and beaver are found in the forest, and there is good fishing in the many lakes and streams in the three southern units.

Some good trails in the forest are limited to nonmotorized use, but many roads penetrate all units of the forest. Cross-country travel is one way to find solitude, especially in the 15,000-acre Savage Run Wilderness and the Snowy Range area. The trails in the westernmost unit along the Sierra Madre would be the next best bet. The season is late spring to early fall in most areas of the forest, with snow lingering on in the higher elevations into summer.

For information and a map (50¢) of the forest, contact the Supervisor, Medicine Bow National Forest, 605 Skyline Drive, Laramie, Wyoming 82070.

Flaming Gorge National Recreation Area

This reservoir with 375 miles of shoreline is located in the southwest corner of the state extending into Utah. It is in an arid area, making for an interesting contrast between the blue waterfront of the reservoir and the bright buttes that surround it. In addition to the trout in the reservoir, deer, antelope, and elk graze in the meadows, and waterfowl and other birds are common.

This area is not developed for backpacking. Used by over 1 million people each year, mostly boaters, the reservoir is by no measure a remote wilderness area. This area provides a different sort of sport for the backpacker who likes to wander through the mostly easily traveled terrain surrounding the reservoir. Often, just over the nearest bluff, wilderness seems to stretch for miles. In this barren, arid country, solitude is often just over the next butte. Season is spring through fall.

For information on the reservoir, contact the Area Ranger, Flaming Gorge National Recreation Area, P.O. Box 157, Dutch John, Utah 84023.

Bighorn Canyon National Recreation Area

See Montana, above.

Seedskadee and Pathfinder National Wildlife Refuges

Two wildlife refuges, the Seedskadee and the Pathfinder, where wild-type camping is permitted, provide an excellent opportunity for the backpacker to observe wildlife, especially birds. The Seedskadee is located on the Green River near the town of Green River in the southwest corner of the state, and the Pathfinder is located in the south-central portion of the state adjacent to the Pathfinder Reservoir north of Rawlins. Both are areas of mostly bottomlands surrounded by arid uplands. Travel is cross-country or along existing roads. Wildlife includes a variety of marsh, water, and shore birds, deer, antelope, even moose, and many smaller mammals. The moderate number of visitors seldom leave the vicinity of their motor vehicles in these areas.

For information on the Seedskadee, contact the Manager, Seedskadee National Wildlife Refuge, Green River, Wyoming 82935, contact the Manager Arapaho National Wildlife Refuge, Walden, Colorado 80480, or The Bureau of Land Management, P.O. Box 2834, Casper, Wyoming 82601 for information on the Pathfinder.

Other Public Lands

Most of the state is in public ownership, with the highest concentration of public land in the western two-thirds of the state. The Bureau of Land Management manages over 18 million acres and backpacking is a recognized use. This public landscape includes forested mountains, rolling foothills, grasslands, rivers, lakes, and deserts, as well as geologic formations such as sand dunes, badlands, granite domes, canyons, buttes, and caves. This land is home for thousands of antelope and other wildlife including elk, buffalo, and the rare black-footed ferret.

One of the most interesting though harshest regions is the Red Desert northeast of Rock Springs in southwest Wyoming. This is a high desert in the Great Divide basin with elevations from 6,000 to 10,000 feet where water drains to the interior to evaporate and percolate away. Wild horses, burros, antelope, and a few rare prairie elk can be seen roaming the sagebrush prairie. Sand dunes, buttes, and fossils are also found in this part of the state. Another area, the Bighorn Basin in the north-central part of the state between the Shoshone and Bighorn national forests, provides a more rugged, scenic environment with arid mountains eroded into beautiful hues and impressive canyons.

None of the BLM land is developed for backpacking, and the visitor is on his own in an environment that can be hostile to the unprepared.

For information and maps of BLM lands, contact The Bureau of Land Management, Wyoming State Office, P.O. Box 1828, 2120 Capitol Avenue, Cheyenne, Wyoming 82001.

8

The Midwest: Illinois, Indiana, Iowa, Michigan, Minnesota, Missouri, Ohio, and Wisconsin

While the Midwest does not have the soaring mountains of the East and West, nor the spectacular canyons of the Southwest, it has instead thousands of acres of primitive forests, thousands of miles of free-flowing rivers, and extensive stretches of magnificent Great Lakes shoreline. Most of the region's backpacking opportunities are found in the northern states of Michigan, Minnesota, and Wisconsin, with only a scattering of backpacking areas in the other states. Terrain is generally flat to moderately rolling, and it is easily traversed. These areas are most attractive, though, because of their proximity to the population centers of the Midwest and East industrial belt.

ILLINOIS

By virtue of this state's excellence for agriculture, there exist few backpacking opportunities. The state is mostly flat, but becomes hilly in its extreme southern tip between the confines of the Mississippi and Ohio rivers. Here, a few out-of-the-way pockets of woods and swamps provide primitive experience, but one is never far from roads.

General tourism information is available from the Illinois Division of Tourism, 222 South College, Springfield, Illinois 62704.

Shawnee National Forest and Crab Orchard National Wildlife Refuge

These two adjacent areas are located near the town of Harrisburg in the southern tip of the state. The forest comprises 241,000 acres and the refuge includes about 44,000 acres, mostly of hardwood forest covering rolling hills with occasional eroded rock outcrops and cliffs. Other interesting features include prehistoric stone forts and Indian mounds, Ohio and Mississippi river bluffs and shoreline, and the LaRue-Pine Hills Ecological area, which contains rare plants and towering limestone bluffs (no overnight camping without a permit). The wildlife refuge includes low, wet areas, as well as several large bodies of water. It is a favorite resting place for migratory waterfowl, game, and songbirds. Fishing is good for bass, catfish, crappie, and bluegill.

Little true wilderness is found in the forest and refuge, with about one-half of the area privately owned. The main attraction is the 120-mile Shawnee Hiking Trail, following woodland paths as well as secondary roads. There are no other long-distance back-country trails in the forest and refuge, but a few abandoned roads are suitable for backpacking. Cross-country travel is easiest in the non-growing-season months. (Camping is permitted only on designated sites in the refuge.)

For information and a map of the forest, contact the Supervisor, Shawnee National Forest, 317 East Poplar, Harrisburg, Illinois 62946. For information on the refuge, contact the Refuge Manager, Crab Orchard National Wildlife Refuge, P.O. Box J, Carterville, Illinois 62918.

INDIANA

Like Illinois, Indiana is well plowed under in the north, but offers limited backpacking opportunities in the extreme south. A

Beltrami Island State Forest
Voyageurs National Park
Pine Island State Forest
Superior National Forest
Koochiching State Forest
Kabetogami State Forest
Isle Royal National Park
Chippewa National Forest
Apostle Islands National Lakeshore
Porcupine Mountains Wilderness State Park
Pictured Rocks National Lakeshore
George H. Crosby Manitou State Park
Brule River State Forest
Ottawa National Forest
Hiawatha National Forest

MINNESOTA

Chequamegon National Forest
Flambeau River State Forest
MICHIGAN
Nicolet National Forest
Huron National Forest
WISCONSIN
Black River State Forest
American Legion State Forest and Northern Highlands State Forest
Sleeping Bear Dunes National Lakeshore

ST. PAUL

Kettle Moraine State Forest
Manistee National Forest

MADISON
MILWAUKEE
LANSING
DETROIT

IOWA

DES MOINES

OHIO

COLUMBUS

ILLINOIS
INDIANA

SPRINGFIELD
INDIANAPOLIS

Zaleski State Forest

MISSOURI

Hoosier National Forest

KANSAS CITY
ST. LOUIS
Shawnee State Forest

JEFFERSON CITY
Crab Orchard National Wildlife Refuge

Shawnee National Forest

Mark Twain National Forest

Mississippi River
Illinois River

✹ Relatively large-acreage area
✶ Comparatively small-acreage area

single small national forest and a few state forests constitute the backpacking resource.

General tourism information is available from the Indiana Department of Commerce, Tourism Division, 336 State House, Indianapolis, Indiana 46204.

Hoosier National Forest

This forest is located in south-central Indiana near the town of Bedford and comprises 180,000 acres. The forest is not outstanding for its natural attributes, but it does have a variety of small mammals and migrating waterfowl, and a magnificent stand of black walnut trees. Rivers, a reservoir, and many small lakes are found throughout these hardwood forested hills.

About three-quarters of the land within the forest boundary is privately owned and there are no good long-distance backpacking trails. However, there are over 50 miles of newly constructed trails. Cross-country travel is best from fall to spring and provides good vistas from the ridges.

For information and a map of the forest, contact the Supervisor, Hoosier National Forest, 1615 J Street, Bedford, Indiana 47421.

Indiana State Forests

The state is currently conducting a backcountry area and trail development program. A 1,000-acre area in the Clark State Forest by Henryville and a 2,500-acre area in the Jackson-Washington State Forest near Brownstown presently provide cross-country travel and backcountry camping opportunities. There are no formal trails, but old roads and fire lanes provide access among the forested hills. A long-distance backpack trail, the Knobstone Trail, is also planned for development.

For maps and up-to-date information on backpack facility development in the state, contact the Indiana Department of Natural Resources, Division of State Forests, 6th floor, State Office Building, Indianapolis, Indiana 46204.

IOWA

Iowa ranks high among the "civilized" states. There are 107 Iowa state parks, forests, and preserves, and none are suitable for backpacking. Primitive camping is permitted with permission in Shimek Forest, near Farmington (3,700 acres); Stephens Forest, near Chariton (4,200 acres); and Yellow River Forest near Mc-Gregor (4,200 acres). If you live near one and are desperate for a short weekend of primitive camping, more information can be obtained from the Iowa Conservation Commission, 300 Fourth Street, Des Moines, Iowa 50309.

MICHIGAN

Michigan shares the spotlight with Minnesota and Wisconsin as the Midwest's showplaces for backpacking. It is blessed with extensive forests, especially in the north, and with water everywhere —around it and in it. The state consists of two peninsulas, the Upper and Lower. The Upper Peninsula is mostly forested, often swampy, and bounded on the north by Lake Superior and on the south by northern Lake Michigan. It tends to get a bit crowded in the summer when it is visited by the inhabitants of Detroit and southern Michigan, but otherwise provides good backpacking opportunities on both state and federal land. The Lower Peninsula is mostly cut-over, farmed, or developed for vacation homes, but some backpacking opportunities can be found in the northern half of this peninsula. The state receives much snow and cold temperatures in the winter, so the season for most backpackers is late spring through fall. Mosquitoes and black flies can be bothersome until about mid-summer.

General tourism information is available from the Michigan Department of Commerce, Tourist Council, Suite 102 Commerce Center, 300 South Capitol Avenue, Lansing, Michigan 48933.

Isle Royale National Park

This island is the wilderness gem of the Midwest, a roadless land of wild creatures, forests, lakes, and scenic shoreline. Its 539,000 unspoiled acres in Lake Superior are accessible only by boat or float plane. More than 30 interior lakes are surrounded by mixed hardwoods and conifers, and the entire island is itself surrounded by the picturesque islets and bays of the island's Lake Superior shoreline. The island is famed for its moose and wolf packs, and it also supports a population of beaver, fox, snowshoe hare, and various birds. Fishing is good both on the 8,500 acres of the interior lakes and along the shoreline. To complete the northwoods environment, there are mosquitoes and black flies in early summer and leeches in the inland waters.

The island is rugged in places, but generally the 160 miles of trails are not difficult. The most popular is the Greenstone Ridge Trail extending down the island's backbone, but all the trails receive heavy use. Cross-country travel and backcountry camping are permitted throughout the park with only a fire permit required. However, dense vegetation and numerous bogs make cross-country travel difficult. Even though the park is heavily used during the summer, this is the only season it is open (May-October). Transportation to the island is available from Copper Harbor and Houghton, Michigan, and from Grand Portage, Minnesota.

For information and a map of the park, contact the Superintendent, Isle Royale National Park, 87 Ripley Street, Houghton, Michigan 49931.

Ottawa National Forest

Being located in the western Upper Peninsula east of Ironwood on the northern border of Wisconsin, this forest is closer to most Wisconsin residents than to those of Michigan. A typically northwoods environment, the 924,000-acre forest has numerous lakes and rivers among the mixed hardwood and conifer stands. There is also a small portion of Lake Superior shoreline. Short trails are found throughout the forest, and additional longer trails are being developed.

A 21,000-acre solid block of public land called the Sylvania Recreation Area is the big attraction for the backpacker. The area contains maple, birch, hemlock, and associated species of northern hardwoods, and scattered pine, spruce, and fir, much of it still virgin timber. The many lakes in the area are exceptionally clear and pure, and a virgin-type fish population has developed in them, as most are relatively large and old. Deer, black bear, raccoon, skunk, beaver, otter, muskrat, porcupine, coyote, fox, mink, and other small mammals, and loon and eagle are found here. Lake fishing is good.

But the best characteristic of Sylvania is that roads only skirt the boundaries and no motors are allowed. Unfortunately, a resource of this quality attracts many users. There are 84 wilderness-type camping units assigned by permit on a first-come, first-served basis. This is an ideal area to visit after Labor Day.

For information and a map of the forest and a brochure on the Sylvania Recreation Area, contact the Supervisor, Ottawa National Forest, Ironwood, Michigan 49938.

Hiawatha National Forest

This forest's 865,000 acres are divided into two units, one in the middle and one in the eastern end of the Upper Peninsula. The dense stands of mixed hardwoods and conifers, intermittent wetlands, and scattered rolling hills are punctuated by streams and many lakes, including portions of shoreline along Lake Michigan, Lake Huron, and Lake Superior. Wildlife includes deer, black bear, pine marten, and other small mammals, sandhill crane, bald eagle, and a variety of game fish. There have been reported sightings of both wolf and moose in the forest. This forest has also earned the unusual distinction of being a good wild mushroom hunting ground.

Two major hiking trails are under construction in the forest (they are planned for completion during 1980; major portions are or will be usable sooner): The Bay de Noc-Grand Island Trail will run from near Rapid River to Christmas (46 miles) and The North Country Trail will cross both units of the forest. The segment crossing the east unit will run from near St. Ignace to Tahquamenon Falls State Park (75 miles). The segment crossing the west unit will run from near Munising to the Rock River Canyon Area (18 miles).

Most of the forest is in public ownership and is well laced with primitive roads. These can be used for planning loop trips of 5 to 10 miles in length. Cross-country travel is difficult because of the dense vegetation and numerous bogs. State fire laws apply to national forest lands, and a fire permit may at times be needed for backcountry travel.

For information and a map of the forest, contact the Supervisor, Hiawatha National Forest, Escanaba, Michigan 49829.

Huron-Manistee National Forests

These two forests are managed jointly. The Huron is located in the northeastern portion of the Lower Peninsula by Tawas City, and the Manistee is in the northwestern portion of the Lower Peninsula by Ludington. Together they equal 901,000 acres. Deer, small mammals, and various birds inhabit the forests, and there is good stream fishing, but these forests have been extensively cut-over and have lost their wilderness character. In addition, they are both heavily used by visitors from the nearby urban centers. The only backpacking opportunities of significance are found on the Michigan Riding and Hiking Trails found in these forests (see below), but even these trails do not offer the secluded natural experience most backpackers are seeking. Plans for the development of good backpacking trails in both of these forests may result in additional opportunities in the future.

For information and maps of these forests, contact the Supervisor, Huron-Manistee National Forests, 421 South Mitchell Street, Cadillac, Michigan 49601.

Pictured Rocks National Lakeshore

Forty miles of multicolored sandstone cliffs and sand and pebble beaches distinguish this national lakeshore along Lake Superior in the eastern Upper Peninsula near Munising Michigan. This is one of the newer additions to the nation's natural recreation estate and is still in the acquisition stage. Resourceful backpackers can find their way along existing trails, logging roads, and cross-country to many secluded woods and shoreline environments. This national lakeshore is not heavily used yet, but there is also much private land that should be respected.

The Superintendent, Pictured Rocks National Lakeshore, P.O. Box 32, Munising, Michigan 49862, can provide information on backpacking. Since the lakeshore is not developed for backpacking yet, it would be wise to drop into the lakeshore headquarters before you begin your trip to inform the superintendent of your plans.

Sleeping Bear Dunes National Lakeshore

This national lakeshore is a composite of dunes, ridges, valleys, plains, streams, lakes, and a few islands located in the northwest corner of the Lower Peninsula near Glen Haven, Michigan. Like Pictured Rocks National Lakeshore, this newly designated national lakeshore has not been developed for backpacking and there is much private land within its boundaries. Five thousand acres of semiwilderness on South Manitou Island offer a rudimentary trail system and primitive camping. Access to this island during the summer is by passenger ferry from Leland, Michigan.

Information and a map of the lakeshore is available from the Superintendent, Sleeping Bear Dunes National Lakeshore, 400 Main Street, Frankfort, Michigan 49635. Any plans for backpacking in this area would best be cleared with the superintendent before you begin.

Porcupine Mountains Wilderness State Park

This outstanding state park is located near Ontonagon in the western Upper Peninsula and is one of the few remaining wilderness areas in the Midwest. Its 58,000 acres contain towering stands of virgin hardwoods, pine, and hemlock, with waterfalls, lakes, rivers, gorges, and spectacular Lake Superior shoreline. It is home for deer, black bear, coyote, with a variety of small mammals, and birds. Fishing for trout and other species is good. What makes this area unique is its elevation—up to 2,000 feet, making it one of the highest land masses between the Appalachians and the Black

Hills. The elevation lends an alpine quality to the environment, making it seem much loftier than it actually is.

Eighty miles of trails wind up the hillsides, and it is frequently steep and rugged traveling. Registered backpackers may camp anywhere along the trails, though designated sites are provided. Like the Sylvania Recreation Area in the Ottawa National Forest, the "Porkies" are popular in summer. The best season to visit them is in the fall when pesty insects and crowds are replaced by gorgeous fall colors.

For information and a map of the park, contact the Superintendent, Porcupine Mountains Wilderness State Park, Route 2, Ontonagon, Michigan 49953.

Michigan State Forests

Michigan has 33 state forests. The area within the forest boundaries in public ownership averages about 60 percent, totaling over 3.8 million acres. Camping is allowed on this state land unless posted otherwise. The many environments of Michigan are represented in these state forests and since they are not publicized for backpacking and primitive camping, there is no problem with overuse by backpackers. Few of these forests are developed for backpacking, though, and the user is often on his own to find trails and logging roads suitable for backpacking. The best state forests for backpacking are found in the Upper Peninsula in the vicinity of the two national forests. A few "quiet areas" have been established for nonmotorized trail use.

For information and location of state forests and quiet areas, contact the Forestry Division of the Michigan Department of Natural Resources, Stevens T. Mason Building, Lansing, Michigan 48926. County maps that show the state forests may be obtained, up to 6 per request, from the Lands Division of the Michigan Department of Natural Resources, same address as above.

Michigan Riding and Hiking Trails

These trails are located in the northern Lower Peninsula and consist of the Michigan Shore-to-Shore Trail (210 miles) and its spur trails. These trails are by no means paths to wilderness adventure, but they are flanked by natural country and public lands. Camping is generally limited to public trail camps, except where the trail crosses public land and trailside camping is permitted. The trails are used by hikers, horseback riders, and, illegally, by motorcyclists.

A map and description of the trail is available from the Recreation Division of the Michigan Department of Natural Resources, Stevens T. Mason Building, Lansing, Michigan 48926.

MINNESOTA

This state, along with Maine, is most representative of the northwoods environment. It evokes an image of birch trees ringing lakes with excellent fishing and of forests stretching almost endlessly. This image is correct. Minnesota has over 15,000 lakes of 10 acres or more and the northern half of the state is almost continuous forests on rolling hills, flatlands, and wet low areas. The many trails, extensive public lands, and mostly gentle terrain make this an excellent backpacking state. Its chief drawback is that mosquitoes and black flies are numerous in the early summer. Also, it rains quite a bit and the many bog areas are often impassable. Summer and early fall are the best backpacking seasons, with abundant snowfall making this state a mecca for snowshoers and skiers in the winter.

General tourism information is available from the Vacation Information Bureau, Minnesota Department of Economic Development, 57 West Seventh Street, St. Paul, Minnesota 55102.

Superior National Forest

This national forest is the showplace of Minnesota wilderness. Its 2,128,000 acres in northeast Minnesota north of Duluth boast over 2,000 lakes with rugged shorelines, sand beaches, beckoning islands, and over 400,000 acres of virgin forest. One of the finest wilderness areas in the country is in this forest, within a day's drive of Chicago. The ever-present granite outcroppings are part

of the southern extension of the Laurentian Shield, which under-
lies over 2 million square miles of Canada. Dating back 2½ billion
years, they are among the oldest rocks on the North American
continent. These lichen-covered rocks are as much a part of this
forest as the trees and lakes, and they seem to literally pile up in
the eastern part of the forest where it is more steep and rugged,
especially along Lake Superior. Nestled within the conifers, birch,
and other hardwoods are numerous lakes and streams supporting
more than 30 species of fish, including musky, walleye, northern
pike, bass, trout, and panfish. In addition to the common small
woodland mammals, deer, bobcat, lynx, black bear, and moose may
be spotted. The forest also provides a refuge for the eastern timber
wolf and the bald eagle, both classified as endangered species. But
because of the abundant water and woods, the most prevalent
wildlife in early summer seems to be the mosquitoes and black
flies, neither of which, unfortunately, is listed as endangered.

The pattern of woods and water has made this forest a wonder-
land for the canoe traveler. The Boundary Waters Canoe Area
(BWCA) within the forest is the most popular canoe area in the
United States and this has resulted in controls on the use of motors
in certain northern areas of the forest. The virtues that make this
a good resource for the canoeist likewise attract the backpacker.
While this area is a site for mining and timber interests, the overall
impact is that of a wilderness just waiting to be explored.

There is no need to travel cross-country in the Superior, unless
that is your inclination. A system of trails penetrates the forest,
with those in the BWCA providing the best opportunities for the
backpacker. The season is year-round for those who backpack
with snowshoes and cross-country skis in the winter. No motors,
including snowmobiles, are allowed on the trails within the
BWCA. Trail lengths range from a few miles to the 36-mile
Kekekabic Trail, with total trail mileage of over 125 miles. To
protect the exceptional wilderness of the BWCA from the heavy
use it receives from canoeists, there are restrictions on group size
and prohibition of carrying nonburnable disposable containers.
A permit is required at all times and reservations are necessary
mid-May to Labor Day. Such special restrictions are not in effect

for the forest proper, where over 200 miles of snowmobile trails and many miles of other designated and undesignated trails comprise less heavily used backpacking resources.

For information and a map of the forest, including the BWCA, contact the Supervisor, Superior National Forest, P.O. Box 338, Duluth, Minnesota 55801.

Chippewa National Forest

The "Chip" covers about 650,000 acres in north-central Minnesota by the town of Cass Lake. This forest is about one-third water, with several large lakes containing walleye, northern pike, and panfish. Several large stands of virgin red pine are found in this mostly coniferous forest, home for deer, black bear, smaller woodland mammals, and a variety of upland birds and waterfowl.

The forest does not have the wilderness attributes of Superior National Forest, and only about one-half of the land within the forest boundaries is in public ownership. Development of intensive recreation facilities on the larger lakes has taken priority in the forest, and this as well as the great amount of private in-holdings has limited backpacking trail development. Many miles of trails do exist, though, and backcountry camping is allowed on public property. However, just about anything this forest has to offer the backpacker, the Superior National Forest has more and better of.

For information and a general map of the forest, contact the Supervisor, Chippewa National Forest, Cass Lake, Minnesota 56633. Detailed forest maps showing recreational trails (indispensable for the backpacker) must be purchased from this address.

Voyageurs National Park

This is one of the nation's newer parks, located on the north-central border of the state just east of International Falls. When formally established, the park will include 219,000 acres, of which about 80,000 acres will be water. The main feature of the park is the Kabetogama Peninsula surrounded by large lakes. Like most of the park, it is an undeveloped forest of fir, spruce, pine, aspen, and birch, broken by bogs and many lakes. These lakes are dotted with islands and are ringed by shorelines of bays, rocky coves, and cliffs. Fishing is good for walleye, northern pike, bass, trout, and panfish. Moose, black bear, deer, fur-bearers, and waterfowl are also among the park's inhabitants.

This is primarily boat and canoe country. However, just as in the Boundary Waters Canoe Area, trails will eventually be developed in the park. Presently, foot access is primarily along old logging roads and game trails. The interior lakes of the Kabetogama Peninsula are only accessible by foot trail, but these trails begin at boat camps along the shore of the peninsula. Backpackers who manage to make their way to this pristine backcountry will be rewarded by excellent campsites among the rock outcrops and cliffs on the shores of the many remote, beautiful lakes.

For information and a map of the park, contact the Superintendent, Voyageurs National Park, P.O. Box 50, International Falls, Minnesota 56649.

George H. Crosby Manitou State Park

This state park covers about 7 square miles and is located near Lake Superior about 50 miles north of Duluth. Although not a large area, it is designed exclusively for backpacking. The 20 or so miles of trails loop and wind their way along the rugged, forested terrain in this surprisingly mountainous part of the state. Backcountry camping is permitted only in established trailside campsites. While this area provides an excellent backpacking opportunity, it is upstaged by the nearby Superior National Forest.

For a trail map, contact the Minnesota Department of Natural Resources, Division of Parks and Recreation, Centennial Office Building, St. Paul, Minnesota 55155. (You may also wish to ask for information on the Recreation Corridor along the North Shore, under development in 1978.)

Minnesota State Forests

The state has 55 state forests encompassing almost three million acres, most of which are in the north and in the southeast along the Mississippi River. Few are specifically developed for back-packing, though all allow backpacking and backcountry camping on public land. Over 1,600 miles of recreational trails of various kinds are found in these forests. The trick is obtaining informa-tion on them. For the experienced backpacker who is interested in traveling cross-country where few others tread, the following strategy is recommended: Obtain a Minnesota highway map from the Minnesota Department of Highways, State Highway Building, St. Paul, Minnesota 55155. This map shows names and location of the forests. When you have chosen one that appears to have potential (the northern forests are the best), write to the Min-nesota Department of Natural Resources, Division of Parks and Recreation, Centennial Office Building, St. Paul, Minnesota 55155, and tell them what you are planning. They will provide informa-tion and/or refer you to the appropriate ranger station. For those interested in trail hiking in the forests, contact the Trail Coordi-nator, 320 Centennial Office Building, St. Paul, Minnesota 55155, for the latest information on the development of trails in the state forests suitable for backpacking.

These large, wild state forests are the most attractive:

BELTRAMI ISLAND STATE FOREST

This pine forest and peat bog just south of the Lake of the Woods in northern Minnesota is one of the wildest areas left in the state. It contains the last remaining herd of caribou and the largest concentration of moose in the United States as well as elk, black bear, many species of birds, fur-bearers, and wolves. There are no backpacking trails as such, but there are old and primitive roads leading into the interior, and cross-country travel is possible.

PINE ISLAND AND KOOCHICHING STATE FORESTS

These are located just east of Beltrami Island State Forest in north-central Minnesota and their environments are similar to it. Both are rather heavily lumbered, but the wilderness quality of the area has remained. Access is via primitive roads and by cross-country travel.

KABETOGAMA STATE FOREST

This forest lies astride the western boundary of the Superior National Forest and is environmentally similar to it. There is more water in it than in those state forests mentioned above, and one loop trail of about 30 to 40 miles to the east of Pelican Lake, half on the roads and half off, provides access. The map of Superior National Forest also covers this state forest.

MISSOURI

It is unfortunate that this state does not have more backpacking trails. The state is rich in natural environments, from hills of dense hardwood forests that burst brilliant with color in the fall to impressive limestone cliffs and caves. Perhaps it is the relative scarcity of backpacking trails and the many rivers that make canoeing the more popular means of exploring this state. Cross-country travel on federal land in the state expands the backpacking options. The warm season is about 8 months long, with cross-country travel best in early spring and late fall.

General tourism information is available from the Missouri Tourism Commission, 308 East High Street, Jefferson City, Missouri, 65101.

Mark Twain National Forest

This forest's 1,455,000 acres are divided into 9 units, generally in the southeastern part of the state. The forest is characterized by karst topography—easily dissolved limestone crust that erodes to form ridges, rolling hills, deep hollows, and underground streams, caverns, and sinkholes. Valley hardwoods provide a spring bloom of dogwood and redbud, and a fall blaze of color. The drier uplands are sheathed in short-leaf pine and oak, with prairie and barren rock outcrops, home for tarantulas and scorpions. The abundant wildlife includes deer, turkey, squirrel, mink, rabbit, bobcat, raccoon, opossum, fox, beaver, coyote, skunk, woodchuck, and quail. Streams contain smallmouth bass, panfish, and walleye.

The Mark Twain is heavily lumbered and there are many hunters in season, but several maintained trails, logging roads, a wilderness and cross-country travel can take one away from these intrusions. The approximately 150 miles of maintained trails consist of trails from 6 to 25 miles long. Some are loops. Although you will have to share these with the horsemen, off-road vehicles are prohibited. In addition, the recently designated 12,000-acre Hercules Glades Wilderness has a good trail system and provides some of the best scenery in the forest. Cedar and oak trees are interspersed with glades of native prairie grasses and limestone outcrops among the steep hillsides. There are limited open water sources and a permit is required for entry. The Big Piney and Berryman trails are loops. Probably the best way to see this forest, though, is to obtain topographic maps and head out cross-country. If you're a novice, go with someone who isn't. In tame forests like those of Missouri, the best way to find wilderness and solitude is by cross-country travel, easiest early spring and late fall (this is the visitation season, however). It takes more research and planning, but if you are successful you can wind your way so deep into the woods that neither the loggers, nor the horsemen, nor the hunters, nor the off-road vehicle users will be able to find you.

For information and a map of the forest, contact the Supervisor, Mark Twain National Forest, P.O. Box 937, Rolla, Missouri 65401. For additional information on trails in the forest, contact the Missouri Department of Natural Resources, 1204 Jefferson Building, Jefferson City, Missouri 65101.

Other Trails

There are four backpacking trails in the state in addition to those mentioned above where motors are prohibited: Lake Wappapello Trail, a 15-mile loop through rugged Ozark upland north of Poplar Bluff in Lake Wappapello State park; Peewah Trail, a

10-mile system on the loess hills above the Mississippi River north of Cape Girardeau in the Trail of Tears State Park; Rockywood Trail, a 10-mile loop through the cedar glades and rock outcrops in Washington State Park; Whispering Pine Trail, a 10-mile figure-8 system in the sandstone/granite outcrops and forests of Hawn State Park 60 miles south of St. Louis. All trail users must register and camp in designated sites on each of these trails.

For information and maps, contact the Missouri Department of Natural Resources, P.O. Box 176, Jefferson City, Missouri 65102.

OHIO

Obviously, one will find little wilderness in Ohio. As in Illinois and Indiana, farms have replaced forests and, except for a few areas in southern Ohio, the backpacker will have to pursue his activity elsewhere (the Wayne National Forest in this state is generally unsuitable for backpacking). The backpacking season in southern Ohio is just about year-round.

General tourism information is available from the Ohio Development Department, 65 South Front Street, Columbus, Ohio 43215.

Shawnee and Zaleski State Forests

Both are located in the hill country of southern Ohio, with the Shawnee near Portsmouth and the Zaleski west of Athens. The hills are not high but surprisingly steep, and cloaked in a mantle of pine and hardwoods that become brilliant in the fall. Wildlife includes deer, small mammals, and many birds.

There is one trail in the Shawnee that, for this part of the country, is excellent. Its 50 miles connect several small lakes. Another good 20-mile trail is found in the Zaleski. A fire permit is required for primitive camping along these trails and camping is permitted in designated sites only.

For trail and forest maps, write the Division of Forestry, Department of Natural Resources, 1952 Belcher Drive, Fountain Square, Columbus, Ohio 43224.

Buckeye Trail

This trail is more of a hiking trail than a backpacking trail, and mostly follows back roads, canals, public and private forest lands. It may be of interest to Ohioans looking for an opportunity for a quick weekender as some sections of the trail traverse public forestlands. The Buckeye Trail Association has established and marked this 1,014-mile trail route encircling Ohio for hiking and bridle use, and it may be used for such by anyone. It traverses a cross-section of Ohio, from forests to cities. Campsites are not yet frequent enough to permit trailside camping every night along the trail, but motor campgrounds often can be found. Every section of the trail is well covered by literature and guidebooks, and maps are available for sale by the Association.

The free pamphlet, "The Buckeye Trail," is available from the Buckeye Trail Association, Inc., P.O. Box 254, Worthington, Ohio 43085.

WISCONSIN

Wisconsin is very similar to its sister across the lake, Michigan, as far as backpacking opportunities go. It is mostly agrarian in the south, but in the northern half of the state, the forest holds its dominance. One must travel to the extreme northern portion of the state, though, to find a quality backpacking experience.

There is little rugged terrain in the state. As one travels north, hardwood forests transform into mixed stands of hardwood and conifers in an undulating rhythm of gently rolling hills. The state is bounded on the east by Lake Michigan and about half of its northern boundary is imposing Lake Superior shoreline. Also like Michigan and Minnesota, Wisconsin is blessed by an abundant water resource, in the form of both interior lakes and rivers, and the shoreline of two Great Lakes. Although it seems that all of Chicago uses Wisconsin as a getaway and the state is rather tourist oriented, unsaturated backpacking havens can still be found. The season is late spring through fall with considerable snowfall in the winter and bothersome insects in early summer.

General tourism information is available from the Vacation and Travel Service, P.O. Box 450, Madison, Wisconsin 53701.

Chequamegon National Forest

These 838,000 acres of northern Wisconsin lakes and woods are divided among 5 Ranger Districts located near the town of Park Falls. The pine and spruce forests support a population of black bear, coyote, deer, snowshoe hare, gray squirrel, ruffed grouse, and other small mammals and birds. Its more than 400 lakes and over 460 miles of streams are home for brown, brook, and rainbow trout; musky; northern pike; walleye; bass; and panfish. The terrain is generally flat to rolling, and it is well drained.

Almost all the land within the forest boundaries in all districts is in public ownership. The forest is popular for outdoor sports year-round, including snowmobiling in the winter, but the backpacker can get away from all this by traveling cross-country in the many large roadless areas or by taking the North Country Trail (closed to motorized use) across the northern unit of the forest or the Flambeau Trail in the middle unit. A portion of the North Country Trail passes through the 6,538-acre Rainbow Lake Wilderness Area, located in the Washburn Ranger District. In addition a forty mile section of the Ice Age Trail has been completed in the Medford Ranger District. This section has recently been designated as a National Recreation Trail and gives the hiker intimate contact with the landforms that were created when the last glacier covered Wisconsin. Unfortunately, none of these long-distance trails have loop possibilities, but they are excellent otherwise.

For information and a map of the forest, contact the Supervisor, Chequamegon National Forest, P.O. Box 280, Park Falls, Wisconsin 54552.

Nicolet National Forest

This forest is found astride the Michigan-Wisconsin border, just east of Rhinelander in the northeast corner of the state. It is smaller than the Chequamegon (650,000 acres), but a little closer to the heavy populations of southern Wisconsin and northern

Illinois. The environment is typically northwoods, similar to that of the Chequamegon, including many lakes, rivers, and streams, and forests of pine, spruce, balsam, cedar, and hardwoods. Trout and musky are found in the lakes and streams and the forest supports deer and smaller wildlife. This country is generally rolling and serves as the headwaters of many of Wisconsin's popular scenic canoeing rivers, including the Pine, Popple, Wisconsin, Peshtigo, and Oconto rivers.

The forest is not quite as attractive for backpacking as the Chequamegon. It is more heavily used by nonbackpacking recreationists, especially snowmobilers in the winter, and there is a bit more private ownership within the boundaries, mostly around the lakes. Abundant backpacking opportunities can still be found in this forest, though. About a half-dozen marked snowmobile trails in the forest, ranging from about 10 to 25 miles each, some loops, make fine spring, summer, and fall hiking trails. Cross-country travel along the rivers, especially the Pine, is also rewarding. Although this forest is relatively heavily used in the summer, it is easy to get away from the bulk of the tourists; the northern portion of the forest offers the greatest solitude. Fall is a beautiful time here when insects, and many of the tourists, are gone.

For information and a map of the forest, contact the Supervisor, Nicolet National Forest, Federal Building, Rhinelander, Wisconsin 54501.

Apostle Islands National Lakeshore

This national lakeshore is very near to the Chequamegon, just north of it off the northernmost tip of Wisconsin. There are 23 islands in the group, 3 of them are state forests and all are part of the national lakeshore. These forested islands of mixed hardwoods and conifers support small mammals and birds, with lake fishing off the sand beach and rocky cliff shoreline.

The isolation that has preserved these islands as the wildest environment in the state also serves to make these islands difficult for the backpacker to reach. The nearest island is within about 1 mile of the mainland, and each island is on the average within about 1 mile from at least one other island, making this an ideal opportunity for island-hopping in a small boat. There is no ferry service, so the backpacker is on his own to find transportation out to them. (Canoes are not officially recommended for inter-island travel.) After reaching them, though, the backpacker has many square miles of virtually unspoiled wilderness reminiscent of Isle Royale to tromp around in. The largest island, Stockton, is about 13 square miles. Travel via primitive trails is supplemented by cross-country travel and backcountry camping is permitted on all public land. Travel to the Apostles takes a little extra planning, but is well worth the effort.

For information on backpacking the Apostles, contact the Superintendent, Apostle Islands National Lakeshore, 1972 Centennial Drive, Bayfield, Wisconsin 54814. The Apostles are also included in the Chequamegon maps mentioned above.

Wisconsin State Forests

Many thousands of acres of public land suitable for backpacking are found in the state's state forests. Most are in the northern part of the state. Hiking and backcountry camping is permitted on any state forest land (except in the Kettle Moraine State Forest) unless posted otherwise. A camping permit is required.

The following selected state forests offer fair-to-good backpacking opportunities:

NORTHERN HIGHLAND STATE FOREST AND AMERICAN LEGION

This state forest is located in north-central Wisconsin, and has lakes, streams, and many miles of backcountry hiking trails. Wilderness camping units have been developed. For information, contact the Trout Lake Forestry Headquarters, Route 1, P.O. Box 45, Boulder Junction, Wisconsin 54512.

BLACK RIVER STATE FOREST

The Black River (actually tea-colored) and a few lakes are found in this state forest in west-central Wisconsin. There are some hiking/snowmobile trails in the forest and hiking along the river on deer paths is possible and quite beautiful in the fall. For information, contact the Black River State Forest, Route 4, Box 5, Black River Falls, Wisconsin 54615.

BRULE RIVER STATE FOREST

The Brule River, in northwestern Wisconsin, is this forest's biggest attraction. Canoe campsites along the river are accessible to the backpacker. A 24½-mile trail also winds through the forest. For information, contact the Brule River State Forest Headquarters, Brule River, Wisconsin 54820.

FLAMBEAU RIVER STATE FOREST

Several loop trails of moderate length are found in this northern Wisconsin forest. The Flambeau River is one of the state's finest, and though there are some boggy areas, hiking along it is possible and campsites can be found along the river. For information, contact the Flambeau River State Forest, Winter, Wisconsin 54896.

KETTLE MORAINE STATE FOREST

Located in southeastern Wisconsin, this forest is most accessible to the large population centers and consequently is heavily used. As the name suggests, the forest lies atop a glacial moraine and contains many kettle lakes, formed when huge buried hunks of ice melted as the glaciers retreated and left large "kettle holes." The forest has two units, with the northern units containing more than a dozen trails. Camping is permitted only in designated areas, though. The Glacier Trail, about 25 miles long, is complete with trailside shelters, which must be reserved in advance. For information, contact the Kettle Moraine State Forest, P.O. Box 426, Cambellsport, Wisconsin 53010.

Wisconsin State Trails

These are by no means wilderness trails, sometimes passing through populated areas, but they do provide the beginner or one who prefers a more civilized trail with a good backpacking opportunity. The Tuscobia-Park Falls Trail in north-central Wisconsin is the best for backpacking, with bicyclists sharing the right-of-way on the Ahnapee Trail on the Door Peninsula and on the Elroy-Sparta and Sugar River trails in southern Wisconsin. Camping is limited to designated sites. The Wisconsin Department of Natural Resources, P.O. Box 7921, Madison, Wisconsin 53707, can provide maps and information.

County Forests in Wisconsin

The state has 28 county forests totaling 2.25 million acres generally open to backcountry camping, but usually providing only a mediocre backpacking experience. Those in the northern part of the state are the most attractive, though all are short on trails. Primitive and abandoned logging roads and cross-country travel provide access. Information on individual county forests is available from the respective county court houses. The location of county forests and county seats (as well as state forests) are shown on the Wisconsin highway map available from the Department of Transportation, Division of Highways, State Office Building, P.O. Box 40, Madison, Wisconsin 53702. Planning a trip to one of these forests requires some research and usually a topo map, but the backpacker won't have to worry about crowds.

9

The South: Alabama, Arkansas, Florida, Georgia, Kentucky, Louisiana, Mississippi, North Carolina, Oklahoma, South Carolina, Tennessee, Texas, Virginia, and West Virginia

The South has an interesting mixture of backpacking environments. The thick southern Appalachian forests of hardwoods and conifers offer the bulk of the backpacking opportunities in this region, but many of the lowland forests on the coastal plain are also suitable for backpacking. Even the coast itself has a few opportunities for backpacking. Finally, West Texas offers a spectacular desert backpacking resource. While the South is not considered one of the country's best regions for backpacking, development of facilities by both public and private organizations is increasing. This, combined with the region's long backpacking season and usually moderate use level, has made the region an increasingly popular area for Easterners.

ALABAMA

This state offers few backpacking opportunities because while there are many beautiful natural areas, especially along several pristine rivers, most of the land is privately owned. Even the 4 national forests in the state have large private inholdings. These forests provide the only significant backpacking opportunities in the state.

General tourism information is available from the Alabama Bureau of Publicity and Information, State Highway Building, Room 403, Montgomery, Alabama 36104.

National Forests in Alabama

From north to south, the state's national forests are Bankhead, 181,000 acres; Talladega, 360,000 acres; Tuskegee, 11,000 acres; and Conecuh, 85,000 acres. With the exception of Tuskegee, which is simply a pine plantation, these forests are mixed pine and hardwood stands on flat plains and rolling hills, with limited sections of rugged terrain. Deer, turkey, small mammals, and various birds are common, and warm water fishing for bass, bream, and perch is good.

Alabama is a better state for water recreation than backpacking. However, the Pinhoti National Recreation Trail, extending about 30 miles in the Talladega National Forest, a 13-mile trail in the Conecuh National Forest, and backpacking in the 12,000-acre Sipsey Wilderness in the Bankhead National Forest will provide good backpacking experiences. Another good bet is striking out along timber access roads or taking short cross-country trips. The season is year-round but the fall, winter, and early spring are the best times to avoid insects and hot, humid weather. Backpacking use is extremely light. ꞌ

For information and very general maps, contact the Supervisor, Alabama's National Forests, P.O. Box 40, Montgomery, Alabama 36101. More detailed maps are available for each national forest (two for the Talladega) at 50¢ each from the same address.

ARKANSAS

This state is Missouri's physiographic twin. It is about 60 percent forested, with 3 distinct regions: the Ozark Plateau of the northwest, the Ouachita Mountains of the west-central region, and the flat coastal and delta plains of the south and east. Like Missouri, the mountainous regions are underlaid by porous limestone, which provides excellent drainage in the extensive forests. But, also like Missouri, there are few developed trail systems and wild areas, with many roads and other civilized intrusions. Two national forests and a wildlife refuge offer the only significant backpacking opportunities in the state.

General tourism information is available from the Arkansas Department of Parks and Tourism, 149 Capitol Building, Little Rock, Arkansas 72201.

Ouachita National Forest

This 1,570,000-acre forest of shortleaf pine, gums, oaks, maples, sycamore, dogwood, hickories, and persimmon covers ridge after ridge of the Ouachita Mountains in western Arkansas northwest of Hot Springs. It is drained by hundreds of miles of streams and rivers, and bass, bluegill, deer, quail, and a variety of small mammals and birds are abundant.

Over 150 miles of trails currently exist in the forest, with many more planned under an active trail development program. Most of the trails, however, are neither remote nor very wild. The trails generally have grades of only moderate difficulty and often follow creek and stream beds or ridge tops. There is a trail going through the Caney Creek wilderness, but the best wilderness experience is found by cross-country travel in the many pockets of roadless areas. The open pine/hardwood forest is well drained by the porous bedrock with few boggy areas to hinder the cross-country traveler. The season is year-round, though winters have occasional cold snaps. Cross-country travel is best in spring, winter, and fall when the undergrowth and insects aren't a problem. Summers are hot and humid. Use is never heavy and is especially light off-season.

For information and a map of the forest, contact the Forest Supervisor, Ouachita National Forest, P.O. Box 1270, Hot Springs, Arkansas 71901.

Ozark National Forest

Located atop the Ozark Mountains in northeast Arkansas by Russellville, this 1,103,000-acre forest is best known for its caverns, but the surface environment is similarly noteworthy for its impressive river bluffs and colorful outcrops. Abundant rivers, backwaters, and lakes are nestled among the hardwood-forested ridges, containing deer, small mammals, and birds with warmwater fishing in the lakes and streams.

Trail backpacking opportunities are very limited, with only a few short (5-to-10-mile) trails and no trail system as such. As in the Ouachita, cross-country travel is good, and the forest is especially easily traversed in the fall, winter, and spring. Good roadless areas are found in the center of the forest, and everywhere there are interesting geological features and picturesque stream valleys. The weather is best in the spring and fall. Winter temperatures can drop below 0°F (though snow seldom remains on the ground long), and summers are hot and humid. Use is never heavy and is especially light off-season.

For information and a map of the forest, contact the Supervisor, Ozark-St. Francis National Forests, P.O. Box 340, Russellville, Arkansas 72801.

White River National Wildlife Refuge

This 113,000-acre refuge is located in southeastern Arkansas above the confluence of the Mississippi, Arkansas, and White rivers. The refuge varies from about 2½ to 10 miles wide and extends for 65 miles along the White River. Bayous, chutes, channels, and

165 lakes are distributed along the floodplain, which may be entirely under water for several months during the spring floods. It is almost entirely timbered with southern bottomland hardwoods: pecan, oak, ash, maple, elm, sycamore, sweet gum, cypress, and tupelo gum. Over 200 birds have been identified in the refuge, as well as deer, otter, mink, raccoon, other small mammals, and a few black bear. Fishing is good for catfish, crappie, bream, and bass.

This refuge is primarily used by hunters and fishermen. However, a system of trails and designated camping areas serve the refuge. Fires are not permitted outside of designated camping areas. While the backpacking itself is not outstanding due to the many roads and lack of developments specifically for the backpacker, the abundance and variety of wildlife makes up for it. The summers are hot, humid, and buggy. The other three seasons are more comfortable, but flooding is extensive in the spring.

For information and a map of the refuge, contact the Manager, White River National Wildlife Refuge, P.O. Box 308, DeWitt, Arkansas 72042.

FLORIDA

As a winter haven, this state attracts millions of visitors. Most flock to the beaches and resorts, though camping in the Everglades National Park and in the national forests is increasing in popularity. Backpacking is not one of the state's big attractions, though there are a few opportunities of significance in federal areas. The backpacking environment is generally flat and monotonous, with no really wild or remote areas. The state's greatest attribute is its weather, which allows a year-round backpacking season with temperatures even in the winter rarely dropping below freezing. Insects also seem to like this climate and are found everywhere in all seasons, but their abundance varies greatly with the environment.

General tourism information is available from the Florida Department of Commerce, 107 West Gaines Street, Tallahassee, Florida 32304.

Ocala National Forest

Just east of Ocala between the Oklawaha and St. Johns rivers in north-central Florida lies this forest's 367,000 acres of sand pines and grassy prairies. The terrain is very flat and consists almost entirely of coarse sand that allows rain water to percolate away rapidly. Few rivers are found here because of this, though there are many lakes and ponds in the low lying areas. As its name suggests, the sand pine is at home in this type of soil and is abundant. In wetter areas along the few streams and in the lower areas, palm, cypress, gum, and live oak are found. Deer are moderately abundant, as are smaller mammals such as raccoon and opossum, with a few black bear. Turtles, alligators, bass, and panfish are found in the lakes and streams. Four poisonous snakes—rattlesnake, copperhead, cottonmouth moccasin, and coral—inhabit the forest, but are seldom encountered.

The highlight of the forest's backpacking resource is the 66-mile Ocala National Recreational Trail, which extends north-south through the forest. All the forest's environments are represented along this trail, including about 60 ponds. None of the trail is steep nor rugged, though spring and summertime insects can be locally pesty. Winter is the most attractive season with average low temperatures in the 50s and average highs in the 70s. Summer average highs are in the 90s and humid with afternoon rain showers just about every day. The trail is moderately heavily used but closed to motorized use. For those who wish to get off the beaten path, the open pine forests offer some cross-country opportunities, though a trek may be cut short by an impassable swamp. Few areas in the forest, other than the swamps, are truly wild and some are closed to motorized use.

For information and maps of the forest and trail, contact the Supervisor, Ocala National Forest, P.O. Box 1050, Tallahassee, Florida 32302.

Osceola National Forest

Located in extreme northern Florida just east of Lake City, this 157,000-acre forest is flat pinelands, with occasional ponds, sinks, and cypress swamps harboring alligators, a variety of waterbirds, bass, perch, and bream. Deer, turkey, and quail are found in the drier uplands. Backpacking opportunities are few, mostly limited to the Osceola Trail, extending for about 20 miles through the forest and closed to motorized use. For those experienced in traveling southern bottomlands, cross-country travel skirting the many swamp areas takes one closest to the wildlife and farthest from civilization's intrusions. Late fall, winter, and early spring are best.

For information and a map of the forest, contact the Supervisor, Osceola National Forest, P.O. Box 1050, Tallahassee, Florida 32302.

Apalachicola National Forest

This 558,000-acre forest is located in the Florida Panhandle just southwest of Tallahassee. Natural pine stands, pine plantations, and swamps of cypress, blackgum, and bay trees blanket the nearly flat landscape. The variety of wildlife is great: the carnivorous pitcher plant, cactus on the drier ridges, orchids, ferns, and a number of rare, endangered, and unique animal species, including the Southern bald eagle, red-cockaded woodpecker, sandhill crane, alligator, osprey, and cougar. Deer and bear are hunted, and fishing is good for bass, bream, warmouth, and catfish. Unfortunately, the forest is poor for backpacking as there are no hiking trails as such, only 33 miles of horseback riding trails. Many secondary roads provide access and cross-country travel is possible in the late fall, winter, and early spring for those experienced in this type of travel. Even then much of the forest is impassable. The trailless, roadless 23,000-acre Bradwell Bay Wilderness is closed to motorized use, and motorized use is restricted to certain roads in two other areas.

For information and a map of the forest, contact the Supervisor, Apalachicola National Forest, P.O. Box 1050, Tallahassee, Florida 32302.

Everglades National Park

This park, one of our finest Eastern wildernesses, is all but useless to the backpacker. It is a watery wilderness, best experienced by canoe. On the 44 miles of trails, backcountry camping is only permitted in designated areas, and only one designated area is reached by trail. This trail is under water from June to December and is often mosquito-ridden.

For those who'll be in the area and are interested in hiking this trail, contact the Superintendent, Everglades National Park, P.O. Box 279, Homestead, Florida 33030 and ask for information on backpacking in the Everglades on the Flamingo-area trails.

Myakka River State Park

Just east of Sarasota, this park offers a limited backpacking experience, or more precisely, a backcountry camping experience. The 3-mile Backwoods Camping Trail meanders through hummocks of live oak and cabbage palm and through pine flats and marshes. Deer, turkey, and less abundant otter, bobcat, cougar, alligator, and bald eagle may be observed. The trail ends at the primitive camping area on Bee Island, an elevated spot in the flatlands. Late fall, winter, and early spring are the best times, as the trail may be quite wet in other seasons. Its proximity to Sarasota causes it to be heavily used.

For information and a map of the trail, contact the Superintendent, Myakka River State Park, Route 1, P.O. Box 72, Sarasota, Florida 33577.

Florida Trail

This proposed 1,300-mile trail will eventually run the length of the state, connecting many of the state's public and natural areas; over 500 miles of the trail are already complete, developed and maintained through the efforts of the private organization, the Florida Trail Association. Much of the trail traverses wild terrain, with the wildest section found along the Ocala Trail in the Ocala National Forest and in the section through Big Cypress Swamp. Developed campgrounds and other camping areas are available along the trail. The trail may be too "civilized" for some, but remember that Florida is a too-civilized state.

The longest portion of the completed trail is the 67-mile Ocala Trail. This, of course, is public land and open to everyone (see Ocala National Forest). All but about 200 miles of the trail are on private land and only members are permitted to hike it. There is a nominal membership fee, and maps are sent only to members. For information, contact the Florida Trail Association, Inc., 4410 N.W. Eighteenth Place, Gainesville, Florida 32605.

GEORGIA

Backpacking opportunities in this state are concentrated in the mountainous, northern portion of the state. Numerous trails are found there in the Chattahoochee National Forest, including the southern terminus and 100 miles or so of the Appalachian Trail. The season is year-round, though the winters are cold. The remainder of the state has little extensive public ownership and few backpacking opportunities.

General tourism information is available from the Georgia Department of Natural Resources, 270 Washington Street, S.W., Atlanta, Georgia 30334.

Chattahoochee National Forest

The two units of this 720,000-acre forest stretches across the northern edge of the state, with more than half of the acreage within the forest being publicly owned. The forest is astride the southern reaches of the Appalachian Mountains and contains the highest peak in the state, 4,784-foot Brasstown Bald. A large number of flowering plant species are found in this heavily forested environment, including spruce, fir, pine, a variety of hardwood, and many wildflowers and flowering shrubs such as violets, trillium, azaleas, and rhododendron. Rainfall is plentiful, creating outstanding waterfalls, and several impoundments and many streams and creeks contain trout and bass. Other wildlife includes turkey, quail, raccoon, and various other small mammals and birds.

The larger eastern unit of this forest contains all the trail backpacking opportunities, including about 86 miles of the Appalachian Trail and its southern terminus on Springer Mountain (for more on this trail, see West Virginia, below). It is possible to make a 60-mile loop trip near this end. The 35,000-acre Cohutta Wilderness abutting the Tennessee border has 18 trails totaling 75 miles over rugged, beautiful terrain. Wild bear, black bear, and trout are found here. There are many more miles of other good trails throughout the forest and in the various wildlife management areas that are entirely publicly owned. These trails, unlike the Appalachian Trail, frequently do not follow the natural contours and are sometimes steep and difficult. None are very long, generally only about 10 miles except for the 40-mile Bartram and 14-mile Chattoga River trails. The forest's outstanding feature is its long season, just about year-round, though wintertime temperatures frequently fall below freezing and the ridge trails are iced over most of the winter. Fall color and spring wildflowers make these especially attractive seasons, and even the summers are not too warm because of the altitude. Late fall, winter, and early spring when undergrowth is light, are especially good times for cross-country travel. Expect rain anytime.

For information and a map of the forest, contact the Supervisor, Chattahoochee National Forest, P.O. Box 1437, Gainesville, Georgia 30501.

Cumberland Island National Seashore

Lying off the southern Georgia coast by St. Mary's, this seashore was designated to preserve at least a remnant of the barrier islands currently under the onslaught by developers. Cumberland

Island is about 20 miles long and averages about 2 miles wide. Like other barrier islands in the South, the sand spits are built up by prevailing winds and currents and stabilized by beach grasses. Farther inland, live oaks and palmettos become established, as well as stands of pine. This environment, the interface between land and sea, supports abundant and varied wildlife. Fish, shellfish, and alligator thrive in the nutrient-rich marsh, while turkey, deer, wild boar, and small mammals inhabit the forest with birds, reptiles, and amphibians found throughout the island.

Trails lead to 4 backpack camping areas, each between 5 and 10 miles from the trailhead. Water is available at only two sites, ground fires are not permitted, camping is limited to 7 days, and advance reservations are required. The island is not particularly wild and the trails are neither long nor very challenging, but the area provides a good opportunity to experience the barrier island environment. Use is not very heavy yet. Late fall to early spring is the most comfortable time of the year. Access is by ferry.

For information on the seashore, contact the Superintendent, Cumberland Island National Seashore, P.O. Box 806, St. Marys, Georgia 31558.

KENTUCKY

Like many Southern states, Kentucky has great backpacking potential, but little of this potential is developed. Vast areas in the state are forested with terrain varying from gently rolling to quiet steep. In addition, the climate is accommodating with short and often mild winters. The state government is making an effort to develop its backpacking potential, and backpacking trails and areas are increasing each year. The existing backpacking resource is mostly in the national forest, with only limited trail mileage and few areas open to backpackers elsewhere. Extensive private ownership, farms, timber, and mining operations close most of the state to the public.

General tourist information is available from TRAVEL, Department of Public Information, Capitol Annex, Frankfort, Kentucky 40601.

Daniel Boone National Forest

This 585,000-acre hardwood forest stretches for 140 miles north and south across the eastern third of the state, with another large unit between this strip and the Virginia border. The steep slopes are punctuated by limestone caves, arches, mineral springs, impressive falls, and sandstone cliffs 100 feet high. Five hundred miles of fishing streams offer bass and pike, with deer, small mammals, game, and songbirds throughout the forest.

While there are over 150 miles of trails suitable for backpacking, no single trail is over about 10 miles long and there are few wild and remote areas. However, trails and logging roads provide access to many excellent areas and backpacking use is light. The trails are mostly of moderate difficulty. Also, cross-country travel is possible just about anywhere in the fall through spring when the undergrowth dies back. The most outstanding area in the forest is the 5,500-acre Three Forks of the Beaver River Area, a proposed wilderness. Here, cliffs and small rock arches emerge from the thick growths of wildflowers, ferns, rhododendron, mountain laurel, and virgin stands of hemlock and yellow poplar (one is nearly 7 feet thick). Rainbow trout inhabit the cool Beaver Creek. Only one forest service road penetrates the area, with a trail following the river. Another good area is the scenic Red River Gorge, outstanding for its many large natural stone bridges. A road follows much of the gorge, but one section is roadless with a good trail along the bottom of the gorge.

For information, brochures, and maps of the forest, contact the Supervisor, Daniel Boone National Forest, Winchester, Kentucky 40391.

Cumberland Gap National Historical Park

This small, elongated 20,000-acre park lies south of the Daniel Boone National Forest on the Virginia-Kentucky line, and encompasses the forested mountain pass of the Wilderness Road, a main artery of the trans-Allegheny migration. The thick hardwood forest is inhabited by deer, mink, flying squirrel, bobcat, and fox. Backpacking opportunities are limited though, with only 42 miles of trails, most open also to horseback riders. Trail hiking can be augmented by cross-country travel for solitude and many grand vistas.

For information and a hiking guide, contact the Superintendent, Cumberland Gap National Historical Park, P.O. Box 840, Middlesboro, Kentucky 40965.

Land Between the Lakes

On the other side of the state in far western Kentucky is the 170,000-acre peninsula between Kentucky Lake and Lake Barkley, formed by damming the Tennessee River. There are 60 miles of developed trails and about 400 miles of other backpacking trails and roads. Much of this area is wilderness, crossed only by old logging roads and game paths. This typical Southern hardwoods forest is home for deer, and a variety of small mammals and birds. Although there are no streams of significant size, small creeks are common. Of course, there is also the lengthy shoreline along the two lakes, providing fishing for bass and other warm-water species.

Travel in this area is partially cross-country, with hikers striking out along the old logging roads and game trails. During fall, winter, and spring months, cross-country travel is easiest and especially good along the shore. Two roads enter the area, one north-south and one east-west, at the junction of which is located the information center. Backpackers are required to register here before heading out into the woods.

For information on the area, contact the Department of Public Information, Capitol Annex, Frankfort, Kentucky 40601.

Mammoth Cave National Park

This 52,000-acre park in north-central Kentucky is located near Brownsville and Cave City. In addition to a variety of guided cave trips, the park offers a system of moderately difficult back-packing trails which wind through the hardwood-cloaked lime-stone hills. Deer, raccoon, opossum, fox, squirrel, copperhead, and rattlesnake, along with a large variety of birds, inhabit the back-country.

Muskellunge, bass, rainbow trout, catfish, crappie, perch, and bluegill provide good to excellent fishing along the 29 miles of the Green and Nolin rivers within the park.

Backcountry camping is by free permit in designated back-country sites or along the river banks and islands. For informa-tion, contact the Superintendent, Mammoth Cave National Park, Mammoth Cave, Kentucky 42259.

LOUISIANA

Only one place in this state provides significant backpacking opportunities, the Kisatchie National Forest. The rest of the state is mostly privately owned and dedicated to making some-one's living. Many of the most pristine wildernesses are found in the floodplains, swamps, and wetlands in the South. The Atchafalaya River in Louisiana has such a floodplain, but it is generally unsuitable for backpacking (good for canoeing, though) and mostly privately owned.

General tourism information is available from the Louisiana Tourist Development Commission, P.O. Box 44291, Baton Rouge, Louisiana 70804.

Kisatchie National Forest

The 595,000 acres of this forest are distributed among several units in the northern half of the state. The units with the most extensive public ownership lie northwest of Alexandria. The terrain is flat to rolling with many rivers, swamps, and an occa-sional gorge cut in the red, sandy soils. The vegetation consists of large expanses of longleaf pine, with mixed hardwoods of sweetgum, cypress, and oak along the river bottoms. Wildflow-ers, flowering shrubs, and yucca are common in the understory. Wildlife is fairly abundant, with several wildlife management areas in the forest. Deer, otter, beaver, raccoon, nutria (a large rodent), and smaller mammals inhabit the forest. Over 250 species of birds have also been identified. As throughout the South, several species of poisonous snakes are found here, but do not pose a serious danger to the cautious visitor.

The forest has no backpacking trails of significant length. However, pine-covered areas generally have little undergrowth, making cross-country travel possible. The best area for cross-country travel is in the Red Dirt Game Management Area in the forest unit south of Natchitoches. The Kisatchie Hills Scenic Area found here provides a panorama of rugged terrain, mesas, buttes, and rock outcrops, among the stands of longleaf pine. Summers are uncomfortably warm and humid with highs in the 90s, making this forest more attractive as a winter haven for backpackers. The best season is in late winter through April when the wildflowers are in bloom. Temperatures are comfortable, and insects haven't yet reached peak population.

For information and a map of the forest, contact the Supervisor, Kisatchie National Forest, 2500 Shreveport Highway, Pineville, Louisiana 71360.

MISSISSIPPI

Like Louisiana, backpacking opportunities in this semitropical state are limited. Physiographically, it is also similar to Louisiana with rolling hills and flatlands, wild floodplains and swamps. The summers are uncomfortably hot and humid with locally heavy insect pest populations. Fall through spring is the best period for visitation.

General tourism information is available from the Travel and Tourist Department, Mississippi Agricultural and Industrial Board, P.O. Box 849, Jackson, Mississippi 39205.

Gulf Islands National Seashore

This seashore will eventually include 125,000 acres but at present is still being purchased by the Park Service. Of interest to backpackers are 3 islands about 10 miles offshore of the Mississippi coast. These islands, Ship, Horn, and Petit Bois, are actually stabilized sand dunes, created by currents and wind in the same way as Cape Hatteras, Cape Cod, and other offshore banks according to one theory. The sand dunes that form the islands are held in place by the sea oats and other grasses, with palmetto, prickly pear, magnolia, and live oak on the more stable soils inland. Slash-pine forests frequently flattened by hurricanes that seasonally batter the islands, grow back quickly in groves on the islands. Wildlife is varied and includes alligator, raccoon, rabbit, other small mammals, osprey, heron, egret, and other migratory birds. The beaches are home for a variety of marine life. Poisonous snakes are present, but not abundant.

Backpacking and camping is permitted on all the islands. Ship Island (actually several islands since a hurricane washed out part of it in 1969) is the only island with camping restrictions that limit camping in a designated area. Motorized vehicles are prohibited on all the islands. Horn Island, about 12 miles long and one-half mile wide, is the largest, with the other two islands about half its size. There are no trails, but most of the islands' forests and beaches are easily traversed. Camping on the beach is idyllic, swimming is fine, and use is extremely light except on the western portion of Ship Island (camping is not permitted here anyway). The only drawback is that all but the western portion of Ship Island can only be reached by private or chartered boat.

For information and a map of the seashore, contact the Assistant Superintendent, Gulf Islands National Seashore, Mississippi District, 4000 Hanley Road, Ocean Springs, Mississippi 39564.

National Forests in Mississippi

There are 6 of them, but each entire forest is equivalent in size to a single unit within an average-size national forest. The forests are scattered throughout the state, and from north to south are: Holly Springs, Tombigbee, Delta, Bienville, Homochitto, and De Soto. The total area is 1,136,000 acres, but few are suitable for backpacking. The forests are mostly pine, with hardwoods in the wet bottomlands. Upland and water gamebirds are common, as are deer, smaller mammals, and some poisonous snakes. Warm-water fishing is excellent.

Two trail backpacking opportunities are found in these forests. The best is the 10-mile Tuxachanie Trail in DeSoto National Forest just north of Biloxi. The trail follows open pine-covered ridges and bottomland hardwood forests along the Tuxachanie Creek. It's not very wild, but is an interesting hike. The other trail is the 23-mile loop Shockaloe Trail in Bienville National Forest by the town of Forest. This mediocre trail is officially a horseback riding trail and has 9 roads crossing it. However, camping is permitted along its length. As for cross-country travel, the pine uplands in these forests are passable, but uninteresting, and the bottomlands are difficult to traverse and snake infested, making cross-country travel in the state's forest generally inadvisable.

For information and maps of the national forests in the state, contact the Supervisor, National Forests in Mississippi, P.O. Box 1291, Jackson, Mississippi 39205.

NORTH CAROLINA

Beginning in the west atop the Smoky Mountains, the state slopes to the Atlantic Ocean, first abruptly, then gently along the coastal plain. The wildest and most spectacular scenery is found in the western mountains, the Appalachians, where a national park, two national forests, and two wildernesses offer excellent backpacking opportunities. The rest of the state is less spectacular and too populated to be of much interest to the backpacker. It is unfortunate that so much of the coastal areas of the state has silpped into private ownership. However, there is a new national seashore here that is a good backpacking resource.

General tourism information is available from the North Carolina Department of Natural and Economic Resources, Commerce and Industry Division, P.O. Box 27687, Raleigh, North Carolina 27611.

Great Smoky Mountains National Park

See Tennessee, below.

Pisgah National Forest

This rugged, 485,000-acre forest on the eastern slopes of the Appalachians is divided into two units, one on either side of Asheville. Many of the peaks in the forest are over 5,000 feet high, with Mount Mitchell, the highest peak in the Eastern United States, reaching 6,684 feet. Moderate climate and heavy rainfall produce lush vegetation. The forest consists mostly of poplar, maple, oak, and black cherry with a scattering of pine. The under-story blooms with dogwood early in the spring, followed by azalea, then rhododendron by early June. Black bear, deer, and various small mammals and birds are found here, and trout can be caught in the many streams. Waterfalls and scenic gorges are among the forest's outstanding natural features.

While it is possible to travel cross-country in the colder months, or follow game trails and old roads and pathways (shown on topo maps), 3 backpacking resources are particularly inviting. The first, the Appalachian Trail, extends for 60 miles through this forest on its western edge by the North Carolina-Tennessee line. As is the case along most of the trail, it is heavily used. For more information on the Appalachian Trail, see West Virginia, below.

Two of the all-too-few Eastern wildernesses are found in this forest—Shining Rock Wilderness and Linville Gorge Wilderness. The 13,000-acre Shining Rock Wilderness takes its name from the erosion-resistant snow-white quartz rock outcrops on the summit of Shining Rock Mountain. Elevations range from 3,500 feet to over 6,000 feet. The 25 miles of trails vary from very steep to gently undulating and they follow a good mix of ridgetop and river-bottom environments of mixed conifer and hardwood forests. The 7,500-acre Linville Gorge Wilderness follows the precipitous river canyon of the Linville River. The main trail follows the river (good for trout fishing) and is flanked on both sides by sheer cliffs and rock outcrops favored by climbers. This is one of the most rugged pieces of real estate in the Eastern United States; fortunately it was too rugged for loggers, who left its virgin forest intact for today's backpacker to enjoy. Both these wildernesses are moderately to heavily used during the summer, when it rains just about every day. Spring and fall are especially good seasons with much lighter use.

For information and maps of the forest and wilderness areas, contact the Supervisor, National Forests in North Carolina, P.O. Box 2750, Asheville, North Carolina 28802 (information on all the state's national forests can be obtained from this address).

Nantahala National Forest

Located in the western tip of the state, this 465,000-acre forest is surrounded by national forests on 3 sides with the Smoky Mountains National Park on the fourth to the north. The flora and fauna are similar to that of the Pisgah. Several especially large, sinuous reservoirs, with extensive shorelines, as well as many rivers and waterfalls, are nestled in the lush valleys. Perhaps the most interesting natural feature in the forest is the Joyce Kilmer Memorial-Slick Rock Wilderness, over 14,000 acres extending into Tennessee and including 3,700 acres of virgin forest wilderness, providing a rare opportunity for Easterners to experience the type of environment that was once common throughout the Eastern United States.

Most backpackers in the forest are found on the Appalachian Trail, which extends for 80 miles north and south through the center of the forest, following the higher peaks and at places reaching elevations of over 5,000 feet. The trail is often steep, but the path is well marked and the scenery includes some of the best in the forest. However, it's heavily used. For more information on the Appalachian Trail, see West Virginia, below. Other trails in the forest are less well known and less heavily used, but are not as long as the Appalachian Trail. The forest is well-supplied with these trails, most serving as side trails of the Appalachian. Also, cross-country travel is possible; it is easiest from late fall to early spring before the undergrowth becomes heavy. Few areas, though, are very remote or wild.

For information and a map of the forest, contact the Supervisor in Asheville (see Pisgah, above). Sufficiently detailed information on trails other than the Appalachian Trail must be obtained from the district rangers, U.S. Forest Service, at the following addresses: P.O. Box 577, Murphy, North Carolina 28906; Route 1, Box 16A, Robbinsville, North Carolina 28771; P.O. Box 749; Highlands, North Carolina 28741; and P.O. Box 469, Franklin, North Carolina 28734.

Uwharrie National Forest

This tiny 46,000-acre forest consists of scattered holdings east of Albemarle in south-central North Carolina. It is more like a state forest; not very wild, but deer and small mammals roam the hardwood hills and warm-water fishing is fair in the Badin Lake Reservoir adjacent to the forest. Small creeks also wind through the woods.

Surprisingly, this forest offers a fair backpacking opportunity thanks to a resourceful district ranger who enlisted the support of the Boy Scouts and the Youth Conservation Corp to construct the 22-mile Uwharrie Trail running north and south through the forest. The trail has moderate grades and very light use year-round. Another large public tract adjacent to Badin Lake contains many short trails and provides an opportunity to mix cross-country travel with travel along a trail or logging road for short distances. Again, the use is extremely light in this area.

For information and various maps of the forest and trail, contact the District Ranger, Uwharrie National Forest, Drawer F, Troy, North Carolina 27371.

Croatan National Forest

Moving across to the other side of the state, this 155,000-acre forest lies on and near the Atlantic Coast south of New Bern. It is one of the few Eastern forests that represent the Atlantic coastal plain with its sandy soil and acid bogs. As is often the case along the interface of two environments—the ocean and the coastal plain—the biological diversity is great. Both hardwoods—mostly poplar, sweetgum, tupelo, and oak—and pine comprise the forest. A large area is covered by bog, home of 3 carnivorous plants: the venus flytrap, the sundew, and the pitcher plant all supplement their intake of nitrogen from the poor soil with the decaying bodies of insects they capture. Hundreds of birds have been seen in the forest, including egret, turkey, osprey, and various hawks. Black bear, deer, smaller mammals, and fur-bearers inhabit the forest, along with alligator, poisonous snakes, and other reptiles. Fishing is not very good in the acid inland waters.

The backpacker visiting this forest should do so because of the interesting biological diversity rather than in expectation of outstanding hiking opportunities. Only one trail, the Neusiok, is found in the forest. No other trails of significance exist. Although much of the forest is bog covered and virtually impassable, the upland pine stands are fairly open and suitable for cross-country travel. Use is light and the season is year-round; fall through spring is a good time to observe bird life.

For information and a map (50¢) of the forest, contact the District Ranger, Croatan National Forest, 435 Thurman Road, New Bern, North Carolina 28560.

Cape Lookout National Seashore

This 58-mile-long chain of barrier islands is a low, narrow ribbon of sand off the coast of North Carolina northeast of Beaufort. It is a young national seashore and has yet few recreational developments. It will probably be managed as a primitive seashore. Beaches, sand dunes, grasslands, and maritime forests of live oak, cedar, holly, loblolly pine, and shrubs greet the visitor. The few native mammals share Shackleford Banks with domestic sheep, goats, cows, and horses which have gone wild. Bird life is abundant, and there are numerous amphibians and reptiles (no known poisonous populations).

There are no backpacking trails on the island, but none are really needed because of the open nature of the islands. All access is by boat; ferry and charter service is available. Water should be carried, although some can be found on the larger islands. The peak insect season is from July to October.

For information and a map, contact the Superintendent, Cape Lookout National Seashore, P.O. Box 690, Beaufort, North Carolina 28516.

OKLAHOMA

While there are a few pockets of wild areas yet remaining in the state, the Ouachita National Forest provides the only significant backpacking opportunities. For a discussion of the Ouachita, see Arkansas, above.

General tourism information is available from the Oklahoma Department of Tourism and Recreation, 504 Will Rogers Building, Oklahoma City, Oklahoma 73105.

SOUTH CAROLINA

This state is physiographically similar to its twin, North Carolina. It slopes from the Appalachian Mountains down to the Atlantic coastal plain, with its best backpacking opportunities found in these mountains. Unfortunately, this state differs from its sister to the north in that it has very limited backpacking opportunities.

General tourism information is available from the South Carolina State Department of Parks, Recreation, and Tourism, P.O. Box 71A, Columbia, South Carolina 29202.

Sumter National Forest

This 346,000-acre forest is divided into 3 units, all in the northwestern half of the state. The forest is mountainous to hilly, with elevations under 3,000 feet. It is mostly hardwood, with scattered stands of pine and heavy patches of rhododendron and other flowering shrubs. Deer, turkey, quail, and other small mammals and birds are abundant. Trout are found in the streams and bass in the warmer rivers and reservoirs.

The Andrew Pickens District, the "gateway to the mountains," comprises the extreme northwest corner of the state abutting the Nantahala National Forest in North Carolina and the Chattanoochee National Forest in Georgia. This unit contains the best backpacking in the state and a good, fairly long-distance backpacking trail, the Foothills Trail, about 20 miles. This trail extends into the Ellicott Rock Scenic Area, the largest, wildest area in the state, and varies in difficulty from easy to very strenuous. The trail is moderately heavily used in the summer and the season is year-round. Camping is at designated points along the trail only. Other less attractive shorter trails and some cross-country opportunities through the pine stands are also found in this unit of the forest.

The other two units of the forest—Enoree, between Newberry and Union, and Long Cane, south of Greenwood—have little to offer the backpacker. Much of the land within the forest boundaries is privately owned. The only trail of significance is the Buncombe Trail, a hiking-horseback riding loop trail, partly on roads, about 25 miles long, in the Enoree unit. Otherwise, the backpacking opportunities are limited to cross-country travel through the pine stands and hiking along the logging roads.

For information and maps of the forest, contact the Supervisor, Sumter National Forest, 1801 Assembly Street, Columbia, South Carolina 29201.

Francis Marion National Forest

Like the Croatan National Forest, this 246,000-acre forest lies on the Atlantic seacoast, north of Charleston. Much of the forest is gum and cypress swamp, laced with creeks, rivers, and dotted with lakes. Bream and bass fishing are good, and alligators are common. The forest is on the Atlantic flyway and over 250 species of birds have been observed. In the 180,000-acres of pine uplands and in the hardwood stands deer, opossum, raccoon, and other small mammals and upland game birds are found.

There are no official backpacking trails as such in the forest; travel by boat is more popular. However, hiking through the pine forests is fairly easy and some of the game trails through the hard-woods and lowlands are negotiable. The variety of environments and wildlife adds interest to an otherwise unexciting forest. The best seasons are late fall and early spring, with use light year-round.

For information and a map of the forest, contact the Supervisor, Francis Marion National Forest, 1801 Assembly Street, Columbia, South Carolina 29201.

TENNESSEE

This state has an excellent backpacking environment along its eastern edge, the Appalachian Mountains. Not only is the season long (year-round for those who don't mind a little snow), but wilderness and trails are plentiful. The Great Smoky Mountains National Park is this state's backpacking gem. A national forest and even some private timber trails round out the state's back-packing opportunities. All are in mountainous, verdant environ-ments, some of the most scenic in the East. Wildlife, though, is not as abundant as one might expect.

General tourism information is available from the State Eco-nomic and Community Development Department, Andrew Jack-son State Office Building, Nashville, Tennessee 37219.

Great Smoky Mountains National Park

One of the finest backpacking areas in the East, this 517,000-acre park lies along the Tennessee-North Carolina border atop the loftiest section of the Appalachians. Sixteen peaks exceed 6,000 feet, with Clingman's Dome the tallest at 6,643 feet. The name "Smoky" is derived from the smoky haze that so often envelopes the mountains. The haze consists of organic compounds released into the air by the luxuriant vegetation, which then react on exposure to ultraviolet light to create a form of natural smog.

The plant life in the Smokies is truly extraordinary. Over 1,400 kinds of flowering plants grow in the forest, including 131 species of native trees—almost more than in all of Europe! Fifty ferns,

330 mosses and liverworts, 230 lichens, and 1,800 fungi also attest to the region's floral diversity. Coniferous forests predominate from about 5,000 feet and above, with thick hardwoods and rhododendron stands lower down. Some of the virgin trees are of record size. Many slopes are covered with "heath balds" of rhododendron and mountain laurel that put on a fantastic color display in late spring and early summer. "Grass balds," grassy forest openings, exist on many of the mountaintops, and their presence is not fully understood. These grassy mountaintops are not merely areas above timberline, because nearby taller mountains will have timber extending much farther up.

The abundant vegetation is due to the heavy rainfall—80 inches annually—and mild climate. Although rainy, these slopes are well drained by many streams and rivers. Fishing is only fair to poor, and trout are present along with about 80 other species of fish, about 80 reptiles and amphibians, over 200 birds, and various mammals including black bear, deer, opossum, mink, fox, bobcat, flying squirrel, and wild boar.

There are 650 miles of designated trails in the park to help the visitor enjoy this remarkable environment, including about 80 miles of the Appalachian Trail (see West Virginia, below, for more about this trail). Experienced backpackers stay off of this section of the trail, one of the most heavily traveled in the country. It's overused, crowded, difficult to find firewood, and stripped of most of its wilderness character. The other trails in the forest are excellent, but they'll steal the wind from anyone not in shape for the long, winding grades. Cross-country travel is also possible, but difficult in the steep terrain. The season is year-round; autumn lasts until December, summers produce rain, moderate temperatures, and a few insects, and winters have occasional snow and temperatures down to the 20s, but spring returns very early in the year, sometimes in January. Use is moderate to heavy in the summer, much less the rest of the year. Raingear is a must.

For information and a map of the park, contact the Superintendent, Great Smoky Mountains National Park, Gatlinburg, Tennessee 37738. Topographic maps are a great help and can be purchased in the park.

Cherokee National Forest

This 621,000-acre forest stretches the entire length of the Tennessee-North Carolina border, except for the portion within the Great Smoky Mountains National Park. The forest is an environment similar to the Smokies with conifers in the higher elevations, hardwoods lower down, with mountain laurel, rhododendron, and a multitude of other plant species interspersed in the lower story of the forest community. Most peaks are in the 2,000- to 5,000-foot range, though some points in the forest exceed 6,000 feet of elevation. Plentiful rains fill the many streams and reservoirs, and fishing for trout and warm-water species is fair to good. Other wildlife includes black bear; deer; game and song birds; wild boar; red and gray foxes; gray, red, and fox squirrels; raccoon; wild boar; and wild turkey.

Almost as many trails serve this forest as the Smokies—about 500 miles closed to motorized use. One hundred ninety-three miles of the Appalachian Trail follow the state line, frequently over 5,000 feet in elevation. This segment of the trail is one of the most rugged, with beautiful ridgetop views and many wild-flower "balds." (For more information on the Appalachian Trail, see West Virginia, below.) Whereas the trail receives heavy use in this area, the many other miles of trail in the forest are much less heavily used. These trails follow the river bottoms as well as ridgetops and provide good opportunities to compare these differing environments. Possibilities for loop trips are few, unfortunately, because the forest ownership is generally limited to strips along the mountain crests. Season is the same as in the Smokies, year-round.

For information and maps of the forest trails, contact the Supervisor, Cherokee National Forest, P.O. Box 400, Cleveland, Tennessee 37311.

Bowater Southern Paper Corporation

This private timber company has taken a unique approach in its land-stewardship role. Several rugged, especially scenic areas in southeastern Tennessee and one in western North Carolina, have been designated by the company as "Pocket Wildernesses" and set aside in their natural state except for hiking trail development. At present, three trails are used for backcountry camping: Virgin Falls (5 miles), Piney River (10 miles), and Bob's Creek (8 miles). While not as extensive as most trail systems on public lands, the program has been successful and may be expanded in the future. Hopefully, other timber companies will do the same.

For information and maps of the trails, contact the Public Relations Department at either Bowater Southern Paper Corporation, Calhoun, Tennessee 37309 or Bowater Carolina Corporation, Catawba, South Carolina 29704.

TEXAS

For a state well known for having the biggest and most of everything, there are surprisingly few wild and natural areas suitable for backpacking. The state is hot and dry desert shrub in the west, and hot and humid forest and parkland in the east, with grasslands in between. The most wild, rugged backpacking environments are found in the desert mountains and canyons of west Texas. Population is sparse here, and even tourists are few. In east Texas, woodlands provide the bulk of the backpacking opportunities. In these typically southern forests, roads and people seem to be everywhere leaving little room for solitude. However, a few good trail systems have been developed recently. In between west and east Texas, cattle seem to outnumber everything else.

General tourism information is available from the Texas Highway Department, Travel and Information Division, P.O. Box 5064, Austin, Texas 78763.

Big Bend National Park

Located on the "big bend" formed by the Rio Grande along the southwest border of the state, this 708,000-acre park contains desert flatlands, impressive river gorges, and mountains to 7,835 feet. In the lowest elevations are found plants typical of the surrounding desert—creosote bush, ocotillo, yucca, and a variety of cacti. Farther up the foothills, grasslands and then a piñon-oak-juniper woodland cloaks the mountainsides, with Douglas fir, pine, and cypress on the cooler, wetter summits. The steep cliffs and rugged canyons that change their hues with the progression of each day typify the park. The Rio Grande, creator of the impressive landscape, is set off by a ribbon of green of the willows and cottonwoods along its bank. Birds are abundant year round, with nearly 400 species observed. A variety of lizards and snakes (some poisonous), cougar, coyote, coatimundi, bobcat, ringtail, gray and kit foxes, pronghorn, peccary, and deer also inhabit the varied environments of the park.

One hundred seventy-four miles of trails and unlimited cross-country backpacking opportunities make this an excellent hiking environment. Its advantages include a year-round season, light use of the backcountry (especially in summer), and a variety of environments in the lowlands. Frequently steep and rugged terrain, and mountain and canyons all too easy for the cross-country traveler to become lost in are the disadvantages. Temperatures frequently exceed 100°F, no supply of potable water can be relied upon and flash floods turn dry washes into torrents, so this is no place for the novice. Spring through early summer is an especially attractive time, but the park is also most crowded then.

For information and a map of the park, contact the Superintendent, Big Bend National Park, Texas 79834.

Guadalupe Mountains National Park

In the western tip of the state just across the border from Carlsbad Caverns National Park, the Guadalupe Mountains rise to 8,751 feet, the highest point in the state. The 76,000-acre park that preserves these mountains contains a wide variety of environments, but the most interesting feature is the mountains themselves. Over 200 million years ago when this part of the state was covered by a warm sea, a barrier reef (corals built up in a large ring-shaped island) was formed. Millions of years later, when the sea subsided, the reef was buried, only to emerge millions of years later as the Guadalupes. This formation is an island once again, an island in the desert. This is the southern and eastern limit of many Rocky Mountains species and the northern limit of many Mexican species. The lower elevations, beginning at about 3,650 feet, support creosote bush, sotol, yucca, and other typical desert plants. The high country contains pine, Douglas fir, and aspen, reminiscent of a Rocky Mountain Forest. In sheltered, moist canyons, rare associations of hardwoods grow in delicate balance that is typical of microcommunities. Elk, deer, bobcat, coyote, a few black bear, and cougar, and smaller mammals are found here, as well as 70 species of reptiles and amphibians and over 200 species of birds.

The greatest limitation for the backpacker is the scarcity of water. Water must be carried, up to a gallon a day in the summer. Otherwise, over 60 miles of rugged desert trails provide excellent backpacking opportunities. The park is in its early development stages, and the trails are poorly marked. Additional trails are continually being developed. Topo maps can be purchased in the park and are a must for the cross-country traveler and advisable for the trail user. The maze of canyons can become a baffling trap for the unwary. Camping is permitted only in designated backcountry sites and wood fires are prohibited. The season is year-round with hot summers, frequently severe storms, and cold winters because of the elevation.

For information and a map of the park, contact the Superintendent, Guadalupe Mountains National Park, 3225 National Parks Highway, Carlsbad, New Mexico 88220.

National Forests in Texas

The state's 4 national forests—Davy Crockett, Sam Houston, Angelina, and Sabine—are all located in east-central Texas and total 663,000 acres. Public ownership within the forest boundaries is spotty and the rolling hills of mixed hardwoods and pine are penetrated by many roads. The several large reservoirs also attract many fishermen angling the bass and catfish. The most common wildlife are small mammals, birds, and a few reptiles.

These forests are not good for the wilderness seeker, but pockets of seclusion can be found in each. While there are many short man-made and game trails throughout the forest, the only trail of significance for the backpacker is the 100-mile Lone Star Trail in the Sam Houston National Forest, built by the local Sierra Club chapter. The trail follows highways, game trails, logging roads, and in places was blazed through the forest. Generally, it is neither remote nor wild, but goes through portions of fine forest timber nevertheless. Hiking is easy, but water must be carried. May through September is a miserably hot season with many tormenting insects.

For general maps and information on the forests and the Lone Star Trail, contact the Supervisor, National Forests in Texas, Box 969, Lufkin, Texas 75901. (Information on lesser trails can be obtained from the district rangers and are shown on topo maps.)

Pedernales Falls State Park

This 4,800-acre state park, located just west of Austin in central Texas, has a single 7-mile backpacking trail winding through the grassland, buttes, mountains and along the Pedernales River. While the park is being managed to allow it to revert back to its natural state, it is by no means wild. The trail is interesting, though, because it provides the backpacker a rare opportunity to experience a high prairie regime of grassland and scattered oak and cedar in its nearly natural state. Some larger forms of wildlife are scarce because the surrounding private land is fenced stock range, but deer, turkey, and raccoon are abundant. The trail has easy-to-moderate grades with a designated backcountry camping area (no wood fires permitted). The season is year-round. Use is heavy.

For information and a map of the park, contact the Texas Parks and Wildlife Department, 4200 Smith School Road, Austin, Texas 78744.

Other Trails

Three other trails in the state provide additional backpacking opportunities. The 24-mile Somerville Trail in the Lake Somerville

State Recreation Area is a multiuse trail for backpacking, bicycling, horseback riding, and nature study. For information, contact the Lake Somerville State Recreation Area, Rt. 1, Somerville, Texas 77879. The 15-mile Cross Timbers Hiking Trail follows the southwest shore of Lake Texoma and is exclusively a hiking/backpacking trail. For information, contact the U.S. Army Corps of Engineers, Southwest Division, 1114 Commerce Street, Dallas, Texas 75202. The 5-mile Fairfield Lake State Park Trail is also exclusively for hiking and backpacking and is complete with primitive camping facilities. Contact the Fairfield Lake State Recreation Area, Rt. 2, Box 171, Fairfield, Texas 75840 for information.

VIRGINIA

This state's backpacking resource is concentrated along the crest of the Appalachians in the western third of the state. Here the peaks are neither particularly high nor wild, but the lush greenery with which they are blanketed for most of the year is very inviting. As the mountains slope to the sea, they become increasingly settled and lose their natural appeal. Unfortunately, there is no seacoast area in this state suitable for backpacking. In the three public areas along the Appalachians, fair to good backpacking is found year-round if one does not mind snow in the winter. It seldom becomes uncomfortably warm in these elevations in the summer either.

General tourism information is available from the Virginia State Travel Service, Ninth Street Office Building, Richmond, Virginia 23219.

Shenandoah National Park

Stretching for 80 miles along the Blue Ridge, the eastern rampart of the Appalachians, this 194,000-acre park is located northeast of Charlottesville in northern Virginia. Only a few peaks exceed 4,000 feet, and the thick, mostly hardwood forest lends a soft, rounded appearance to the park. Ironically, this is an area that becomes wilder every year. Before the park was established, the area was home for mountain people and lumberjacks, who exhausted the soil, depleted the forest, and caused the wildlife to become increasingly scarce. Today, several decades later, the forest is well on its way to reclaiming the land, an excellent example of environmental succession. Pines and locusts are reclaiming cut-over areas, nurse trees for further hardwoods that will eventually take their place. The wildlife, too, follows this succession. Black bear, deer, beaver, raccoon, opossum, turkey, and other small mammals and songbirds are regaining their previous numbers. On the other hand, animals adapted to open environments—rabbit, quail, and red fox—are declining in number. Streams, though, have cleared with the more stable natural ground cover, and trout can be found in many of them.

The backpacker may encounter an old fence or other remnant of a preceding human inhabitant, but on many of the 370 miles of trails the visitor will more likely encounter other backpackers. The Appalachian Trail traverses the length of the park and it is very heavily used. After first trying to concentrate all backcountry campers around 25 or so shelters along the trail, the Park Service now allows camping anywhere in the backcountry, except in a few natural areas such as the Limberlost, to disperse camping's impact on the environment. A backcountry camping permit is required. For more information on the Appalachian Trail, see West Virginia, below. The trails farthest from the Appalachian Trail are the best for the solitude-seeker and for anyone else who still wants to be able to find downed firewood. On these less popular trails, the backpacking experience can be very rewarding. For those so inclined, topo maps show old trails that are even better for getting away from it all. Cross-country travel is difficult because of undergrowth during the growing season and because of the steepness of the terrain. Winter backpackers must register before entering the backcountry.

For information and a map of the park, contact the Superintendent, Shenandoah National Park, Luray, Virginia 22835.

George Washington National Forest

Between Shenandoah National Park and the border of West Virginia lies this 1,028,000-acre forest. It is divided into several units on either side of Harrisonburg and includes the major ranges of the Appalachian Mountains in the northern half of Virginia, extending slightly into West Virginia. The natural environment is similar to that of Shenandoah National Park, with peaks to 4,500 feet, dense mixed forests, and a variety of wildlife including black bear, deer, turkey, grouse, and small mammals, and bass and trout in over 200 miles of cold-water streams. From the many ridgetops and mountains, the scenery is outstanding. Waterfalls, limestone caverns, sinkholes, and a profusion of wildflowers grace the mountainsides. Hepatica, bloodroot, and may apple begin blooming in April, then azaleas and rhododendron, with mountain laurel blooming until the end of July.

This is one of the best and least known forests for backpacking in the Southeast. Most who backpack here take the Appalachian Trail, which extends for 70 miles through the southernmost unit of the forest (see West Virginia, below, for more on the trail). There are almost 840 additional miles of trails in the forest, though, and none of these is as overused as the Appalachian Trail. The larger northeastern unit of the forest has many long-distance trails that follow ridges as high as those the Appalachian Trail follows and offers the same impressive vistas. Trips of a week and longer could easily be planned. Most of the forest is in federal ownership and there is generally unrestricted use of the backcountry. Cross-country travel is difficult during the growing season, and grades both on and off the trails frequently are steep. Motorized use is prohibited on some trails. While the forest map shows the major trails adequately, topo maps would greatly increase one's backpacking enjoyment in the forest.

For information and a map of the forest, contact the Supervisor, George Washington National Forest, Harrisonburg, Virginia 22801.

Jefferson National Forest

South and west of Roanoke along the Appalachians, this 677,000-acre forest includes the forested ranges of southwestern Virginia and partially extends into Kentucky. Like the George Washington, its mixed forests and streams provide a home for black bear, deer, various game and song birds, bass, trout, and other wildlife. Wildflowers and forest undergrowth flourish in the abundant rainfall and long growing season. This forest differs in one respect, though. As one moves south in the state, the elevation of the Appalachians increases until in the southern portion of the southernmost unit of this forest, the highest point in the state, is reached, 5,729-foot Mount Rogers. Here above the timberline is an environment strangely out of place in the lush greenery common to the southern Appalachians. Trees are sparse and stunted, and the rocky hearts of the mountains emerge through the topsoil to cap the peaks. The view is spectacular and unhindered except for cloud banks rolling up the slopes.

Mount Rogers might be a silent alpine retreat if it were not for the Appalachian Trail, which skirts its crest. The portion of the trail threading through this forest is very heavily used, a common situation at the AT. For more information on the Appalachian Trail, see West Virginia. Although not as abundant as in the George Washington, there are good long-distance trails off the AT. The southern unit of the forest, the Mount Rogers National Recreation Area, has the best system, but it is also the most heavily used. On the higher peaks in this area, there is easy cross-country travel in the alpine areas. The forest map is adequate, but topo maps are much more useful. Another good area is the small, 8,000-acre James River Face Wilderness at the north end of the forest which is closed to motorized use.

For information and a map of the forest, contact the Supervisor, Jefferson National Forest, Roanoke, Virginia 24001.

WEST VIRGINIA

This state consists entirely of forested hills with farms nestled in the valleys, except where coal mining has stripped them both away. A few wildernesslike areas in the single national forest provides the best backpacking opportunities in the state. While the Appalachian Trail does not enter West Virginia, the Conference's headquarters is in Harpers Ferry, as discussed below.

General tourism information is available from the State Department of Commerce, Travel Department, State Capitol, Charleston, West Virginia 25305.

Appalachian Trail

The Appalachian Trail is the first of the country's long-distance foot trails. From its inception in 1921 to its official designation as a National Scenic Trail by Congress in 1968, over 2,000 miles of the trail had been constructed in 14 states by private groups. Generally, the trail follows the crest of the Appalachian Mountains from Mount Katahdin in Maine to Springer Mountain in Georgia. It reaches an elevation of 6,641 feet in the Great Smokies after dipping down almost to sea level where it crosses the Hudson River in New York. Over 230 lean-to shelters are strung along the trail, with no distance greater than 35 miles between any two.

While hundreds have hiked the entire length, most pick and choose the sections that appeal to them. The 279 miles of the trail in Maine is the wildest. Unlike much of the remainder of the trail, it does not follow a crest, but passes separate peaks, lakes, and follows streams. The peaks are still tall and rugged as it turns west and crosses the White Mountains in New Hampshire, but then the environment begins to tame a bit as the trail heads south through the Vermont Green Mountains. The terrain is the least rugged and the environment most civilized as the trail heads south through Massachusetts, Connecticut, and the corners of New York and New Jersey. As the trail enters Pennsylvania, it follows a discernible ridge. Here, though, the trail follows secondary roads to take it over to the Blue Ridge where the trail again follows a ridge through southern Pennsylvania, Maryland, and into Virginia. As the trail extends through Virginia, North Carolina, and northern Georgia to its southern terminus, it remains mostly within national parks and forest. This southern half

of the trail has outstanding scenic vistas and remains in fairly remote, forested mountain ranges. In places, it becomes quite wild,
almost regaining the wilderness character of its Maine portion.

The Appalachian Trail has earned a certain mystique. It repre-
sents a grand volunteer effort of planning and cooperation. It has
its own heroes who have hiked it—the first, the oldest, the
youngest, etc.—and reams have been written about it. But it
seems to mesmerize more than anyone the novice backpackers
who, perhaps because of its fame, seem to flock to it in greater
numbers each year. But the trail's fame and proximity to the
eastern populations have been its undoing. It is now the super-
highway of the backcountry. Trail-side shelters become backpack
ghettos along the most popular segments of the trail, and downed
firewood is nowhere to be found. When one escapes to the Appalachian Trail for a little peace and solitude, all too often one is
confronted by wilderness rush-hour instead.

There are ways to avoid this madness, and take home from the
trail the rejuvenation it was meant to deliver. First, don't rely on
finding a trail-side shelter. It may seem romantic and a good way
to save the weight of a tent, but the concept of shelters developed
when there were no light-weight backpack tents available. The
shelters now tend to concentrate the campers and magnify their
impact on the environment. In addition, you may find no room
at the inn when you finally do arrive. Second, try to use the less
popular sections of the trail. While none of the trail receives light
use, the portions in Maine and in the national forests in the southern states are less heavily used than, say, the sections in the Great
Smoky Mountains and Shenandoah National Parks. Third, be
familiar with the side trails off the section of the trail you are
going to visit. Then, if the trail is overcrowded when you arrive,
you can amend your trip to include the side trails. Fortunately,
the most heavily used sections (those in the national parks) have
the best side-trail systems. Finally, try to visit the Appalachian
Trail off-season. True, firewood will still be hard to find and the
trail will still be well trodden, but the shelters are more likely to
be vacant and some of the best vistas can only be seen when the
leaves are off the trees.

Information and trail maps of the Appalachian Trail are available from the Appalachian Trail Conference, Incorporated, P.O. Box 236, Harpers Ferry, West Virginia 25425. Most of the material is for sale, but trail maps of sections of the trail are offered for free by many of the public agencies mentioned elsewhere in this book that administer lands it crosses.

Monongahela National Forest

This 840,000-acre forest stretches across the Allegheny Range of eastern West Virginia, south and east of Elkins. Like other southern Appalachian forests, it is mostly hardwoods with conifers in the higher elevations that reach 4,860 feet on Spruce Knob, the highest point in the state. The forest is well watered and has many streams and rivers, some containing trout. Black bear are common, and there are also turkey, deer, gray and red foxes, and many smaller mammals. Hundreds of species of game and song-birds have been sighted in the forest, which is a favorite spot for birdwatchers observing fall migrations. Caves, waterfalls, rock outcrops, and wildflowers are also among the forest's attractions.

Only a little more than half of the forest is in public ownership, but the public ownership is concentrated in blocks that provide good backpacking opportunities. Total developed trail mileage is over 675 miles. Three areas provide the best. The 53,000-acre Cranberry Backcountry area in the southern portion of the forest is high, mountainous country well served by 75 miles of trails, and 8 shelters are available. This is the most popular backpacking area in the state. Within the area is the interesting Cranberry Glades, a bog area suggesting more northern environments. In the northern portion of the forest there are two other good areas, the Dolly Sods and Otter Creek wildernesses. The 10,000-acre Dolly Sods Wilderness is a high plain and sphagnum bog with elevations of about 4,000 feet. The area is curious because the environment is more similar to those of northern Canada than those of the southern United States. There is a good trail system of over 25 miles, and cross-country travel here, as well as in the Cranberry Backcountry, is possible. The 20,000-acre Otter Creek Wilderness is a different environment from the two other areas mentioned above. The Otter Creek plunges through a steep mountain valley, cascading over tall waterfalls and passing many limestone caves and outcrops. The approximately 50 miles of trails are good, but cross-country travel is impractical most of the year. Poisonous snakes are found throughout the forest, though they are not particularly abundant. Heavy snowfalls can be expected in the winter.

For information and a general map of the forest, contact the Supervisor, Monongahela National Forest, Elkins, West Virginia 26241.

West Virginia State Forests

A total of 79,000 acres is included in the state's 9 forests scattered throughout the state. None are developed for backpacking, but old roads, game trails, and cross-country travel provide access, and backcountry camping is permitted. While the backpacking resource offered by these forests is only fair, some of the forests are quite rugged and wild. All types of use in most of these forests are extremely light.

The publication *West Virginia State Parks and Forests* provides a general description of each of these forests, and is available from the State Department of Natural Resources, Charleston, West Virginia 25305. More specific information can be obtained directly from the addresses supplied in the above publication. The best forests for backpacking are Cal Price, Dunmore, West Virginia 24934; Kumbrabow, P.O. Box 10, Huttonsville, West Virginia 26273; Panther, Panther, West Virginia 24872; and Seneca, Dunmore, West Virginia 24934.

10

The Northeast:
Connecticut, Delaware, Maine, Maryland, Massachusetts, New Hampshire, New Jersey, New York, Pennsylvania, Rhode Island, and Vermont

The Northeast's backpacking resource is concentrated in Maine and in the inland states along the Appalachian Mountain system; the smaller coastal states are too densely populated and too civilized to offer the backpacker much of interest. The major wild and natural areas remaining in the Northeast, though, are among the best in the country. These large areas of northwoods lake and forest environment and sprawling mountain chains attract many Easterner visitors, as does the Appalachian Trail. A curious phenomenon in the East is the abundance of long-distance hiking trails like the Appalachian Trail developed and maintained by private organizations. Unfortunately, many of these trails lack the wilderness and natural attributes sought by most backpackers. These trails are best where they cross public land.

Baxter
State Park

MAINE

Appalachian
Trail

Long
Trails

Groton
State Forest

White Mountain
National Forest

Adirondack
Forest Preserve

MONTPELIER

AUGUSTA

Green Mountain
National Forest

PORTLAND

Calvin Coolidge
State Forest

NEW
HAMPSHIRE

NEW YORK

CONCORD

Hudson River

Connecticut River

MASSACHUSETTS

BOSTON

Catskill
Forest Preserve

Allegheny
National Forest

HARTFORD

PROVIDENCE

PENNSYLVANIA

NEW
JERSEY

NEW YORK CITY

Appalachian
Trail

PITTSBURGH

HARRISBURG

PHILADELPHIA

TRENTON

Susquehanna River

Batona Hiking Trail,
Lebanon and Wharton
State Forests

Savage River
State Forest

MARYLAND

BALTIMORE

DOVER

Chesapeake and
Ohio Canal

Assateague Island
National Seashore

✸ Relatively large-acreage area
✴ Comparatively small-acreage area

CONNECTICUT

This rolling, forested state has no significant wild areas that might interest the backpacker. However, over 500 miles of hiking trails, including part of the Appalachian Trail, are maintained by private trail organizations represented by the Connecticut Forest and Park Association. These trails pass through many scenic areas on both public and private land, with some camping opportunities. This is generally not a trail system for the wilderness seeker, though, frequently crossing roads and passing through areas that are quite civilized.

For information on the Appalachian Trail, see West Virginia, chapter 9. The *Connecticut Walk Book* describes hiking trails in the state in detail (including the Appalachian Trail) and can be purchased from the Connecticut Forest and Park Association, P.O. Box 389, East Hartford, Connecticut 06108.

DELAWARE

There are no significant backpacking opportunities in this small and densely populated state.

MAINE

Maine is one of the finest states in the East for backpacking, but its backpacking resource is limited to just a few areas, with much of the remainder of the state a canoeist's paradise. It is entirely northwoods country, plagued by mosquitoes and black flies from late spring to mid-summer and beset by heavy snow and cold temperatures in the winter. The coast is one of its most valuable resources, but it has unfortunately been largely lost to private landowners. Instead, backpackers must be content with wilderness spruce forests, mountains, lakes, and rivers, and surprisingly few trails for a state with such a great trail potential.

General tourism information is available from the State Publicity Bureau, Gateway Circle, Portland, Maine 04102.

White Mountain National Forest

See New Hampshire, below.

Baxter State Park

This park of over 200,000 acres is located in north-central Maine northwest of Millinocket and is one of the country's finest state park backpacking areas. Besides numerous lakes and streams in the dense mixed hardwood and conifer forest, many peaks and ridges march across the rugged landscape. The highest point in the state, 5,267-foot Baxter Peak, is in the park, as is the famous Mount Katahdin, northern terminus of the Appalachian Trail. Black bear are numerous, and moose may be spotted. Deer, various smaller northwoods mammals, and birds are also abundant. Fishing is excellent.

One hundred forty miles of trails penetrate the park, forming a good system connecting peaks, ridges, lakes, and streams. Some of the trails are steep, but many others are limited to easy grades. This forest contains the wildest and one of the least used sections of the Appalachian Trail. See West Virginia, chapter 9, for more information on this trail. Camping is at designated sites only. Use is moderate on the trails, and cross-country travel is not recommended because of the terrain and dense vegetation. Early fall when the leaves are changing is delightful. Late spring and early summer are beset by insects.

For information and a map of the park, contact the State Publicity Bureau, Gateway Circle, Portland, Maine 04102.

Appalachian Trail

Perhaps the finest portion of the Appalachian Trail is found in this state, both in and out of Baxter State Forest. For more information, see West Virginia, chapter 9.

MARYLAND

Not surprisingly, this heavily populated state has a backpacking resource of limited quantity and generally poor quality. But it's not completely devoid of backpacking areas, even if most tend to be small and overcrowded.

General tourism information is available from the Department of Economic Development, Suite M-69, State Office Building, Annapolis, Maryland 21401.

Appalachian Trail

A short segment of the Appalachian Trail crosses the western neck of the state. For more information, see West Virginia, chapter 9.

Maryland State Forests

There are 9 state forests in the state, totaling 120,000 acres, and backpacking and backcountry camping are permitted in a few of the larger ones. The best by far, and the only one with developed trails, is the Savage River State Forest in the extreme western portion of the state west of Cumberland. This rugged, 53,000-acre forest is the wildest part of the state, with elevations to slightly over 3,000 feet. It's mostly hardwoods—oaks, hickories, birches, maples, beech, cherry, basswood, poplar—with a few pine and hemlock. Wildlife includes deer, turkey, grouse, small mammals, and about 100 species of songbirds. Fishing for trout is good in the Savage River and its many tributaries. The main hiking trail is 16 miles long along a mountain crest, and there are at least twice as many miles of shorter trails throughout the forest. The forest is not well known and about 150 miles from the large urban centers, so use is only moderate. A camping permit is required.

For information and a map of the forest, contact the Superintendent, Savage River State Forest, Grantsville, Maryland 21536.

General information on other state forests is available from the Maryland Park Service, Tawes State Office Building, Annapolis, Maryland 21401.

Chesapeake and Ohio Canal

This 185-mile trail extends from Washington, D.C., to Cumberland in western Maryland. It is a unique hiking facility, an old canal towpath built in the early 1800s, abandoned in 1924, and slowly being reclaimed by nature ever since. The natural environment includes small mammals and birds, young hardwoods, shrubs, and weedy banks. The unnatural environment includes ruins of past settlements and polluted water.

If you're looking for a place to backpack without really leaving civilization, this is the place. Where else can you backpack right into a major metropolitan area? Campsites are spaced about 5 miles apart along most of the trail, and the grades are flat. Most backpackers wouldn't give this trail a second thought: it's shared by bicyclists, horseback riders, and night travel alone is not recommended (trail crimes?). The most attractive portion is near the western end.

For information and a map of the trail, contact the Superintendent, Chesapeake and Ohio Canal National Historic Park, P.O. Box 4, Sharpsburg, Maryland 21782.

Assateague Island National Seashore

This slender, 37-mile-long island extends from Chincoteague to Ocean City off the coast. It is a barrier strand composed of wind and sea-drifted sand, anchored first by beach grass, then colonized by shrubs, pines, and hardwoods in the more stable areas. One of the big attractions of this seashore are the wild horses that have inhabited the island since the 1600s. The visitor frequently observes roaming bands of these stunted, shaggy animals. Other wildlife includes deer, fox, rabbit, peregrine falcon, osprey, various other birds, and clams and other marine life along the shore.

Backpacking here is rather unusual. Camping is allowed in only three sites, and these are strung out along the shore at distances of 4.5, 9.5, and 13.5 miles. The park service describes the trail thus: "This is not a fun trail. Barrier Island backpacking can be unexpectedly rugged even for the most experienced hiker. Each year a number of hikers have become physically sick from insect bites." However, this facility never fails to attract capacity crowds and many backpackers cannot get reservations during the summer. The best way to see the island, but to avoid the insects and crowds, is to visit it from October to May. Take a camp stove, long wooden or sand tent pegs, and make reservations.

For information and a map of the seashore, contact the Superintendent, Assateague Island National Seashore, Route #2, P.O. Box 294, Berlin, Maryland 21811.

MASSACHUSETTS

See West Virginia, chapter 9, concerning the Appalachian Trail, the only significant backpacking resource in the state.

NEW HAMPSHIRE

The backpacking resource of this state is concentrated in one area, the White Mountains. While the northern tip of the state is also an environment of low mountains, lakes, and coniferous forests, it is privately owned and undeveloped for backpacking. Fortunately, the White Mountains have one of the finest trail systems in the country, one that is able to satisfy most backpackers' needs.

General tourism information is available from the New Hampshire Division of Economic Development, P.O. Box 856, Concord, New Hampshire 03301.

White Mountain National Forest

This 730,000-acre forest is located in the northern third of the state by Berlin. It contains some of the tallest mountains in the East, including the highest point in New England, 6,288-foot

Mount Washington. Scattered stands of hardwoods in the lower elevations put on a spectacular color display in the fall in contrast to the dark green of the conifers that dominate up to timberline. Sizable alpine areas are found on the higher peaks. Six hundred fifty miles of streams and 39 lakes and ponds provide fair fishing, and deer, black bear, bobcat, and a variety of small mammals and birds also inhabit the forest.

This forest is notable in several respects. It has the most extensive trail system to be found in the country: more than 1,000 miles packed into this modest-sized forest. No area of the forest has been left out of this system. Forty-seven lean-to shelters are found along the trails, as well as 9 "huts" (trail-side hotels that feed and house the hiker—not an establishment the purist backpacker would likely have much use for) managed by the Appalachian Mountain Club. This is the oldest and one of the most active trail clubs in the country, maintaining over 350 miles of trails in this forest alone. There are two wildernesses in the forest, the 6,000-acre Great Gulf Wilderness and the 20,000-acre Presidential Range-Dry River Wilderness. Both require permits. Heavy use is a problem throughout the forest, and finding a place in trailside shelters is difficult in the summer. Early fall is the best season to visit the forest, when leaves are changing and the insects and crowds of summer are gone. Winters are merciless and snow in the high areas lasts until June. Many trails are steep, but in good shape. Cross-country travel is difficult.

For information and a map of the forest, contact the Supervisor, White Mountain National Forest, Laconia, New Hampshire 03246. Detailed maps and descriptions of the trail system can also be purchased from the Appalachian Mountain Club, 5 Joy Street, Boston, Massachusetts 02108.

Appalachian Trail

The best portion of this trail in the state is in the White Mountain National Forest, described above. See West Virginia, chapter 9, for more information on the trail.

NEW JERSEY

Two backpacking opportunities are found in New Jersey, one in the north and one in the south. As is to be expected, neither area is very wild. In this densely populated state, any backpacking resource is a treasure, though.

General tourism information is available from the State Promotion Section TR, P.O. Box 1889, Trenton, New Jersey 08625.

Appalachian Trail

The Appalachian Trail follows the northern border of the state and then heads south along the western border until it enters Pennsylvania near Stroudsburg. The trail traverses two state forests and two state parks, with 11 campsites along its length. The environment includes some of the most rugged New Jersey landscape of forested hills, lakes, and streams. However, this is not a particularly wild section of the trail, and roads are usually nearby. Use is heavy. For more about the Appalachian Trail, see West Virginia, chapter 9.

Maps of the route of the Appalachian Trail in the state are available from the Department of Environmental Protection, Bureau of Parks, P.O. Box 1420, Trenton, New Jersey 08625.

Batona Hiking Trail, Lebanon and Wharton State Forests

These two forests are located northwest of Atlantic City. The 100,000-acre Wharton State Forest is connected to the 27,000-acre Lebanon State Forest by the 30-mile Batona Hiking Trail, built by the Batona Hiking Club. The trail crosses mixed forests, many streams, and a number of roads. Although not wilderness, the variety of wild fauna and flora along the trail provides a good opportunity for nature observation. Backcountry campsites exist along the trail. Use is heavy.

For information and a map of the trail and forests, contact the Department of Environmental Protection, Bureau of Parks, P.O. Box 1420, Trenton, New Jersey 08625.

NEW YORK

Most of this state is city, suburb, and farm. Two large areas
are exceptions: the Adirondack and Catskill forest preserves. By
far the best backpacking in the state, and some of the best in the
East, is found in the Adirondacks. State trail development activity has centered on these preserves, but several other long-
distance trails—the Appalachian, Finger Lakes, and Long Path—
have been developed by private groups. However, except for
the portions of these trails that traverse large public holdings,
they lack the wild qualities and remoteness most backpackers
seek. Even much of the Appalachian Trail in the state skirts cities
and farms.

General tourism information is available from the State Department of Commerce, 112 State Street, Albany, New York
12207.

Adirondack Park

The Adirondack Park consists of nearly 6 million acres covering much of northern New York State and is unique in its concep-
tion and administration. Formed in 1855 before conservation
policies in this country were firmly established, the area is a curious
mosaic of public and private land. Pristine wilderness as well as
Coney Island-type developments are all found within its approximately 100-mile-by-100-mile boundary. If the park had not been
established as early as it had, development would have no doubt
been much more disastrous. Now, public and private land in the
park is managed according to a master plan that strives to recon-
cile public and private development activity with the preservation of the area's outstanding wilderness and natural attributes.
In any case, the first-time visitor is usually struck by the contrast
between gawdy tourism developments and the beauty and
quality of the backcountry behind the billboards.

The environment consists of mountains to 5,344 feet (Mount
Marcy, the highest point in the state), mixed forests, bare mountaintops and rock outcrops, rushing streams, and thousands of

lakes. This type of environment is found in several areas in the Northeast and nearby portions of Canada. In these areas, domes and mountain areas were scraped clean down to the bedrock during the last period of glaciation. The remaining basins cut in the bedrock capture and hold the ample precipitation to form a maze of interconnected lakes and streams, each a link in the water's journey to the Atlantic Ocean. Very little water manages to percolate into the thin topsoil. This water network makes the region as good for canoeing as for backpacking. The thick forest thrives in this rocky soil and harbors black bear, deer, otter and other fur-bearers, various smaller mammals, and over 200 species of birds. The streams and lakes provide good trout fishing. This is also an ideal habitat for bothersome insects, with mosquitoes breeding in still water and black flies breeding in the many fast-water streams.

About one-third of the land enclosed by the park's boundary is in public ownership, and provides hundreds of miles of excellent backpacking trail systems. Lean-tos are provided along most of the trails, but camping is not limited to them. Campsites are frequently on scenic lakes and along streams. Because of the mountainous terrain, most trails are rather steep, but that doesn't discourage the hordes of hikers who flock to the Adirondacks. Since use is so heavy, many rely on cross-country travel to find solitude. Although difficult because of the steep terrain, the higher elevations are a bit easier for cross-country travel because of the sparser undergrowth. Frequent bogs are a problem, though. Another significant consideration is the mosquito and black-fly population in early summer. If you are not experienced in dealing with these pesty swarms, stay out until at least July. To avoid both people and insect problems, visit the preserve in early fall. The first light snow arrives in October when colors are at their peak.

For information and maps of the best areas in the park for backpacking, contact the State Department of Environmental Conservation, Division of Lands and Forests, Albany, New York 12233. Additional information can also be purchased from the

Adirondack Mountain Club, Inc., 172 Ridge Street, Glen Falls, New York 12801.

Catskill Park

This park comprises 675,000 acres west of Kingston and is a miniature of the Adirondack Park with fewer of the assets and more of the liabilities for the backpacker. About 241,000 acres are state owned. There are many tall mountains, but only a few rise a bit over 4,000 feet, and there is not nearly the density of lakes that is in the Adirondacks. The mixed forests and other plant life is similar, as is the wildlife, though animal life is not as abundant. Also, there are fewer backpacking opportunities, with only a little over 200 miles of trails. The greatest problem here for the backpacker, though, are the sheer numbers of people. As it is so close to the New York metropolitan area, the park is flooded with tourists, and wilderness preservation does not seem to be a priority in the park's management. It would be wise for the wilderness-seeker to travel to the Adirondacks instead. Otherwise, fall is the best season, or try cross-country travel. Many have made it to the summits of the taller peaks up mountains where no designated trails exist. A permit is required for all back-country camping.

For information and a map of the park, contact the State Department of Environmental Conservation, Division of Lands and Forests, Albany, New York 12233.

Appalachian Trail

See West Virginia, chapter 9.

PENNSYLVANIA

This state provides a curious combination of backpacking opportunities, unique among the states. While there is one national forest, the bulk of the backpacking resources is managed

by the state and private organizations on state land. These areas
are found mostly in the rolling forested hills and the Allegheny
Plateau in the north-central portion of the state, and along the
series of mountain ridges that extend across the southeastern
quarter of the state. The state's environment combines characteristics of the northwoods with the more moderate climate of the
central-eastern seaboard states. The early summer insect populations are not as preponderant nor the winters as fierce as farther
north. In addition, the rolling-to-mountainous terrain has preserved large tracts of near-wilderness in an otherwise highly in-
dustrialized state.

General tourism information is available from the State Department of Commerce, Bureau of Travel Development, Harrisburg,
Pennsylvania 17120.

Allegheny National Forest

This 508,000-acre, predominantly hardwood forest is located
in northwestern Pennsylvania south of Warren. While few lakes
are found in these well-drained rolling hills, about 350 miles of
streams and rivers contain trout and bass. Black bear, deer, various small mammals, turkey, and many other species of birds are
common. Deer are especially abundant in this forest, as in much
of the state. A few virgin timber stands remain protected.

The forest is generally not very wild, with many roads, scattered dwellings, and small towns throughout. However, there
are several moderate to long-distance trails through the forest,
including a portion of the North Country Trail, which may one
day stretch across the Midwest as an addition to the National
Scenic Trails System. These trails occasionally follow roads
briefly, but otherwise provide a good backpacking experience
through natural terrain with gentle grades and frequent streams
with good campsite potential. Use of the trails is moderate. Cross-
country travel is fairly easy except during the growing season.
The 4,131-acre Tionesta Scenic and Research Area and the 120-
acre Hearts Content Scenic Area are national natural landmarks
and closed to motorized use.

For information and a map of the forest, contact the Supervisor, Allegheny National Forest, Warren, Pennsylvania 16365.

Other Trails

Pennsylvania has one of the best nonfederal trail systems in the country, which includes many long-distance trails running throughout the state. Much of this trail mileage is through areas too populous and civilized to be of much interest to the backpacker, but the hundreds of miles of these trails that traverse the millions of acres of state forests and game lands found on the Allegheny Plateau and mountains of the southeast portion of the state are more suited to backpacking. Perhaps the best is the Susquehannock and Black Forest trails in north-central Pennsylvania on state forest land. These two connected loop trails and their side trails equal over 125 miles. The wildest trail in the state is the 55-mile Mid-State Trail a little farther south, also on state forest land. A large portion of the Appalachian Trail cuts through the state from Stroudsburg to Waynesboro, mostly following state forests and game lands. See West Virginia, chapter 9, for more information on this trail. Another long-distance trail, the Tuscarora Big Blue Trail, extends for 400 miles from near Harrisburg all the way down to Shenandoah National Park in Virginia. Most of its distance in Pennsylvania is on public land and is one of the better segments for backpacking. Camping by permit is permitted on public land.

For information on these state trails, contact the Department of Environmental Resources, Office of Public Information, P.O. Box 1467, Harrisburg, Pennsylvania 17120. The state highway map, available from the address of the State Department of Commerce given above, shows these trails and state land.

Pennsylvania State Natural and Wild Areas

Pennsylvania has an excellent system of natural and wild areas mostly found in the state forests. Backcountry camping is permitted on designated sites in the natural areas and in the general backcountry of the wild areas. All motorized use of these areas is prohibited. The size of the areas ranges from 10 acres to over 46,000 acres. Trail development is not extensive, and cross-country travel opens up many possibilities in these mostly lightly used areas. Perhaps the best area (but also the most heavily used) is the 46,000-acre Quehanna Wild Area on the Allegheny Plateau of north-central Pennsylvania, where a backpacking trail is being developed.

For information on these areas, contact the Department of Environmental Resources, same address as above.

RHODE ISLAND

There are no backpacking opportunities in this tiny state.

VERMONT

Like New Hampshire, this state typifies the New England environment with its rolling mountains, mixed forests, and scattered towns in the valleys. Public land is not abundant, and two long-distance trails, the Long and the Appalachian, form the basis for the state's backpacking resource. Even though the state itself is sparsely settled by Eastern standards, tourists flock in year-round from the nearby megalopolis, putting somewhat of a strain on the state. Late spring and early summers have a moderate insect problem, and the tourists are thick throughout the summer. Fall is brisk and colorful with far fewer visitors. Winters are cold and snowy.

General tourism information is available from the Agency of Development and Community Affairs, Information and Travel Division, Montpelier, Vermont 05602.

Green Mountain National Forest

This 264,000-acre forest is divided into two units north and south of Rutland, running through the central portion of the southern two-thirds of the state. About 30 lakes and ponds, and about 400 miles of fishing streams are nestled in these low mountains (generally under 4,000 feet). The thick forest cover of spruce, pine, birch, and other hardwoods and conifers provides habitat for black bear, deer, grouse, fox, and other small mammals and birds.

The main attraction in this forest for the backpacker is the Long-Appalachian Trail, which runs the length of the forest. This is discussed more fully below. Some of the trails in the forest are open to motorized use, making them less attractive for the backpacker. The 19,000-acre Lyle Brook Wilderness has a trail system and is closed to motorized use. The 4,000-acre Bristol Cliffs Wilderness also has no motorized use, but no trails either. Both require permits. Unfortunately, all trails in the forest are heavily used in the summertime, which is also a difficult time to attempt cross-country travel because of the undergrowth. Although only about half of the land within the forest boundary is publicly owned, it is concentrated into blocks. Cross-country travel in these areas is best in the fall because of the colorful scenery and the less troublesome undergrowth and insects. Trail hiking is also best during this season because of the lower use.

For information and a map of the forest, contact the Supervisor, Green Mountain National Forest, 151 West Street, Rutland, Vermont 05701.

Long and Appalachian Trails

The Appalachian Trail enters this state from New Hampshire near Hanover in midstate and picks up with the Long Trail near Rutland in central Vermont. The Appalachian and the Long trails then run together south to Massachusetts. See West Virginia, chapter 9, for more on the Appalachian Trail. The Long Trail (including part of the AT) extends for 263 miles from the southern boundary of the state to Canada. It is one of the finer privately developed and maintained trails in the country, with 70 shelters along its length. A significant portion of the trail is on public land, principally in the national forest. The grades are not terribly steep, and the environment is generally wild, with many beautiful vistas from mountain and ridgetops. Of course, roads are crossed along the route and one is never actually very remote, though one often feels so. The major problem with the trail is overuse during the summertime. For both the user's enjoyment and the sake of the trail, one should opt for using the trail off-season if possible.

For general information and a map of the Appalachian and Long trails in Vermont, contact the Green Mountain Club, P.O. Box 889, Montpelier, Vermont 05602. More detailed information can also be purchased from this club.

Groton and Calvin Coolidge State Forests

Neither of these forests has much of a trail system, but they do have backcountry campsites. Calvin Coolidge is the better, located on the southern boundary of the northern unit of the Green Mountain National Forest near Rutland. It has trails connecting its camping areas with the Long Trail. Groton is located near Montpelier, but it has no trails of any significant length. Camping in undesignated areas on state land is prohibited.

For information and maps of these forests, contact the Park Regional Supervisor, Gifford Woods Maintenance Shop, Killington, Vermont 05751 concerning Calvin Coolidge State Forest, and the Park Ranger, Groton State Forest, Marshfield, Vermont 05658 concerning the Groton State Forest.

Physiographic Cross-Reference

The entries in this book are organized geographically by region and state. The following list of these entries is organized on the basis of principal environmental characteristics to assist you in identifying those areas with a particular backpacking environment. Entries in each group are listed in the order they appear in the book, with multiple entries for areas with significant multiple backpacking environments.

High Elevation Mountains found in the western United States are generally rugged and forested with alpine areas and glacial activity on the summits in all but the southernmost ranges. The scenery is spectacular and most of the country's designated wildernesses and primitive areas are found here, making these environments the most attractive to backpackers. Trail hiking and cross-country travel are often steep and difficult, and weather conditions can be severe.

Mid-Elevation Mountains are found throughout the country. Most are forested and few extend beyond the timberline. Less designated and de facto wilderness is found here than in the high elevation mountains, but the scenery is excellent and traveling is generally less strenuous.

Low Elevation Forests of the eastern United States occur on flat to rolling topography. Few are remote and untouched by man-made intrusions, but most have good vegetation cover and easy trails.

Deserts occur throughout the western United States on both flat and mountainous terrain. Some of the most pristine de facto wilderness is found in the large desert areas, along with interesting and varied life forms. Generally, desert areas contain few trails and special precautions must be taken because of the extreme climate.

Canyons and River Gorges are generally found in wild, arid zones of the western United States. The scenery is imposing, but travel is frequently made difficult by the terrain, climate, lack of trails, and danger of flash floods.

Coastal Areas and Islands have environments ranging from the glacial fjords of the Alaskan coast to the sand beaches of the southeastern barrier islands. Similarly, they vary widely in their attractiveness for backpacking.

Grasslands, Marshes, and Floodplains are generally less attractive to back-packers because of less imposing scenery and limited quality backpacking opportunities. These areas are frequently outstanding for wildlife observation, though.

Outdoor Recreation Suppliers

These are some of the better known general backpacking suppliers. Most will send catalogs on request.

Alpine Designs, P.O. Box 3561, Boulder, Colorado 80303

Eddie Bauer, 417 E. Pine at Summit, Seattle, Washington 98122

L. L. Bean, Freeport, Maine 04032

Bugaboo Mountaineering, 689 Lighthouse Ave., Monterey, California 93940

Camp and Trail Outfitters, 21 Park Pl., New York, New York 10007

Camp Trails, P.O. Box 14500, Phoenix, Arizona 85031

Eastern Mountain Sports, 1041 Commonwealth Ave., Boston, Massachusetts 02215

Eiger Mountain Sports, P.O. Box 4037, San Fernando, California 91342

Frostline, P.O. Box 2190, Boulder, Colorado 80302

Gerry, 5450 North Valley Highway, Denver, Colorado 80216

Great World, Inc., 250 Farms Village Rd., West Simsbury, Connecticut 06902

Holubar, P.O. Box 7, Boulder, Colorado 80302

JanSport, Paine Field Industrial Park, Everett, Washington 98204

A. I. Kelty Manufacturing Company, 1801 Victory Blvd., Glendale, California 91201

Mountain Master (Denali), 1947 W. Dayton Ave., Fresno, California 93705

Mountain Traders, 1711 Grove St., Berkeley, California 94709

North Face, P.O. Box 2399, Station A, Berkeley, California 94702

Ocaté Corporation, P.O. Box 2368, Sante Fe, New Mexico 87501

Recreation Equipment, Inc., 1525 Eleventh Ave., Seattle, Washington 98122

Sierra Design, Fourth and Addison Sts., Berkeley, California 94710

The Smilie Company, 575 Howard St., San Francisco, California 94105

Trail Tech, 108-02 Otis Ave., Corona, Queens, New York 11368

Trail Wise (Ski Hut), 1615 University Ave., Berkeley, California 94703

Bibliography

Listed below are just a few of the many books available on backpacking. Most are "how-to" books; one deals with equipment exclusively.

Abel, Michel, *Backpacking Made Easy*. Healdsburg, California: Naturegraph Publishers, 1972. General information with many helpful hints.

Backpacking Magazine (editors of), *Backpacking Equipment: A Consumer Guide*. New York: Collier Books, 1975. Definitive guide to buying backpacking equipment.

Broner, David, ed., *The Sierra Club Wilderness Handbook*. New York: Ballantine Books, 1968. General information, equipment and food lists, wilderness outings.

Fletcher, Colin, *The New Complete Walker*. New York: Alfred A. Knopf, Inc., 1975. A classic, both literary and entertaining.

Manning, Harvey, *Backpacking: One Step at a Time*. Seattle: Recreation Equipment, Inc., 1972. Good general introduction on all aspects of backpacking.

Rethmel, R. C., *Backpacking*. Minneapolis: Burgess Publishing Co., 1974. Good introductory book for the beginner.

Welch, Mary Scott, *The Family Wilderness Handbook*. New York: Ballantine Books, 1973. Advice for families who take to the trails.

Woods, Robert S., *Pleasure Packing: How to Backpack in Comfort*. San Francisco: Condor Books, 1972. Discusses all aspects of backpacking. Many helpful hints on techniques and equipment.

These two magazines will also be of interest to the backpacker:

Backpacker Magazine, 65 Adams St., Bedford Hills, New York 10507. The one magazine devoted to backpacking alone.

Wilderness Camping, 1654 Central Ave., Albany, New York 12205. Covers backpacking, ski touring, canoeing, and bicycle camping.

Index

Index